(Mis)managing Migration

The publication of this book and the SAR seminar from which it resulted were inspired and generously supported by Eric and Barbara Dobkin through their commitment to scholarly enterprises that foster positive social change in our world.

The School for Advanced Research gratefully acknowledges the co-sponsorship of the Society for Applied Anthropology in developing this volume.

School for Advanced Research
Advanced Seminar Series

(Mis)managing Migration

Contributors

Diane Austin
Bureau of Applied Research in Anthropology, University of Arizona

Micah N. Bump
Institute for the Study of International Migration, Georgetown University

Ricardo Contreras
Atlas.ti

Elżbieta M. Goździak
Institute for the Study of International Migration, Georgetown University

David Griffith
Department of Anthropology, East Carolina University

Cindy Hahamovitch
Department of History, College of William & Mary

Melanie Hamilton
Department of Anthropology, East Carolina University

Christine Hughes
Department of Sociology and Anthropology, Carleton University

B. Lindsay Lowell
Institute for the Study of International Migration, Georgetown University

Philip Martin
Agricultural and Resource Economics, University of California, Davis

Juvencio Rocha Peralta
Association of Mexicans in North Carolina

Kerry Preibisch
Department of Sociology and Anthropology, University of Guelph

Josephine Smart
Department of Anthropology, University of Calgary

Pablo Valdes Villareal
Department of Anthropology, East Carolina University

(Mis)managing Migration

Guestworkers' Experiences with North American Labor Markets

Edited by David Griffith

SAR PRESS

School for Advanced Research Press
Santa Fe

School for Advanced Research Press
Post Office Box 2188
Santa Fe, New Mexico 87504-2188
www.sarpress.org

Managing Editor: Lisa Pacheco
Editorial Assistant: Ellen Goldberg
Designer and Production Manager: Cynthia Dyer
Manuscript Editor: Merryl Sloane
Proofreader: Kate Whelan
Indexer: Catherine Fox
Printer: Versa Press

Library of Congress Cataloging-in-Publication Data
(Mis)managing migration : guestworkers' experiences with North American labor markets.
    pages cm. – (School for Advanced Research advanced seminar series)
 Includes bibliographical references and index.
 ISBN 978-1-938645-03-7
1. Foreign workers–Government policy–United States. 2. Foreign workers–Government policy-
-Canada. 3. Labor market–United States. 4. Labor market–Canada. I. School for Advanced
Research (Santa Fe, N.M.)
 HD8081.A5M57 2013
 331.5'440973–dc23

                           2013013737

 This book was printed on paper containing 30% PCW.

Cover illustration: Mexican workers await legal employment in the United States, Mexicali,
Mexico. *Los Angeles Times,* February 8, 1954. (Source: http://commons.wikimedia.org/wiki
/File:MexicaliBraceros,1954.jpg.)

*The School for Advanced Research (SAR) promotes the furthering of scholarship on—and public
understanding of—human culture, behavior, and evolution. SAR Press publishes cutting-edge scholarly
and general-interest books that encourage critical thinking and present new perspectives on topics of
interest to all humans. Contributions by authors reflect their own opinions and viewpoints and do not
necessarily express the opinions of SAR Press.*

Contents

Figures and Tables

Managing and Mismanaging Migration

An Introduction

David Griffith

On March 9, 2007, six welders from India employed at a Pascagoula, Mississippi, company that overhauls offshore oil rigs were fired and imprisoned for forty-eight hours in the TV room of their dormitory, ostensibly for threatening to incite fellow Indian workers to protest the company's recruitment practices, labor relations, and worker housing. More than half a century earlier, on January 22, 1954, crowds of Mexican men gathered at the border town of Mexicali, hoping to be legalized as agricultural workers in the United States after US employers and the immigration service announced plans to recruit Mexican labor at the border. Blocked by the Mexican police, the men dodged wherever they could to cross the border, aided by the US Border Patrol; in some cases, prospective Mexican workers ended up as human ropes in tugs-of-war between Mexican and US authorities. In August 1992, a Florida state judge ruled that South Florida's sugar producers had underpaid Caribbean sugar workers for several years, ordering the companies to pay each sugarcane cutter between $1,000 and $1,500 per year in back wages. During the summer of 2009, a Mexican woman contracted to pick meat from blue crabs in North Carolina, after weeks of practically no work, due to a shortage of crabs, visited a friend in a nearby city. During the visit, she was hired by a labor contractor to work for two weeks, illegally, painting condominiums in Myrtle Beach,

South Carolina. Following the end of her contract, instead of returning to Mexico, she remained, still illegally, in the United States. In Toronto, Canada, on Father's Day 2010, the United Food and Commercial Workers sponsored a forum to call attention to the plight of temporary workers from the Caribbean and Mexico who live and work in Canada for months on end without their families.

Each of these incidents occurred because a nation-state—either the United States or Canada—developed an alternative to human trafficking and unregulated labor migration across international boundaries. This alternative is commonly known as managed migration. Called other names—such as guestworker, temporary worker, or temporary visa programs—managed migration involves arranging, legally, for the immigration of foreign nationals into domestic labor markets to perform designated economic services—most commonly, seasonal work in economic sectors like agriculture and food processing. The above examples constitute a fraction of the locations and jobs in which guestworkers work, but they highlight some of the more persistent problems that plague guestworker programs: excessive labor control, persistent wage theft, the contradictory roles of sending and receiving governments, guestworkers becoming undocumented, and the separation from children that is required of most guestworkers. Abuse of guestworkers is particularly common when they are recruited for perceived emergency circumstances or enter economies during periods of unique social or environmental circumstances—following declarations of war, for example, or after a natural disaster—and the conditions they face reflect exceptional labor market developments. Yet, over time, even as labor market conditions change, guestworkers often become a preferred labor force, colonizing specific industries and occupations in ways that effectively bar citizen workers from domestic jobs.

"There is nothing so permanent as a temporary worker," observers of guestworker programs quip, yet guestworker programs and the numbers of guestworkers entering North American labor markets have fluctuated significantly over time. These fluctuations may be because of changing federal positions toward managed migration as much as shifting labor markets, economics, and politics. The best-known North American guestworker program, the bracero program, ran for more than two decades and brought millions of Mexicans to work on US farms, but it was abolished in the mid-1960s because of social movements, shifting political sentiments, and the increasingly elaborate methods of farm labor contracting. Another large-scale guestworker presence in US farm labor, in the Florida sugar industry, succumbed to the legal challenges mentioned above and mechanized sugar harvests after half a century of bringing to South Florida, annually, 8,000 to 15,000 West Indian men.

Yet, today, managed migration is growing across North America (the focus of this volume) and around the world, and the current volume represents a baseline of North American managed migration practices at the dawn of this expansion. An increasing number and variety of North American employers and an increasing number of sending states are becoming interested in or are experimenting with managed migration, allowing employers of guestworkers access to a wider variety of types of migrants— women and men from different national, cultural, and social backgrounds. Hahamovitch (chapter 1, this volume; 2011) considers this a kind of "global shape-up," referring to an international labor market designed to recruit and deploy labor swiftly, pitting workers from many nations against one another and leading, over time, to wages falling to levels that only the poorest are willing to accept.

The growth of managed migration may reflect the general growth of migration from poorer to richer countries occurring around the world, with upward of 200 million people now living outside their natal country. Faced with this phenomenon, managed migration offers nation-states a method of regulating those population movements, directing foreign nationals to specific, identified economic sectors that citizens are less likely to care about, matching employers who claim labor shortages with workers who are highly motivated to work, and offering people from poorer countries the opportunities of higher earnings abroad through temporary absence from their families and homelands. Characterized like this, managed migration sounds like the ideal alternative to unregulated, undocumented migration, which too often results in families separated for years at a time, in wage theft and other abuses, in interior bordering and anti-immigrant sentiments, in increased state expenditures for border patrols and immigration enforcement, and in the orphaning of immigrants' children when their parents are deported.

Unfortunately, as the examples above suggest and the chapters in this volume demonstrate more comprehensively, managed migration does not usually work on the ground as well as it does on paper. Wage theft, excessive labor control, sexual and physical abuse, bribes and kickbacks to labor recruiters and contractors, and broken promises of work guarantees are a few of the problems that plague guestworker-dominated labor markets. At the same time, cases have been documented (e.g., Bump, Goździak, and Lowell, chapter 8, this volume) of guestworker labor forces seeming to function to the mutual (if imbalanced) benefit of employers and workers over long time periods.

DAVID GRIFFITH

Although organized, instituted, and legitimized by nation-states, the actual day-to-day and season-to-season management of guestworkers and guestworker programs usually falls to the employers of the migrants or to their representatives—growers associations, labor contractors, small-scale recruiters, employer-contractor partnerships, and the like. Organizations and individuals from these backgrounds often actively oppose state oversight, characterizing it as a regulatory burden or bureaucratic nightmare, and vehemently oppose efforts to unionize guestworkers or provide them with any means to bargain collectively or negotiate for higher wages, improved working conditions, or other workplace changes that would result in safer or more humane work experiences. Only in isolated cases (Preibisch, chapter 4, this volume) have labor unions begun making inroads into organizing guestworkers, and these have come at great cost, including the death of labor organizer Santiago Rafael Cruz. Cruz worked for the Farm Labor Organizing Committee (FLOC), which in 2004 was successful in organizing North Carolina cucumber guestworkers with H-2A visas; during the campaign, Cruz was found bound and beaten to death in the FLOC office in Monterrey, Mexico, next door to the US consulate (Griffith 2009b). Even when the state plays an active role in managing migration, as in the Canadian Seasonal Agricultural Worker Program, the tendency over time has been for state agents to transfer management responsibilities from public to private control. The changing players and economic interests involved in different phases of guestworker programs—their formation, maintenance, and oversight—often result in contradictory roles of the state in managing migration and in uneven consequences for different regions, industries, and workers' lives.

The contradictions, discussed more thoroughly below, occur at and between many levels. Internationally, even states with government-to-government agreements may have differing expectations and interests in managing migration. Sending states' representatives may desire certain wage levels, work guarantees, and protections from occupational injury and abuse for their citizens, yet receiving states' representatives are reluctant to promise such provisions. Within the sending and receiving states, federal and local interests may clash regarding recruitment of workers, enforcement of protections, methods of establishing wage rates, worker transportation and housing, or other factors. In terms of labor-management relations, rarely are the interests of guestworkers and those of employers and their representatives the same, however much both are involved in joint production processes that generate income they share. Divergent interests derive from a variety of sources, including different national, ethnic, and gender backgrounds, but ultimately become complicated by different social class backgrounds and the vastly different relationships to political-economic power associated with class.

Although some guestworkers are highly skilled individuals, recruited for talents ranging from superior intelligence to athletic prowess to artistic virtuosity, the majority of guestworkers are recruited into the lower-paid and lower-skilled segments of labor markets—in far lower classes than the employers who hire them. Originally used in agricultural harvests in the United States and Canada, today guestworkers are imported into North American labor markets as seafood workers, fast food counter and kitchen help, chambermaids, shepherds, mates on shrimping vessels, race horse stable attendants, and other low-wage workers. The roots of managed migration in agriculture are notable, however, in that agricultural labor practices often become models for other sectors of the economy. Faced with the difficulties of attracting labor to work that is seasonal, sporadic, variable from year to year, and regularly interrupted by inclement weather, US and Canadian farmers and agricultural companies have had to pioneer innovative methods of recruiting and retaining workers. Added to these challenges is the desire to release workers from service as soon as the harvest or processing season ends, without having to compensate them during the off-season. These conditions have underwritten the development of a multilayered, socially and culturally complex workforce of which guestworkers form a small, significant, and growing part. Indeed, one of the questions addressed in this volume is how relatively small numbers of guestworkers influence far larger numbers of both immigrant and native workers.

With the demographic and economic changes that occurred across North America in the century following the US Civil War, resulting in fewer but larger farms and fewer people directly employed in agriculture, the exodus of former slave labor from rural areas meant that agricultural labor markets began relying more on non-slave workers who were disadvantaged because of ethnic origins or legal status, marginal to the labor force, sifted into labor markets through social networks linking labor contractors to specific immigrant and ethnic populations, or working under sharecropping or tenant farming arrangements. At various times and in various locations across North America, farmers have used as farmworkers prisoners of war and prisoners out on work release, convict leasing, child labor, high school students on summer break, drifters, casual workers, the mentally challenged, and, of course, legal and undocumented immigrants. Most people who work in agriculture do so only for a brief part of their lives, moving on to less seasonal, more highly paid, and less dangerous jobs as quickly as they can. This has led observers such as Philip Martin (chapter 2, this volume) to characterize the seasonal farm labor market as a "revolving door," as a labor market that workers move through rather than stay in. This metaphor is significant. Others have characterized workers in agriculture and similar occupations as "disposable" (Stull, Broadway, and Griffith 1995), implying that these industries, which are often hazardous, burn through workforces after a few seasons, disposing of workers after injuring them. The high turnover rates in agriculture, food processing, and similar employment sectors have led employers in these sectors to use political, technical, social, cultural, and physical mechanisms to secure labor that is—in addition to productive—captive and hence reliable.

The characteristics of farm and related labor markets have been critical to the argument that temporary foreign workers are needed to stabilize workforces that fluctuate seasonally and from year to year, generally shrink during periods of economic expansion, and suffer from instability in other ways. As part of the increasing erosion of job security in capitalist economies as contracts between workers and employers become less binding and shorter term, several features of farm labor processes have become more common in other sectors of the economy. Temporary, insecure, and seasonal work environments, in and out of agriculture, are predisposed to receive immigrant workers, including guestworkers. Three processes influencing North American labor markets seem particularly relevant to the growing interest in managed migration among employers, politicians, and potential sending nation-states. Together, they act as three pillars of a theory of key factors leading to or encouraging managed migration: (1) the growing use of temporary, contingent, and subcontracted workers and contract production in North American economies; (2) the contradictory state positions toward labor unions and other worker rights initiatives and toward employers, fluctuating within political regimes and from one regime to the next; and (3) the increasing influence and penetration of global political and economic processes into local production settings in North America and around the world. The three processes are related to one another in dynamic ways and have led to a fourth phenomenon: an increasing number of nation-states are interested in supplying guestworkers to US and Canadian labor markets, as well as to the labor markets of other powerful economies. We deal with each of these below.

TEMPS, CONTRACTS, AND MICROMANAGED MIGRANTS
The use of temporary workers in agriculture, recruited and supervised by labor contractors, has a long history, dating at least to the abolition

of slavery around the world and in some settings much earlier, and the practice has had multiple benefits and drawbacks nearly everywhere it has become institutionalized. At its most basic, labor contracting involves recruiting workers for specific, usually temporary tasks, with labor contractors negotiating with employers such things as wage and piece rates, payment systems, and working conditions. Yet, labor contracting can also involve transporting, housing, and feeding workers; providing cultural and linguistic brokerage services; and developing relations of credit and debt between labor contractors and crew members for services such as filing visa applications or for provision of transportation, loans, and goods such as food, drugs, alcohol, and equipment needed for work.

These are the more concrete dimensions of the growth in labor contracting, but it also raises issues related to labor and migration policies in sending and receiving nations, the degrees of formality or informality of agreements and contracts, and the role of reproductive labor in labor markets. In the Canadian Seasonal Agricultural Worker Program (SAWP), for example, government-to-government agreements have provided some degree of oversight regarding how workers in Mexico and the West Indies are recruited to work in Canadian agriculture, although the Canadian state has been phasing back on this oversight in the past few years. Similarly, once the workers are in Canada, liaison officers in the consulates of guestworker-sending states can respond to worker complaints or employer contract violations, guaranteeing some (albeit limited) protection against exploitation and abuse.

In the US H-2A (agricultural) labor markets, however, recruitment has been privatized, with partnerships between labor-contracting organizations in the United States and in the sending states creating several layers of social relationships between workers and employers that reach deeply through Mexico, the West Indies, and Central America and create opportunities for exploitation and abuse at various social locations in the networks (e.g., between local recruiters and workers, between recruiters and employers, and between supervisors and workers). These conditions are by no means uniform across guestworker settings but vary from one recruiter to another, across employers, and between H-2A and H-2B (non-agricultural) labor markets. Most seafood-processing workers arriving with H-2B visas, for example, have been recruited through their home community, family, and friendship networks rather than through state offices or large labor-contracting companies (Griffith 2006; Griffith and Contreras, chapter 6, this volume). Although conditions for abuse remain, these workers enjoy some protections because they and their families interact with the family members of the contractors in their home communities, where they may be able to exert peer pressure when abuses occur. By contrast, large labor contractors in the shipbuilding industry have been responsible for wage theft and other abuses of H-2B workers along the US Gulf Coast (Austin, chapter 5, this volume).

Behind these examples are a growing number of private labor-contracting firms and the tendency for states to delegate more and more recruiting, labor contracting, and managed migration oversight to private hands. Today in the Canadian SAWP, the federal and provincial governments have been attempting to transfer the responsibilities for recruiting and managing migration from public to private sectors, in line with global neoliberal trends that have shaved away the state's responsibility for its citizens, making work more precarious for many groups of workers but especially for guestworkers (Preibisch, chapter 4, this volume). Liaison officers who might have formerly advocated for workers, however weakly, are becoming increasingly obsolete. This is occurring along with the dismantling of state programs designed to protect workers' rights in agricultural labor markets and other economic sectors that have relied heavily on immigrant labor, including guestworkers. With the dismantling of state protections, increasing privatization of the management of guestworker programs, and decreasing job security, limiting guestworkers' and other low-wage workers' employment prospects, labor unions and others, including churches and NGOs, have stepped forward to advocate on labor's behalf, working with guestworkers in both sending and receiving countries. As the murder of Santiago Rafael Cruz made clear, this advocacy can be daunting, especially when organizers' efforts threaten the continued ability of labor recruiters and contractors in sending countries to sell access to managed migration opportunities.

How these processes play out is best understood through specific cases, given that local circumstances and specific commodity production regimes influence the management of migrant labor as well as related political-economic factors, such as markets, regulatory environments, and community involvement. To illustrate the contradictions in state processes as nation-states both withdraw from industry support and continue providing foreign, temporary, and reliable labor, below we profile the US tobacco industry and fishing and seafood industries. Both industries have used guestworkers since the late 1980s, after the Immigration Reform and Control Act (IRCA) of 1986 expanded opportunities for employers and their associations to import temporary foreign workers using H-2A (agricultural) and H-2B (non-agricultural) visas. Even as they have expanded their use of foreign labor, however, both industries have been experiencing decline.

CONTRACTION AND EXPANSION OF THE STATE
PRESENCE IN US TOBACCO PRODUCTION

In the United States, tobacco was protected by an allotment and price support system from the 1930s to 2004—what one tobacco farmer called "the longest running drug cartel in history" (Griffith 2009a). Guaranteeing prices to tobacco farmers, strictly controlling production amounts, dictating the regional distribution of tobacco varieties, and instituting other controls on the economics of tobacco production, the tobacco program allowed many small farmers to remain in business with relatively small acreages. The degree of government control over production stifled capital concentration in tobacco and made the concomitant displacement of small farmers by large farmers difficult. At the same time, collectively, tobacco farmers became one of the agricultural producer groups most commonly using guestworkers during the period immediately following the passage of the IRCA, when a growers association began marketing the program across tobacco-growing regions. Like the Florida Fruit and Vegetable Association (Hahamovitch 2011) or the Frederick County Fruit Growers Association (Bump, Goździak, and Lowell, chapter 8, this volume), the North Carolina Growers Association (NCGA) became a large labor contractor. Much of the tobacco H-2A labor force was hired by means of the NCGA and labor contractor called Del Al Associates. Del Al recruited workers in Mexico, and the NCGA, along with marketing the program (in part, by spreading fear that farmers hiring undocumented workers would experience workplace raids), handled government paperwork requirements, recruited growers, distributed incoming workers from processing centers to tobacco and other farmers in the southeastern United States, moved guestworkers among farms and crops, and handled employer complaints about workers (usually by deporting and blacklisting any workers causing problems).

From the late 1980s to 2004, therefore, two state developments—the first focused on tobacco prices and production and the second on labor—supported the production of a commodity that many (including many courts of law) view as detrimental to society. In 2004, the longest running of the two supports—the allotment and price support program—succumbed to pressure from tobacco companies like Philip Morris and Universal Leaf, and tobacco marketing through auctions was replaced with contract production arrangements between tobacco companies and eligible tobacco farmers. Production contracts in tobacco now replicate those in the hog and poultry industries, in which "integrators" like Purdue, Butterball, Smithfield, and Hormel contract with individual farmers to raise chickens, turkeys, and hogs according to standardized industry specifications. The withdrawal of the US government from the field of tobacco production has resulted in an accelerated process of structural change in tobacco similar to that which occurred over the twentieth century in agriculture in general: fewer tobacco farms now exist than prior to 2004, but those still producing tobacco tend to be larger than before.

The remaining state presence in tobacco, involving the management of the H-2A labor force, tends to be relatively tame: the NCGA files the same paperwork year in, year out, without any appreciable interaction with the federal and state agencies that exercise oversight over wage rates, working conditions, housing, and other parts of the contracts. As has been the experience of other growers associations that function as labor contractors, the state does not exercise much oversight of tobacco labor contractors' activities. The Florida Fruit and Vegetable Association managed the migration of Jamaicans during the sugar program, and the New England Apple Council and the Frederick County Fruit Growers handled Jamaican labor contracting after the sugar season ended. None of these organizations was heavily regulated, and, occasionally, their actions were challenged by worker advocates like Farmworker Justice, the Southern Poverty Law Center, FLOC, or Oxfam America.

Increasingly, in Canada, the provincial governments give free rein to labor contractors who import guestworkers, their representatives arguing that things have evolved to the point where governments do not want to be involved in that level of detail, do not want to be concerned with the nitty-gritty. The model of privatization is preferred to a managed model, with its memorandums of understanding and legal arrangements (Preibisch, chapter 4, this volume).

INCREASING INSTABILITY IN US FISHERIES

In the US seafood and fishing industries, the state's presence has been complex, with periods of state support of fisheries through research to improve technologies for catching fish or handling seafood interspersed among periods of increased regulatory measures that have reallocated fishing stocks, restricted fishing practices, closed waters to fishing temporarily or permanently, and protected species of fish and other marine life, such as sea turtles or whales, to a degree that has disrupted commercial fishing. The complex state intervention in fisheries has been accompanied by an increase in low-cost imported and farm-raised fish and shellfish and by increased coastal gentrification, with working waterfronts being replaced by pleasure craft marinas, yacht basins, restaurants, resorts, and other facilities oriented toward recreation and leisure.

These developments have combined to make commercial fishing liveli-hoods more temporary, sporadic, and irregular—along with constricting the US fishing fleet in general—resulting in fluctuating supplies of fish and shellfish to the seafood-processing and marketing sectors. For the seafood processors that have remained in business, the increased irregularity of supply of raw materials has led them to supplement domestic seafood sup-plies with imports or farm-raised products, phase back on business, rely more heavily on workers who can be marshaled at a moment's notice yet who can remain idle for long periods without work, or combine these strat-egies. Griffith and Contreras (chapter 6, this volume) found that the few remaining blue crab processors along the mid-Atlantic coast have been able to stay in business primarily due to access to H-2B workers from Mexico—a labor force that can spend many weeks idly in labor camps if supplies of crab fail to materialize.

Tobacco and fisheries are industries that, in decline for the past few decades, have relied on guestworkers as they face ever-greater uncertainty. Their conditions suggest that immigrant labor may compensate partially for a market sector's uncertainty and instability and that, conversely, with-out such a readily available, captive labor force, neither tobacco nor fish-eries would survive as currently constituted. In other words, if market mechanisms were allowed to function without government intervention in tobacco and fisheries, these industries might well not survive. Low-cost or highly productive immigrant labor often functions to support enterprises that, without access to such labor, would either have to change their pro-duction methods—say, mechanize operations, as some industries have done (Martin, chapter 2, this volume)—or go out of business.

THE CONTRADICTORY ROLE OF THE STATE

The labor market distortions that often result from the use of immi-grant labor, in general, and guestworkers, specifically, underscore a cen-tral contradiction of the state's role in regulating a nation's labor supply with guestworkers. As states around the world move to support more free market, neoliberal policies, the deterioration in the conditions of work has encouraged industries to appeal for labor market interventions that reduce workers' access to the labor market. Many writers have emphasized the cap-tive nature of guestworkers, who are legally confined by their contracts to work for individual employers. Preibisch and Encalada Grez argue that the "availability of migrant labor, regardless of the mechanism under which it is made available, has resulted in labor market distortions and the structural dependence of growers on migrants, particularly as farmwork becomes socially constructed as undesirable through the persistence of low wages and poor working conditions" (2010:289). Similar observations could be made of most low-wage labor markets, especially those for seasonal employment, as North American governments at all levels phase back protections for low-wage workers.

The state's contradictory positions toward guestworker programs are not restricted to promoting free market mechanisms and expanding access to captive labor at the same time. Mexican and Caribbean liaison officers and consulate officials in Canada and the United States, supposedly in place to advocate on behalf of workers, routinely engage in disciplining workers from their home countries on behalf of foreign employers, primarily to ensure the workers' continued participation in managed migration. This derives from the power disparities that exist between the sending and receiving countries, emphasizing the ever-present possibility that employers will dismiss workers from one nation only to replace them with foreign nationals from another.

States receiving managed migrants often adopt policies and enforce or ignore regulatory measures that at once encourage and discourage employers from seeking guestworkers. Some US employers of H-2A and H-2B workers, for example, have been able to access foreign nationals by certifying to the US Department of Labor that no domestic laborers are available—completing what are called "clearance orders"—yet they have been sued by rural legal aid organizations funded by the US government: first, for importing foreign nationals when, legal aid attorneys claim, domestic workers were available for those jobs, and, second, for the abuse of foreign nationals in those jobs. In Canada, although binational agreements with countries supplying guestworkers to Canada are negotiated at the federal level, provincial ministers of labor are responsible for monitoring the use of managed migrants, a situation that often renders binational agreements irrelevant to employment conditions, housing, or occupational health. Similarly, the enforcement of housing, wage, and other provisions of H-2 contracts are left up to a combination of federal and local authorities in the United States, with the federal government enforcing the Migrant and Seasonal Agricultural Worker Protection Act and the local authorities inspecting housing, resulting, as in Canada, in a hodgepodge of government oversight behaviors that vary according to the sympathies and budgets of local inspectors. This is not unique to employers of guestworkers, however, but characterizes the conditions facing many low-wage, seasonal workers.

Contradictory policy initiatives have always swirled around debates over immigration, including managed migration. The trade-offs between humanitarian and economic immigration policies have been at the core of immigration debates at least for several decades, challenging both labor advocates interested in protecting workers' rights and friends of capital who want streamlined programs unburdened by bureaucratic oversight. In this volume, US policy positions discussed by Martin (chapter 2) and by Hahamovitch (chapter 1) and Canadian policy positions discussed by Preibisch (chapter 4) and by Smart (chapter 3) show that the questions surrounding managed migration reach right and left across the political spectrum and engage advocates and critics from all walks of life.

The contradictory roles of states in guestworker programs and policies surely have contributed to the tendency for guestworker programs to expand and contract over time. Some of this, of course, has been due to shifts in the balance of power between labor and capital, but developments in specific regions and labor markets also have swung employers toward and away from using guestworkers. Threats of enforcement of immigration law in their neighborhood often prod employers of undocumented immigrants toward managed migration, for example. Conversely, crises such as the 2008 financial debacle, which resulted in increased numbers of workers displaced from construction, have encouraged some former employers of H-2 workers to replace H-2 workers with the displaced. Managed migration, in other words, does not occur in a social or historical vacuum but is much influenced by the political economy of the day.

POLITICAL ECONOMY, THE RISE IN LABOR-SUPPLYING STATES, AND THE GLOBAL PENETRATION OF NORTH AMERICAN LABOR MARKETS AND COMMUNITIES

Political-economic developments are part of global realities, affecting both the households and communities that supply migrants to international labor markets and the industries that rely on migration to meet their labor needs. The economic and political developments that have altered sending states' political and economic systems range from civil war and debt restructuring to microfinancing and fair trade initiatives, the crises often pushing people into labor markets as wage workers and toward the economic alternatives attempting to create opportunities for people to stay in their home regions. For those displaced from peasant and other small-scale, home-based production systems, the push into domestic rather than international labor markets is far more apt to occur. Many more people work as wage laborers within their home countries than join international labor migrations. The estimated 12 million undocumented immigrants in the United States, for example, constitute about 11 percent of Mexico's estimated population of 109 million, and the undocumented hail from many more countries than just Mexico.

Yet, the lack of economic and political initiatives to provide viable livelihoods in sending states has created a climate in which working for wages in factories or factory-like regimes has become the economic alternative of necessity or choice for the majority of the world's peoples. Through this process, they become available for international labor migration, acquiring the workplace discipline required of most capitalist production regimes. Social scientists have written extensively on how people, over time, learn to perform difficult labor and evolve, with their fellow laborers, into working classes, considering it legitimate and just (or at least common) for people to submit to production regimes in which they are paid wages or piece rates for their work. In many parts of the world, wages (or money) as the object or goal of one's work have been a rare and recent phenomenon; most of the world's peoples for most of human history worked not to earn wages but to raise crops and livestock, build shelters and tools, mine minerals, and apply their talents to other useful goods and services, relegating money not to a goal in and of itself but to a medium of exchange and measurement. In Sinaloa, Mexico, Griffith and Contreras (chapter 6, this volume) found that women who want to migrate into the US mid-Atlantic states to pick crab meat must first gain skill in seafood handling in similar crab plants in Sinaloa, learning not only how to pick blue crab meat but also about the many procedures and practices of factory food production: schedules, equipment needs, food safety guidelines, payment systems, supervision, and the like.

Once they are part of the wage labor forces, workers in poor countries begin to hope for improvements in life chances through higher pay and better working conditions, and it does not take long for them to turn their gaze abroad. They learn of wages easily five to ten times higher in wealthy countries than they could, under current conditions, earn at home. Remittances from relatives working abroad further confirm this, as does the tendency for returning migrants to use their overseas earnings to build houses and otherwise conspicuously display their success. The desire for overseas employment is particularly powerful if other paths toward higher-paying and more fulfilling employment, such as education or apprenticeship programs, fail to yield better positions or recede further from reach due to their cost. As opportunities for education and highly paid, skilled positions constrict in poor countries and as the possibility of earning a decent living from independent production or self-employment shrinks, more and more people see their future tied to access to higher-paying jobs far from home.

The increased interest in overseas jobs among people in poor countries has had several consequences in sending and receiving states and in the political-economic geographies that link them—especially the elaborate migration industry of labor smugglers, recruitment companies, and transportation and communication services and the growth of transnational communities. First, in sending states, more and more people are considering migration as a principal path toward improving their life chances, leading to increased emigration and the growth of a migration-facilitating social infrastructure, such as networks of labor recruiters and contractors linked to employer associations. Bump, Goździak, and Lowell (chapter 8, this volume) show how the Frederick County Fruit Growers, an association of apple producers in Virginia's Shenandoah Valley, has developed a managed migrant labor force, a large labor camp, and long experience with the government paperwork required to import Jamaicans; access to this workforce has given many apple growers in the region a buffer against international competition, particularly from China. Second, migration from poorer countries leads to migration to other, usually richer countries and to those intermediate locations and social spaces along migration pathways. Such demographic movements create further demand for the social and physical infrastructures that people rely on to migrate, from transportation and communication networks to official documents to unwritten agreements between labor recruiters and migrants about debts, collateral, and repayment schedules—often particularly nagging aspects of the managed migration experience. In labor-receiving countries, these increased population flows have led to growing immigrant communities whose members occasionally come from managed migration backgrounds. In eastern North Carolina, for example, several Latina-owned businesses—part of a growing number that have revitalized small town downtowns and blighted areas in larger cities—were founded by former guestworkers who either dropped out of managed migration illegally or married local men and settled in or near the small rural communities where they were formerly crab pickers (Griffith 2006).

As immigrant communities grow and become more settled, immigrants begin enrolling students in school, joining and establishing churches, founding businesses, and engaging in the civic life of small towns and large cities, becoming more and more politically active. Leaders emerge, some from the ranks of guestworkers, developing bases for challenging local institutions, employers, and other sources of power that too often violate or fail to protect immigrants' human rights. The profile of the life of Juvencio Rocha Peralta (chapter 9, this volume) in North Carolina shows how leadership can emerge from humble and modest roots to join in transnational activism for immigrants' rights while not losing sight of the local, grassroots base. As immigrant communities mature, guestworkers have more and more opportunities to find work outside their contracts, learn local transportation systems, access new networks, reconstitute families, and, eventually, settle permanently or for long time periods in receiving nations.

Such developments inevitably pose problems for those policy makers who view managed migration as a preferred alternative to undocumented immigration—in part, because of its tendency to avoid the many perceived problems that attend a growing immigrant population. These perceived problems have led to local and state initiatives restricting immigrants' movements and rights in order to appease those who oppose immigration, whether that opposition is due to racism, xenophobia, or concern over the prospect of immigrants taking US citizens' jobs, draining social services funds, or importing poverty, violence, and crime. Yet, guestworker programs offer viable solutions to the problems associated with undocumented migration only if the guestworkers themselves comply with the terms of their contracts: to live for months every year without their families, return home at their contract period's end, and, while in the host country, perform only the services specified in their contracts. Canada's SAWP is often cited as a model program specifically because most guestworkers return home at the end of the season, yet the program is slowly being overtaken by a less highly regulated temporary worker program, in which employers can shop the world for low-wage workers. Will this result in more guestworker settlement or less? What do such trends tell us about managed migration? Is it possible to design a managed migration program that is just, equitable, efficient, and palatable to forces opposed to and in favor of immigration? And what relations are likely to exist between managed migration and other forms of migration from poorer to wealthier nations, between managed migrants and the undocumented, or between the citizens of sending and receiving states and the guestworkers whose status, for a portion of their lives, seems lodged somewhere in between?

As noted earlier, these three dimensions of managed migration—its coincidence with the labor flexibility inherent in the use of temps and contingent workers, its contradictory position in state political and regulatory agendas, and its embeddedness in the globalizing of local labor markets and communities—compose the basic ingredients of a theory of managed migration that, in this volume, we support with historical material, case studies, and comparative analysis. Again, we emphasize that the experiences of workers, employers, industries, and nations that participate in managed migration have been uneven across industries, regions, and national backgrounds; this is to be expected, given that managed migration constitutes a complex project involving nations (always plural), growing numbers of economic sectors, and employers and workers coming from a variety of class, ethnic, gender, regional, and national backgrounds. Nevertheless, nearly everywhere, the design of managed migration is subject to local, regional, and industry manipulation and adaptation. Hahamovitch (chapter 1, this volume) illustrates this particularly poignantly by contrasting the treatment of Jamaican guestworkers during World War II in the US Midwest and the US South, with many midwesterners treating Jamaicans like war heroes and most southerners treating them like convicted felons or slaves. One contribution of this volume, discussed further below, is exactly that its breadth and scope has allowed us to capture the varied, uneven ways that guestworker programs have played out across different labor markets, nations, and regions and also to point out common features that unite them across these different social spheres.

POTENTIAL CONTRIBUTIONS OF THE CURRENT VOLUME

From the above questions and discussion, it should be clear that the complexities and intricacies of managed migration programs, along with the systems and networks they spawn, recommend studies conducted at multiple locations across time and from several disciplinary perspectives. The chapters in this volume evolved out of a short seminar held at the School for Advanced Research in Santa Fe, New Mexico, in August 2010, at which nine of the volume's fourteen authors (Austin, Contreras, Griffith, Hahamovitch, Lowell, Martin, Peralta, Preibisch, and Smart) met to discuss papers they had written about managed migration. The seminar brought together individuals from Canada, Mexico, and the United States in an effort to understand managed migration from multiple points of view. Their chapters, which were revised in light of the discussion at the seminar and additional feedback, address important historical moments and trends in managed migration, develop case studies of managed migration, and provide overviews and analyses of managed migration's relationships to other developments in North American societies and economies.

Managed migration programs have attracted the attention of a broad range of scholars and activists. Reflecting this, here we bring the views of a grassroots leader in a state that imports large numbers of guestworkers together with the views of scholars from anthropology, agricultural economics, history, political science, and sociology. This multidisciplinary team considers the multiple problems associated with managed migration, the costs and benefits such migration brings to employers, workers, and industries, and the factors that have led to its expansion and contraction over time. This volume is being published at a time, moreover, when managed migration programs are evolving in new directions, becoming more privatized, drawing on more female workers and workers from more nations, in many cases increasing the vulnerability of workers to employers' whims, and posing special challenges to labor unions and others interested in worker and human rights. Its special contribution to the literature on managed migration lies not only in its multidisciplinary, multinational, and multisite character but also, as noted above, in demonstrating how uneven have been the consequences of guestworker programs as they are experienced at various scales of human experience, from the highly personal, individual level to the community, regional, national, and global scales.

From such a multiplex perspective, we have nevertheless gleaned common themes. In addition to the three theoretical pillars discussed above, we have found that guestworkers increasingly compete in what historian Cindy Hahamovitch calls a global shape-up, after the infamous methods that farm labor contractors use to form their crews, offering daily wages from the doorways of shuttle buses carrying workers to and from the fields. Guestworkers usually work for wages that are low relative to those of domestic workers but high relative to the wages they can earn in their home countries. These two conditions often lead to guestworkers setting productivity standards that domestic workers have few incentives to match; they also lead to guestworkers (and their nation-states) competing against one another to accept the world's lowest wage. With increasing economic instability worldwide, the race to the bottom has become an avalanche, with labor-contracting firms growing in number and in their ability to promise ever more pliant, willing, and reliable workers.

Yet, the economic sectors that most managed migrants enter are usually particularly sensitive to labor market developments in which sufficient numbers of domestic workers are available only when other economic alternatives have evaporated for them. Such economic sectors are often characterized, as noted earlier, as revolving doors, suffering from chronic high labor turnover. After employers in these sectors become used to guestworkers, they often impose productivity standards that effectively bar domestic workers from these jobs; subsequently, they argue that domestic workers are of poor quality, as well as in short supply. Through such practices, employers construct the labor shortages they use to justify importing guestworkers.

Most of the authors assembled here concur that managed migration has become increasingly privatized and that, with the withdrawal of state protections, guestworker employment has become more precarious and unstable. At the same time, increasing efforts by labor unions, NGOs, and community groups have begun to fill the vacuum left by state withdrawal as they advocate for both worker and human rights. New social spaces have developed for resistance to excessive labor control, wage theft, human trafficking, and other problems associated with managed migration.

Finally, this volume shows how guestworker programs play out differently in the lives and experiences of women and men. Most managed migration is associated with specific commodities and specific tasks required by producers of those commodities and is heavily gendered, drawing on either women or men but rarely both sexes equally. The consequences of this for home communities and families are explored in this volume with the nuanced understanding required to make sense of the intimate places of people's lives.

The volume is organized into three groups of chapters, a conclusion, and an appendix outlining the chronologies and characteristics of US and Canadian guestworker programs. Part I deals with key moments and broad trends in North American and global guestworker history, with chapters by historian Cindy Hahamovitch, agricultural economist Philip Martin, and anthropologist Josephine Smart. Hahamovitch's chapter 1 focuses on the first forty years of the US experience with Jamaican workers carrying H-2 visas, examining in particular the role of the Jamaican state in protecting (or failing to protect) workers' rights. She traces the evolution of protections for H-2 and other guestworkers from official privileges granted to temporary foreign workers—better than those accorded to US citizen farmworkers—to the highly variable conditions guestworkers faced on the ground, which ranged from receiving near heroes' welcomes in some midwestern states to wage theft, debt peonage schemes, racism, and physical abuse in Florida, New Jersey, and Michigan. Jamaican state officials who attempted to prevent their citizens from entering US geographical regions where they suspected abuse would occur, especially the US South, endured intense pressure from US interests and Jamaican legislators to back away from their concerns. Hahamovitch's work places the origins and growth of Jamaica's involvement in US managed migration within the broader political economy of Jamaica and its relationship to the United States.

Philip Martin's analysis (chapter 2) overlaps with Hahamovitch's in its focus on US sugar production, in which the vast majority of Jamaicans worked following World War II. His particular contribution lies in his insight into the relationships between the H-2 visa and bracero programs and the complex payment schemes developed in the Florida sugar industry that ultimately led to legal action against Florida sugar companies. He concludes with a consideration of current policy proposals to supply guestworkers to agricultural industries.

With Smart's chapter 3, the focus shifts from the United States to Canada's long and complex history of guestworker programs. After an initial overview, she discusses thoroughly the Temporary Foreign Worker Program (TFWP) begun in 2002. Since the TFWP's implementation, Canadian employers have enjoyed access to global labor, importing guestworkers from more than twenty countries to meet alleged labor shortages in agriculture, meatpacking, fast food, and other economic sectors. Canada's ever-tightening economic relationship with China, including as a source country for guestworkers, concludes this chapter and this section.

The two chapters in part II—by sociologist Kerry Preibisch and by anthropologist Diane Austin—offer national and regional analyses of fluctuations in guestworker programs over time, emphasizing the relations between capital's attempt to control guestworkers and workers' abilities to organize and marshal resistance to those practices. Preibisch (chapter 4) focuses on Canadian agribusiness, arguing that as Canadian food industry employers utilize more guestworkers from a wider variety of countries—a trend coinciding with the gradual transfer of program administration from public to private hands—work for all farm and food workers in Canada has become more precarious. At the same time, the increasing insecurity and other problems facing workers have captured the attention of worker rights organizations, in particular the Agriculture Workers Alliance (AWA) and the United Food and Commercial Workers (UFCW). Together, the AWA and UFCW have created a multipronged campaign to organize foreign and domestic farm and food workers, a development that has met with heavy and, at times, highly effective opposition, causing them to redirect their efforts and organizing strategies.

Austin's chapter 5 focuses on guestworkers in the US Gulf of Mexico shipbuilding and petroleum industries, chronicling the rapid growth of the use of guestworkers following the human and environmental crisis of Hurricane Katrina and the equally precipitous decline of the hiring of guestworkers after reports of guestworker abuse. Her work situates the H-2B visa program in relation to US strategic interests in shipbuilding and oil production, offering a brief recent history of both industries and showing how their use of guestworkers was consistent with their long experience with various forms of government intervention. As in Canada, the cases of abuse of workers caught the attention of organizations interested in workers' rights and, eventually, led to widespread denials of requests for additional guestworkers. Three years after bringing in more than 10,000 guestworkers, virtually no shipbuilders or oil companies were hiring workers with H-2B visas.

Three of the chapters in part III focus on the families and communities of guestworkers in various regions. The fourth traces the social activism of a grassroots organizer in eastern North Carolina—a region where employers have been heavy users of guestworkers since the 1980s. The section's first chapter (6), by anthropologists David Griffith and Ricardo Contreras, discusses the shared and divergent experiences of women working in the mid-Atlantic seafood-processing industry, who annually leave their families for as long as eight months to pick meat from blue crabs and live in dormitory-like conditions. The paradox of leaving their families to support their families rises to the surface of their narratives along with a generalized ambivalence about how the experience of guestwork has shaped their families and their lives.

In chapter (7), sociologist Christine Hughes offers an account of Guatemalan women working in Canadian agriculture, drawing on Peggy Levitt's concept of social remittances to review how much female guestworkers alter their gender roles as a result of their work and observations in Canada. Perhaps not surprisingly, most prefer to slip back into traditional roles while at home, however progressive their travels and independence abroad may be. A very few, however, have begun questioning gender roles and convincing their husbands to accept more domestic responsibilities.

Chapter 8 by Bump, Goździak, and Lowell tells a story of the evolution of dependence on guestworkers in Virginia's Shenandoah Valley, locating the use of guestworkers in the broader context of the changing apple industry—including increasing national and international competition in apple products like juice from China and fresh apples from Washington and Oregon. In their case, the use of Jamaican guestworkers has not resulted in the permanent settlement of workers in Virginia, unlike the growing Latino population that has emerged in concert with the growing use of H-2A and H-2B workers in North Carolina tobacco, cucumbers, and forestry work and in mid-Atlantic seafood processing. This growing Latino population lies at the heart of the grassroots organizing efforts of Juvencio Rocha Peralta, the executive director of the Association for Mexicans in North Carolina (AMEXCAN) and an ever more highly recognized leader in the transnational community connecting North Carolina with regions across Mexico and Central America. His chapter 9, based on a life history interview conducted by Contreras and Griffith, tells of his growing leadership as more and more Latinos have poured into agriculture and food processing in eastern North Carolina. These industries are among the heaviest users of guestworkers, and Juvencio's story draws connections among the undocumented, legal, and guestworker segments of eastern North Carolina's Latino community.

Together, the fourteen contributors to this volume relate the complexity of managed migration from slightly different disciplinary perspectives and by drawing on a variety of historical and contemporary cases. What unites them is their interest in the curious population flows of legal temporary foreign workers across the Americas and, in some cases, around the world. The potential for managed migration programs to offer legal alternatives to human trafficking and undocumented labor migration across borders, despite their historically poor track records, holds out the promise of forging just, lasting, and mutually beneficial connections among nations, communities, and families. By dissecting managed migration with the varied scalpels of disciplinary methods and by opening guestworker programs from their origins in policy to the viscera of their operation on the ground, we enter twenty-first-century debates about social justice and economic formations that reach back hundreds of years. The continued difficulties and challenges facing the management of migration are liable to increase and grow more complex as these programs incorporate more nations, more regions, and more peoples from diverse cultural and linguistic backgrounds into capitalist political economies. If from our scholarship arises even a modicum of the activism necessary to prevent the further deterioration of managed migration into veiled indentured servitude or outright slavery, or even to reverse these trends, we will have become the hosts that the guests who work beside us would like to revisit.

PART I

Critical Moments in Guestworker Program History

1

"Risk the Truck"

Guestworker-Sending States and the Myth of Managed Migration

Cindy Hahamovitch

Guestworker programs have long been touted as an alternative to illegal immigration, as a way to manage migration both for the protection of citizens in the receiving country, who do not want to be overrun by unregulated immigration, and for the protection of the guestworkers themselves, who might otherwise be vulnerable to exploitation. Sending states have played a large role in managing migration by setting the terms under which workers labor, by licensing the agents who do the recruiting, by sending liaisons or consuls abroad to respond to workers' complaints, and by denying workers to recruiting countries that fail to keep employers in line. Yet, as a group, sending countries have proved feeble guardians of their citizens' rights abroad. Managed migration, this chapter suggests, is a myth.[1]

This chapter reveals sending countries' essential weakness in advocating for their workers abroad by considering one representative example: the US guestworker program known as H-2. The H-2 program, which began in 1943 (though not under that name), currently brings Mexicans, Jamaicans, Thais, Indians, and others to the United States on temporary work permits for everything from harvest work to welding. This chapter focuses on the first forty years of the H-2 program's history, during which 80–90 percent of guestworkers were Jamaican farmworkers and all but a few were agricultural workers. In that period, the British Colonial Office and the Jamaican government played signal roles in setting and monitoring the terms of the H-2 program, crafting a model contract to protect Caribbean workers in the United States. Yet, they had little real power to advocate for workers in disputes with US employers and, once the program was established, little inclination to rock the boat.

A MODEL CONTRACT

When guestworkers began coming to the United States during World War II, there was not one guestworker program but several. Mexicans and Bahamians began arriving in early 1943, Jamaicans a few months later. Barbadians and other West Indians followed in the last year of the war. Although each arrangement was officially separate, all the contracts were based on the Mexican agreement, which was negotiated first. That remarkable document made guestworkers in the United States the most privileged farmworkers in the country, if not the world.

The bilateral agreement required that growers pay a minimum wage (set at thirty cents an hour in 1943) or the prevailing wage, whichever was higher. Guestworkers were guaranteed work or wages for three-quarters of the contract period, a remarkable benefit, given that farmworkers frequently lost days and even weeks of work to cold snaps, droughts, or downpours. US officials would screen imported workers, have them examined by doctors, transport them on US ships and planes, house them in federal labor camps, feed them, treat them when they were sick or injured, and subcontract them to US employers—all at US taxpayers' expense. Mexico required that the United States take responsibility for enforcing the terms of workers' contracts with employers. Most surprising, perhaps, given employers' past treatment of Mexican migrants, the contract contained a nondiscrimination clause and a provision prohibiting the use of Mexican guestworkers as strikebreakers (Calavita 1992:19–20).

The terms of the agreement were all the more impressive because farmworkers were among the *least* privileged workers in the United States, having been excluded from all the benefits brought by the New Deal, including Social Security, minimum wage and maximum hour rules, collective bargaining, and child labor legislation. The depression in agriculture had begun a full decade before the 1929 stock market crash, and by the start of World War II, wages were still well below subsistence levels, and hundreds of thousands of US farmworkers remained homeless.

It was no accident that the contract offered unprecedented protections. The New Dealers involved in the negotiations were not at all convinced that US growers really needed foreign workers. Those assigned the task of estimating the labor supply and labor needs on US farms admitted that there were pockets of labor scarcity around cities and military bases, but they concluded that many regions of the country were still glutted with farm labor. The officials of the Farm Security Administration (FSA), which was the most liberal of the New Deal's agencies, were in the process of addressing that imbalance by transforming migrant labor camps built during the Depression to shelter homeless farmworkers (the only New Deal program to address farmworkers' concerns) into migrant supply centers that would house domestic farmworkers relocated by the government from areas of surplus to areas of scarcity. The camp managers were gratified to see that farmworkers—even black farmworkers in the Deep South—were using those camps as bases to organize for higher wages. They were thus disinclined to undermine that effort by flooding the market with foreign labor (Hahamovitch 1997). To ensure that the presence of foreign workers did not depress already abysmal local conditions, they strove to create a model guestworker program so that the presence of foreign workers would elevate rather than undermine the conditions under which domestic farmworkers labored. To that end, they required growers hiring guestworkers to offer the same terms to US farmworkers.

Mexico's government played a major role in the guestworker program's creation. Still angry about the United States' mass deportations of Mexican citizens (and many Mexican Americans) during the Great Depression, Mexican officials acted essentially as union negotiators for Mexican nationals. They insisted that US officials do the recruiting, that the United States commit to enforcing the terms of workers' contracts, and that guestworkers not be sent to states—most notably, Texas—that were notorious for treating Mexicans terribly. The model contract that resulted infuriated growers who had been demanding access to Mexican and Caribbean workers. They wanted foreign workers and were happy to have taxpayers foot the bill, but they did not expect so many strings to be attached. They certainly did not expect their workers to finally get a New Deal, let alone one brought to them from south of the border!

Despite employers' complaints, the contract negotiated in Mexico stood. US negotiators immediately came to a similar agreement with the governor of the Bahamas, and a few months after that, British colonial officials agreed to a similar arrangement for Jamaicans. The US-Jamaican agreement had one crucial difference: due to the colonial secretary's fear that Jamaicans—unaccustomed to a formal system of segregation—would react virulently to southern segregationists, Jamaicans could only be placed north of the Mason-Dixon Line (Hahamovitch 2011; Henderson

1945:612–614).[2] (The colonial secretary was less concerned about Bahamians working in Florida because the Bahamas had its own sort of Jim Crow system and because Bahamians had been working in Florida for many years.) By the last year of the war, the "migration scheme," "farmworker programme," or "the contract," as it was known in the Caribbean, was extended to include men from other West Indian island colonies, including Barbados, St. Kitts, and St. Vincent. (Women had originally come on the Bahamian contract, but all women were excluded after some of the Bahamians became pregnant and had abortions when threatened with deportation.) It was that West Indian initiative that would morph into the H-2 program in the postwar period.

For a few months, it looked as though this would really be a New Deal and guestworkers would really be treated as honored guests. By the summer of 1943, thousands of Mexican men were at work in the Southwest, where many lived in architect-designed labor camps and the FSA organized fiestas for their entertainment. Mexican *braceros*, as they became known (for *brazo*, or arm), would eventually be placed in all but four states. Thousands of Bahamian men were picking beans and other truck crops in Florida, and Jamaicans were at work in northern communities from Iowa to Connecticut. There, they were welcomed by farmers, feted by rural communities, and even taken to church by white people, who were surprised and bemused by the sight and sound of black farmworkers with "almost Oxfordian" accents, as one reporter put it.[3] Many farmers seemed willing to entertain the notion that Jamaicans were, if not quite their equals, an exotic and superior sort of "Negro" who required and deserved special treatment (Hahamovitch 2011).

Most Jamaican guestworkers who left a record of their arrival in northern communities recalled the thrill of their first encounters with Americans. Rupert Holn wrote from Burlington, New Jersey, "We have found the Americans a very fine lot. I am feeling very homely [feeling very at home] and would not mind if [my] stay could be for all times.... The experience that I have gathered could never be bought in a lifetime in Jamaica." A recruit from nearby Bridgeton wrote his relatives, "[We] got over safely and have started to work. We are now in a place where the people are very fine and courteous to the Jamaicans." On arrival in Randolph, Wisconsin, in May 1943, Ernest Pendley and his thirty-four compatriots were surprised to be greeted by a military band and offered full use of the local country club for as long as they were in the area picking the peas that had been planted on the golf course's fairways and greens. To their amazement, townspeople invited them to attend their churches the following Sunday. Sent to Michigan, Leaford Williams recalled that sometimes, in the evenings, they would hike to town with an entourage of locals, who pressed them for information about where Jamaica was and what it was like (Hahamovitch 2011:60). Expecting white Americans to be hostile, C. W. Creightney reported with surprise, "[They] were willing to come from miles with their cars to take us around and show us a good time." "They were not expecting us to be such fine fellows," he noted. "We never expected to rub shoulders [with them in restaurants and stores]." "It is just like a honeymoon to me," another Jamaican wrote home from Wisconsin. "Please tell them that life is given away in [the] United States."[4]

Jamaicans also marveled at their pay. On their arrival at a farm outside Reece, Michigan, Leaford and Enoch Williams were each given the princely sum of $100 as a cash advance, from which they bought supplies in town, five miles away. Leaford recalled, "[I would] get 50 cents a week in Jamaica, and that was big money. Here, I was able to get 50 cents an hour" (Hahamovitch 2011:61–62). He had $3,000 saved by the end of the war.[5]

Not all recruits were as content with the conditions they found on northern farms and in hastily built farm labor camps, but Jamaican liaisons, Mexican consuls, and US officials worked hard to resolve their problems, despite the fact that there were tens of thousands of guestworkers spread across the country. George Pitt enjoyed the long but "pleasant train trip" from New Orleans to Hebrant Camp in New Jersey, but once there, he worked for three different employers, only two of whom paid him, despite his protests (Hahamovitch 2011:60). In cases like these, when US officials could not get growers to redress conditions, they would move the guestworkers to new locations, as they did with Pitt. Although some discontented, disappointed, or homesick men opted to return home early in those first few months, no Jamaicans were involuntarily repatriated from northern states for refusing to work under the conditions proffered.[6] This was the pinnacle of the US guestworker programs. It was downhill from there.

JOHN BULL MEETS JIM CROW

As long as the program placed Jamaicans only in the North and as long as Jamaican liaisons and officials of the FSA and its parent agency, the War Food Administration, responded promptly to workers' complaints, the scheme seemed useful to all concerned and, at least to some, a promising experiment in interracial cooperation. However, after the WFA forced the British colonial secretary to abandon his decision to boycott the US South, the program's high standards began a rapid decline. For a few months, the colonial secretary held fast to his ban on the Jim Crow South, but before long, Jamaicans were on their way there.

The pressure on Oliver Stanley, the colonial secretary, to break his boycott of the US South had begun to build even as the first boatloads of war workers departed Jamaica's shores. The source of the pressure was Florida's US Sugar Corporation, which was the largest sugar plantation in the country. "Big Sugar," as the company was known locally, had been having difficulty securing local workers to do the dirty and dangerous work of cutting sugarcane since the company's creation during the Great Depression. US Sugar's labor recruiters had taken to enticing black workers from other states to come to Clewiston, by making false promises of high wages, and then locking them in at night to keep them from leaving. After being indicted by the Justice Department on peonage charges in 1942, US Sugar officials decided that guestworkers were the solution to their problem. They were frustrated, then, when Bahamians refused work there. The Bahamians, who had worked seasonally in Florida for generations on an informal basis, knew enough about conditions at US Sugar to refuse cane cutting in favor of better paying and easier work picking beans. US Sugar therefore demanded Jamaicans, who had no experience living and working in Florida. (Jamaica was also a sugar-producing island, so it seemed like a good fit, but US recruiters learned to exclude experienced cane cutters, who were likely to be union members.) The only obstacle to importing them was Oliver Stanley's boycott of the Jim Crow South.

US Sugar enlisted the help of the WFA to persuade Stanley to change his mind. The WFA tried a carrot-and-stick approach. First, its officials dangled the prospect of 100,000 US jobs for unemployed Jamaicans under Stanley's nose. When that did not work, the WFA announced that, unless Jamaicans worked in Florida, the recruitment program would be canceled and Jamaican guestworkers already in the United States would be repatriated. When Stanley held firm, the WFA kept its promise. In May 1943, just as the first Jamaican farmworkers began arriving in northern fields, the WFA suspended the distribution of new recruitment tickets in Jamaica and stopped transporting new recruits to the United States. Men already holding recruitment tickets were left stranded in Kingston "in a state of despondency."[7]

The pressure on Stanley to allow recruitment to resume was enormous both because Jamaicans were desperate to find work and because Jamaica's white rulers were desperate for the political patronage that might keep them in office. At the outbreak of the war, the vast majority of Jamaicans (about a million people out of a total population of 1.2 million) still eked out a living in the countryside, though they owned little of it (Richards 2002:342). Half of all the cultivated land in Jamaica was divided among just 1,400 mostly foreign landowners, the bulk of them American and British corporations (Taylor 1993:37–43; Williams 1942:49). Those who worked for these corporations earned wages so low and suffered conditions so dire that they were forced to supplement their meager wages with food they themselves grew, just as their slave forebears had done. Hired farmworkers were far outnumbered by small farmers who eked out a living on tiny plots—usually two acres or less. They produced most of what Jamaicans ate (Edwards 1961:26–34; McCoy and Wood 1982:15–18, 31–32, 70n9), but Jamaicans had to import everything else. That fragile economy was devastated when the war interrupted commercial shipping. The British government purchased the entire British West Indian sugar, coffee, citrus, and cocoa crops—salvaging the fortunes of Jamaica's foreign-born plantation owners—but it prohibited the use of scarce ships to transport bananas, which was the principal export crop of the island's peasant farmers (Matthews 1952:52–53). Jamaicans, who had to buy goods at inflated wartime prices with decreasing earnings, were desperate for cash.[8]

With land so inequitably distributed, Jamaicans had long sought work abroad. Indeed, leaving for opportunities in the United States, Cuba, Panama, and elsewhere had been practically a rite of passage, but those doors had long been shut (Putnam 2002 ; Thomas-Hope 1978:68). After the canal was completed in 1914, Panama wanted no more West Indians and even expelled some. A decade later, the United States passed the Johnson-Reed Act, which reduced the flow of US-bound immigrants to a trickle. The law restricted colonies to 1,000 immigrants each, effectively reducing Jamaican migration to the United States by 97 percent. Panama and Venezuela followed with restrictive legislation banning West Indians entirely. The Great Depression only made matters worse because many thousands of Jamaicans abroad were forced to return home, where few jobs awaited them (Blanshard 1947; Marshall 1987; Matthews 1952; Post 1978; Thomas-Hope 1978).

Returning migrants put pressure on Jamaican politicians both because they increased unemployment rates and because they brought trade union experience, nationalist ideas, and even revolutionary sentiments home with them. In 1938, on the heels of mass strikes in other parts of the British Caribbean, Jamaican plantation workers, dockworkers, and the urban unemployed launched full-scale rebellions for pay hikes, collective bargaining rights, and the franchise. Their protests were quickly and violently crushed, but news of the uprisings and the repression that followed strengthened anti-colonial forces in England. The result was the 1940 Colonial Development and Welfare Act, which, among other things, required colonial administrations to legalize trade unions in order to qualify for imperial assistance.

Jamaican unions soon spawned two new political parties—the Labour Party and the People's National Party—both of which called for more reforms and, in the case of the PNP, independence from Great Britain (Bolland 1995; Darwin 1988; Feuer 1984; Munroe 1983[1944]; Post 1978). Buoyed by this rapid change, black Jamaicans' expectations rose, but their hopes were soon dashed by the outbreak of war. "Conditions there are terrible," one man lamented. "The government is not interested in the poor man."[9]

Jamaica's wartime government was, in fact, far removed from the cares of "the poor man." The tiny electorate, which represented whites and the small "brown" middle class, chose only half the members of Jamaica's legislative council, who were known as "electives." The remaining "officials" were appointed by Jamaica's white governor, and only "officials" served on the governor's executive council, which saw its job as preserving the interests of its members' class. In 1942, the government's response to the wartime economic crisis was to restore public flogging for men caught stealing vegetables and fruit. It invoked the new statute nearly seven hundred times over the next three years (Blanshard 1947:90–91; Munroe 1983[1944]).[10]

The writing was, nonetheless, on the wall. The appointment of Oliver Stanley as the secretary of state to the British colonies signaled more reforms to come. A Tory and an imperialist, Stanley nevertheless believed that reform was essential to the survival of the empire. In the case of Jamaica, he demanded constitutional amendments requiring secret balloting, universal suffrage, and an increase in the number of elected seats on the legislative council. When these reforms went into effect in 1944, universal suffrage would increase Jamaica's electorate from 70,000 to 750,000, and those new voters would owe Jamaica's white rulers nothing (Blanshard 1947:94–97 ; Darwin 1988:3–68; Munroe 1983[1944]:25–26).

That prospect made Jamaica's wartime rulers positively gleeful at the idea of temporarily exporting as many as 100,000 unemployed black workers to the United States. Stanley may have been reluctant to agree to send Jamaicans to the US South, but Jamaica's electives, who were hanging on to power by the skin of their teeth, jumped at the idea of relieving Jamaica's growing social pressures without bringing lasting change. The migration scheme also appeared to be an ideal way to curry favor with the soon-to-be black electorate. Thus, in a last-ditch effort to hold on to political power, Jamaica's oligarchy formed a party, disingenuously naming it the Jamaican Democratic Party, and began courting the affections of Jamaica's black majority by personally distributing the tickets that entitled the holders to apply for farmwork in the United States (Blanshard 1947:94–97; Munroe 1983[1944]:36, 38).[11]

For all these reasons—destitution, a lack of outlets for emigrants, high expectations, and political patronage—the suspension of recruiting resulted in intense pressure on Stanley. The Jamaican press published heartbreaking tales of men who had secured recruitment tickets and spent what little money they had in order to travel to the port at Kingston for departure, only to discover that the program had been called off. Even the People's National Party, whose party organ, *Public Opinion*, had kept up a steady barrage of criticism against the program over the previous months, could not help but note how important it was as a relief measure. *Public Opinion* reported that workers still in the United States had collectively sent home £20,000 (US$100,000) in remittances in the month of June alone. The *Daily Gleaner* editorialized about the "real and serious difficulty" of sending Jamaicans to the US South: "[They were] bred and reared in an environment of flexible and subtle but illegal discrimination [and] may react to ironbound racial discrimination in a variety of ways, some of them unpleasant or even alarming." But, the *Gleaner* reasoned, "if the men who volunteer for such a trial are made fully aware...of the realities of 'down South' conditions...the experiment might end satisfactorily." "Perhaps, too, as a racial experiment," the *Gleaner* added, "it may prove instructive, certainly enlightening."[12]

After four months of holding his ground, Stanley began to weaken. Not only were Bahamian guestworkers already laboring in Florida under a separately negotiated contract, Stanley learned, but US citizens in Puerto Rico, also a sugar-producing island, were clamoring to be included in the temporary importation scheme. Concerned that failure to comply with US demands might mean the loss of all opportunities for Jamaican guestworkers in the United States, Stanley finally relented in September 1943. Colonial Office officials met secretly with Jamaican and US officials to negotiate an agreement under which Jamaicans would be allowed "to proceed south" to Florida's sugar plantations.[13]

The change in the program was immediately evident. Transferred from northern farms to Clewiston, Florida, to cut sugarcane for US Sugar, Jamaicans were greeted not by marching bands and curious townspeople but by gun-toting labor bosses who threatened guestworkers with physical violence. One carried a swagger stick, Leaford Williams recalled, which later proved to be a folded whip. "You boys come on over heya," Williams recalled the man saying. "I am trouble." "We had just met our enemies," he later wrote. "We were just a few more 'negras' joining farm hands on the sugar plantation" (Williams 1996:97). In Florida, it was soon apparent, a "Negro" laborer was a "Negro" laborer, funny accent and British citizenship notwithstanding. No longer were Jamaicans told to expect "a friendly English-speaking people," with habits and customs "somewhat different" from their own. In Florida, they were warned to adapt to the dictates of Jim Crow.[14]

To ensure that the first 800 Jamaicans shifted southward did in fact abide by the customs of the Jim Crow South, the chief liaison insisted that the men agree to what New York's *Amsterdam News* dubbed the "Jim Crow Creed." "A distinction is made in Florida with colored people," chief liaison Herbert MacDonald warned Jamaicans on their way to Florida, "and you must be careful and endeavor to help the position, as by your conduct you will be judged." Implicitly warning them away from interactions with white women, he noted, "There will be ample opportunity for you to make friends among the colored people, as every city, town and village has its colored section." "You are free to purchase wherever you wish," he added, "but there are certain places of amusement, restaurants and bars where you will not be allowed." Instead of noting the nondiscrimination clause in their contracts, MacDonald informed the men of the new "misconduct and indiscipline clause," which gave the US government the right to terminate the contract "if the worker misconduct[ed] himself." Those who refused to behave, he warned, would be turned over to the Immigration and Naturalization Service (INS) for "repatriation."[15]

After spending five months in communities all over the US North, where they were treated more like Allied soldiers than black farmworkers, Jamaicans were horrified by the conditions they faced in Florida. In some camps, men discovered that they needed passes to leave camp, and bells summoned them to daily roll calls (Reid 1998:197). The parallels to slavery were hard to miss.[16] Arriving at the hot, squalid barracks built to house them in Clewiston, Stanley Wilson and fifty-eight other Jamaican men discovered that they were expected to sleep on bare mattresses, without sheets, pillows, or blankets. When they complained, the camp superintendent did not scramble to find linens. His response was, "Pillows!... You aren't serious! This is the first time in my life that I ever heard niggers slept with pillows, too." Mosquitoes, flies, snakes, and "deadly insects" plagued the camp, Wilson wrote home to *Public Opinion*, the Kingston newspaper published by the democratic socialist People's National Party. Their living quarters were "absolutely intolerable," and the latrine was in an "unimaginable" state of filth. While hard at work cutting sugarcane, moreover, men were given rank water to drink. If they wanted the same water that the company's white mill workers drank, Wilson wrote, they had to pay thirty-five cents a gallon for it—almost an hour's pay. "Workers made the strongest representations" against these conditions, Wilson reported, "but could secure no redress."[17] When nothing was done, Wilson and his co-workers went on strike, which got them thrown into the Palm Beach County jail and then deported. In the North, Jamaicans' British citizenship and "almost Oxfordian" accents resulted in special treatment; in the South, guestworkers' foreignness just meant that they could be threatened with deportation.

Wilson and his fifty-eight co-workers were not the only Jamaicans who refused to "abide by southern customs." In October 1943, ninety-three Jamaicans "refused to get off the busses," according to Herbert MacDonald, and when they did, "they refused to carry their own luggage." When they got to the mess hall, "they scraped their food on the ground & trampled on it" and "abused everyone & everything in sight." The men were quickly shipped off to the Dade City jail to await deportation. Within two weeks, the number of Jamaicans sitting in Florida jails rose to 700.[18] The *Pittsburgh Courier* reported that, in October, 800–900 Jamaican workers were taken to INS offices and were later transferred to common jails in Miami, Tampa, and Raiford, Florida, for refusing "to sign the Jim Crow agreement forced upon them."[19]

Workers' protests did not, however, result in reform, or an end to US Sugar's access to Jamaican workers. Those slated for repatriation were quickly replaced by new Jamaican transfers from the North, and in 1944, Jamaicans harvested 65 percent of Florida's sugarcane. Still, the fact that the program continued did not mean that those who stayed were content with the treatment they received. Fitzroy Parkinson recalled that when a white supervisor threatened to kick one of them, "everybody said no and everybody stopped working." The workers demanded that the head liaison officer come down from Washington, DC, asserting that the supervisors "could not treat the Jamaicans as they treated the natives." Instead of resolving the conflict, however, the liaison who arrived told the men that nothing would be done. After the sugar crop was in, they could go home or go north (Johnson 1995:38–39). Indeed, despite Jamaicans' continued militancy, there is no evidence that their complaints in Florida were ever redressed. A liaison would be summoned if one were available, but US Sugar's field bosses were not accustomed to negotiating with black workers and they were not about to start.

In early 1944, when the importation program expanded to include other southern states, Jamaicans discovered that the problems they were experiencing were not confined to Florida. Nathaniel Allen wrote to his mother from Delaware that work was scarce and dust plentiful: "No latrines, no water to bathe, no beds to sleep in, no lights to sleep with and see at nights [*sic*] and worse than all, no work to do." The most he had earned was $2.50 a day, out of which $1 was deducted for meals and $.50 for rent. Since another $1 a day was withheld as "voluntary" savings, he received no money at all. He was sleeping "on a bit of board on the floor with only a blanket to put on it." "What this thing is going to lead up to I don't know," he wrote, "but what I can tell you is that every one is getting panicky." "Mam, you can't imagine," he wrote in closing. "This is a one man's place. Every where you look belongs to no one else but him, so then he runs the place and fixes the rates the people must work for.... I am not working because working here is only putting money in some one else's pocket."[20]

DEPORTABLE LABOR

Like domestic workers before them, foreign workers tried to organize to protest conditions, but their attempts were aborted by arrest and deportation. When a white camp manager reported Jamaican James Morrison to the local police as an "agitator," Morrison was arrested and held at the Vienna, Maryland, police station without so much as a warrant or a hearing. Though he was eventually released, he noted that two other Jamaicans had been deported as "trouble-makers."[21] George Winston reported from the Pahokee Labor Supply Center in Florida in April 1944, "Approx. 75 workers held a strike at one celery packing house demanding 75 cents/hour against the 50 cents/hour paid them which was the prevailing wage at that time." But the "strike was caused by 3 workers only," he wrote, so after "a hearing was held for the 3 workers involved...they were turned over to the Border Patrol for deportation." No other trouble had occurred since, he noted tellingly.[22]

Increasingly, US officials acted not as defenders of foreign war workers, as they had just a few months earlier, but as suppliers of labor and enforcers of workplace discipline. The WFA blacklisted those accused of "indiscipline" (a term left undefined in guestworkers' contracts), and the INS took responsibility for apprehending and repatriating guestworkers who tried to change farms or to leave farmwork altogether. "We have had quite a few workers go A.W.O.L, leaving one camp and going to another and being taken in w/o official transfer from either ext. or management of the area from which they go," reported Roy Litchfield, the manager of the Goulds, Florida, Federal Labor Camp in January 1944. "In this area," he noted, "we happen to be fortunate in having immigration officers to help us out on this problem."[23]

Within months of Jamaicans' arrival in the United States, in other words, their status had sunk, from exotic British war workers to "alien negro laborers," and their citizenship, their liaison officers, and US responsibility for their welfare did not protect them from the perils of farm labor relations in the southern countryside.[24] By the end of the war, federal negligence and employer recalcitrance had begun to fashion the perfect immigrant, Jim Crow–style: the sort of immigrant who knew from day one that deportation was the price of protest.

THE WEAKNESS OF STATE ADVOCACY

The colonial officials who served as liaisons still traveled from farm to farm, trying to redress workers' complaints, but with thousands of unemployed Jamaicans desperate to get into the program, Jamaican officials at home tended to dismiss those complaints. So many men were clamoring to get into the program that in April 1944, "bedlam, and minor damage to property" resulted when police used batons to beat back 3,000 people trying to get the 180 available tickets at the Port Maria recruiting station in Jamaica (Reid 1998:171–172). As Jamaica's unemployment problems worsened and as remittances flowing back from the United States grew, jobs seemed far more important to Jamaican officials than justice. It was simply easier to replace "troublemakers" than it was to identify and eliminate the cause of the trouble.

A new constitution, universal suffrage, and the first democratic elections in Jamaica's history did nothing to undermine the political and economic importance of the labor recruitment program in Jamaica. The Jamaican Labour Party, the political wing of the Bustamante Industrial Trade Union, swept the polls in 1944, completely unseating the Democratic Party and winning twenty-two seats to the PNP's five.[25] Although the Labour Party had earlier complained about the Democratic Party's control of the recruitment ticket distribution process, the Labour Party readily assumed control of the system as it was. The migration program and the patronage system it had spawned became permanent features of Jamaican political life (Munroe 1983[1944]:42).

Though Jamaica's first black government happily inherited the patronage system that the Democratic Party had built around the recruitment system, it did try to improve conditions in the United States. In April 1946, the Labour government responded to Jamaicans' complaints of racist treatment in Florida by withdrawing all Jamaican contract workers from the state, but its protest collapsed when the government of Barbados quickly offered to take up the slack.[26] There seemed to be little the Jamaican government could do in guestworkers' behalf, short of removing all Jamaican workers from the principal industry that employed them.

Cindy Hahamovitch

GOING PRIVATE

The US Emergency Farm Labor Supply Program was supposed to have ended when World War II did, but the nation's largest producers of fruit, cotton, vegetables, and sugar were unwilling to give it up. Exiting the war far better organized than they went into it, agricultural employers' organizations lobbied Congress, which extended the emergency program and allowed it to grow. By 1947, there were some 220,000 Mexican guestworkers in the United States (up from 62,000) and some 50,000 British West Indians and Bahamians (up from 43,800).[27] Jamaicans and Bahamians had been supplemented by Barbadians, British Guyanans, British Hondurans, and others.

Change was coming, however. In 1947, Congress privatized the migration program, voting to dismantle the War Food Administration and with it the Emergency Farm Labor Supply Program. However, the various labor importation schemes were not dead, but transformed.[28] Congress had not banned the importation of foreign farmworkers; it had simply banned the federal government from footing the bill. The ninth proviso of the 1917 Immigration Act still gave the INS the authority to admit unlimited numbers of "otherwise inadmissible" foreigners on a temporary basis, so long as the secretary of labor gave his assurance that local workers were unavailable and so long as employers were prepared to put up bonds to ensure that foreign workers' stays would indeed be temporary.[29] Jubilant, US Sugar shared the good news with apple, tobacco, and other producers who relied on large numbers of Caribbean workers, and together they launched the privately run but federally sanctioned guestworker program that the United States still has today (Kramer 1966:1–3).[30]

In the summer of 1947, the federal government disposed of the fifty-two permanent and seventy temporary migrant labor camps it had built to house domestic workers during the Depression and the war, selling them to growers associations for just $1 apiece. "All of the farm labor camps built by the government for the use of farmworkers and their families, [are] now in the hands of the big farmers," noted the *Union Labor News*. "Rents have greatly increased, health and sanitation services have been abolished, and all child care services are at an end" (Kramer 1966:51).[31] In December, federal officials stopped recruiting and transporting foreign workers, washing their hands of responsibility for negotiating, signing, or guaranteeing the terms of foreign workers' contracts. In their place, growers associations began bargaining directly with foreign governments, which recruited workers for them. Instead of being contracted by the federal government, guestworkers were now bound to the particular employers or employer associations that advanced their fares. Classified as "non-immigrants" by

16

the INS, postwar guestworkers had no right to stay in the United States, nor could they be reclassified as permanent immigrants. Temporary workers would be permanently temporary.

Any hope that the guestworker programs would help to uplift conditions for domestic farmworkers in the United States died with the birth of federally sanctioned, private recruiting. With Uncle Sam out of the foreign labor supply business, growers negotiated new contracts that passed costs formerly paid by the US government onto the workers themselves. Instead of traveling to the United States on navy ships at US taxpayers' expense, for example, Caribbean workers now came to the United States on chartered planes, working off their fares in the fields. Employers paid workers' return fares, but only if they completed the season without incident, which made airfare a tool of labor discipline. Housing was no longer free either. Growers made payroll deductions for housing and food, plus 3 percent for medical insurance and another 3 percent to pay the salaries of the Caribbean liaisons and to defray employers' own recruiting and management costs. Another 10 percent of workers' pay was withheld for them in government banks at home to encourage the workers to return at the end of their contract. Jamaican workers collected their money with great difficulty because their government wanted to hold it as long as possible. Jamaica's government, not the workers, got the interest (Kramer 1966:21–22).[32]

Caribbean guestworkers were neither party to these new terms nor happy with them. George Winston, the federal manager of the Clewiston, Florida, camp, noted in one of his final reports, "The Jamaican workers are very anxious concerning their new contract, a copy of which has been read and explained to them by supervisors in each camp. There has been a great deal of discussion of this matter, the general feeling being one of dissatisfaction as to [the] contents of the contract." Some Jamaican sugarcane cutters went on strike to protest the new contract; others jumped their contracts and took their chances as illegal immigrants. "It is my opinion," Winston concluded, "that if this document is presented in its present form there will be a wholesale movement of Jamaicans being repatriated who might otherwise remain and work."[33] But Winston underestimated just how much Jamaicans needed the work. If some laborers quit and returned home in protest, others would be waiting to take their place.

Indeed, with Jamaica's population swelling by 30 percent between the census of 1943 and the next in 1960, the Jamaican countryside was crowded with willing recruits. Many rural people were migrating to Kingston and its urban environs, looking for work in construction, new assembly plants, or domestic service and hoping for amenities like running water and flush toilets. But most "country people" lived in the parish of their birth, and most had only a few years of formal education, if any. Their prospects of earning enough money to pay their children's school fees or to buy more land or livestock were slim. Nearly half of all men working in agriculture earned less than £50 a year (approximately US$250) (Francis 1963:1–22).

It is no surprise, then, that when radio stations announced that recruiters were coming to a regional recruitment center on a specific day, ten men would arrive for every job available, and those were just the ones who had managed to secure recruitment tickets from a local MP (or buy one off someone who had) (Kramer 1966:35). In 1960, one in forty Jamaican men between the ages of eighteen and thirty-nine headed for the United States through the farmworker program, a far cry from the one in six who had done so during World War II. But out in the country, the program's impact was even more profound. Perhaps one in twenty Jamaican agricultural workers spent part of 1960 in the United States under contract, and fully half of all Jamaican farmworkers lined up for a chance to go (Kramer 1966:12).[34] For rural Jamaicans, the farmworker program was their best and possibly their only chance of getting a little ahead, of earning wages three times higher than they could make at home doing similar work, of "paying some smalls," as one man put it.[35]

RACE TO THE BOTTOM

Jamaicans were not the only ones dependent on agricultural work in the United States. Jamaican farmworkers found themselves in competition with domestic workers: the white, black, Puerto Rican, and Mexican Americans who still made up the vast majority of the US agricultural workforce. They also vied against other guestworkers: Mexican braceros; vegetable workers from the Bahamas; experienced sugarcane cutters from the unionized islands of Barbados, St. Kitts, Nevis, and Antigua; and British Guyanans from the South American coast.[36] And they competed with undocumented workers, whose numbers were exploding as discontented braceros skipped their contracts or returned without authorization.

As guestworkers, domestic workers, and undocumented immigrants fanned out across the United States in search of work, the competition increased. Four and a half million Mexicans came to the United States as guestworkers—braceros—from 1942 to 1964. As the number of Mexicans exploded in Texas in the 1950s, when Mexico lifted its boycott of the state, Texans of Mexican descent—known as tejanos—were forced to leave the area in search of less crowded fields. The tejanos headed north along well-worn routes to the Midwest but also east to the Atlantic coast's "migrant stream," where they competed against black and white native farmworkers and Caribbean guestworkers.[37] Braceros competed with undocumented Mexicans, many of whom were former braceros who had walked away from their contracts in frustration. In 1949, the INS reported that it had "located" almost 280,000 unauthorized immigrant farm laborers, at a time when there were just 107,000 braceros in the country. The following year, the number of braceros was only 67,500, whereas the total number of "wetbacks" located had reached almost half a million. By 1954, the number of known unauthorized immigrants exceeded a million, outnumbering braceros threefold (Craig 1971:58). In the East, Jamaicans and other British West Indian guestworkers monopolized Florida's sugarcane harvest, but they also made inroads into apple orchards along the Appalachian Trail, pushing out white "fruit tramps."

Growers' ability to switch workforces rapidly served as a form of labor discipline. For example, growers chased the National Farm Labor Union (NFLU) out of the citrus industry by hiring 2,000 Bahamian guestworkers. History repeated itself in 1951 when Bahamians were used a second time to undermine a union campaign.[38] In most cases, however, it was not so much real competition as the threat of competition that gave growers the upper hand in negotiations with sending governments and individual farmworkers. In 1953, for example, A. G. H. Gardner-Brown of the Colonial Office of the Bahamas reported that growers responded to his efforts to negotiate on behalf of Bahamians by pointing out "the ease of getting labour from Puerto Rico."[39] This sort of competition undermined the ability and willingness of individual state actors to advocate for their citizens. Jamaican liaisons who had been quite vigilant in workers' defense during the war began to spend at least as much time trying to protect "Jamaicans'" jobs as they did advocating for their rights. In May 1952, Herbert MacDonald reported gleefully, "The experiment to use Puerto Rican workers in Connecticut was…backfiring. Over twenty of these workers have gone AWOL within the last few days, and they have called a strike and have demanded hot lunches." "We shall be watching this with much interest," he added.[40] It did not seem to occur to MacDonald that he might have demanded hot lunches too.

In 1951, the various British West Indian governments closed ranks to improve their bargaining position vis-à-vis US growers. After the Windward Islands of Grenada, St. Lucia, St. Vincent, and Dominica joined the farmworker program that year, the sending governments of the British West Indies organized the Regional Labour Board, charged with representing British West Indian workers in negotiations with US employers (Kramer 1966:7–8). They also consolidated the various liaison services into the

British West Indies Central Labour Organization (WICLO). Instead of each government going its own way and trying to secure more jobs for its citizens by underbidding the others, the Regional Labour Board negotiated one contract for all and divided the jobs among the sending nations based on an agreed-upon formula (as the most populous country in the British West Indies, Jamaica got the bulk of the jobs).

The advent of the Regional Labour Board prevented British West Indian nations from undercutting one another, but the problem of competition among farmworker groups persisted. The Bahamas, which is not in the West Indies, remained outside the Regional Labour Board's "trust," as did Puerto Rico and Mexico, the colossus among guestworker-sending nations. Thus, growers' ability to play one national group off against another remained long after the Regional Labour Board's formation. In 1952, for example, when an employer refused to dismiss two white supervisors on a Florida farm who had assaulted some guestworkers, Brigadier Buxton Randall, the head of the Bahamian program, withdrew all the Bahamians employed by that grower and refused to send more. Instead of apologizing and promising better behavior, the grower simply contacted Herbert MacDonald, who sent West Indians in their place. When Randall complained to MacDonald, MacDonald refused to withdraw the West Indian workers, arguing that the employer had "no doubt" learned "his lesson." Though MacDonald noted in his report that he regretted the incident, he could not help bragging, "Our B.W.I. workers are…superior workers to the Bahamians."[41]

Like MacDonald, the liaison officers under him got into the spirit of competition and spent an increasing amount of time trying to get their charges to work harder and more efficiently. Liaison Charles Browne found the 340 men at "Mr. Hoyt's" in Leachville, Arkansas, to be "in high spirits," but when Hoyt complained that "the men were not making an effort to learn to pick cotton," Browne checked the payroll records and determined that the men were marking time until their transfer to Florida. To get them to work harder, Browne suggested that Hoyt send the best pickers to Florida first, so as not to reward the slackers. "This notice caused an immediate jump in production the following day," he reported.[42]

Fear of losing "West Indians' jobs" to competing groups of workers made the liaisons desperate to settle disputes, even if that meant settling them in employers' favor. In 1952, Joffre C. David, the general manager of the Florida Fruit and Vegetable Association, wrote to Herbert MacDonald, thanking him for resolving "the incident" at the Harlem Heights Labor Camp in Winter Garden, Florida, "before the CIO or other opponents of the foreign labor program could capitalize on it." There would always be a "small number of workers...temperamentally unfit or emotionally unstable [who will] create trouble," David remarked, "[so it was] important that these men be weeded out as soon as they are found, because they are the ones who aggravate the employers or their foremen and who create dissatisfaction among the other workers." "It has been our experience," he continued, "that the longer these types of individuals are permitted to remain among the rank and file of workers, the worse the situation gets, and their removal invariably clears the atmosphere and everybody is happy again." Listing the four men "properly repatriated for cause," David reminded MacDonald that they were to be barred "forever" from future recruitment for work in Florida.[43] Rather than support workers' militancy, in other words, West Indian liaisons had become enforcers of labor discipline.

The more liaison officers defended their charges' jobs against encroachment, the less inclined they were to take on growers who were abusive or who violated workers' contracts, though the workers were paying the liaisons to do precisely that. The liaisons could have withheld offshore workers from growers who behaved badly, but this almost never happened. Interviewed in 1966, Herbert MacDonald's successor, Harold Edwards, could recall only three occasions when WICLO withdrew workers from particular employers (two of which involved growers threatening workers with guns). WICLO did sometimes ask growers to remove particular foremen, but if WICLO did not take the workers' part, the workers had no other avenues of appeal (Kramer 1966:22–23).

Rapidly, the liaisons lost what little credibility they had with workers, an advent that growers happily abetted. Employers never involved liaisons in disputes unless the employers knew that they were in the right, explained a section foreman for the Sugar Cane Growers Cooperative in 1966: "The liaison officer is the worker's man...he has no choice except to back us in disputes. If we've messed up, we won't call him. Since he's got a contract to uphold, the liaison officer ends up backing us." As a result, workers tended to see the liaisons as company men. "Most of the workers we employ won't deal with a liaison officer," the foreman continued, "because they know when he comes he's going to back us. The liaison officer is a man caught in the middle" (Kramer 1966:23). Workers tended to be less forgiving: "The liaison officer, who...should...stand by your side...the[y] do not care."[44]

By the mid-1950s, farm employers were enjoying a sort of international variant of an early morning shape-up, at which workers vie to get on growers' trucks. If one nation's workers refused to get on board, another's would. Each group of workers—braceros, unauthorized immigrants, West Indians,

Bahamians, Puerto Ricans, and domestic workers—competed against the others, all in a race to the bottom.

MAKING TEMPORARY WORKERS PERMANENTLY TEMPORARY

In 1952, this system was institutionalized as the H-2 program, part of the McCarran-Walter Act, which further restricted the flow of immigrants to the United States (Jamaica's quota shrank from 1,000 to 105) and which relegated unskilled workers to a long list of excluded categories. Yet, the law reauthorized growers' private recruiting of temporary farm laborers under Title I General, section 101, 15(H)(ii). From 1952 on, non-Mexican temporary workers in agriculture were known as H-2 workers (the *A* and *B*, which now indicate agricultural and non-agricultural programs, would not be added until 1986).[45] Nothing in the new law changed the terms of workers' contracts or the imbalance of power between sending countries and US employers.

Jamaica's separation from Great Britain a decade later only increased the importance of the guestworker program for ordinary Jamaicans and for Jamaica's government. Jamaica's black majority celebrated its new independence with jubilation, but England left the infant nation with few resources besides pride and people. There was little industry, no social security system, no unemployment insurance, not even a public school system beyond the first few grades of elementary school. The sugar industry was moribund, and agriculture—the nation's biggest employer—still relied primarily on small peasant farms. Jamaicans were proud of their new university and the island's infant bauxite industry, but both made little difference to the average citizen. The unemployment rate was estimated at 25 or 50 percent of the workforce—depending on whether one counted subsistence farmers and woefully underemployed casual laborers as unemployed. More than ever, Jamaica needed the jobs created by the guestworker program and the dollars guestworkers sent home.[46]

To make matters worse, Britain's Parliament celebrated Jamaican independence by passing the restrictionist Commonwealth Immigrants Act, which shut England's doors to immigrants from former colonies in the Caribbean and South Asia, except for the immediate relatives of those who had already made it under the wire. Migrants from white former colonies, like Ireland, were not restricted by the act, but Jamaica lost a key outlet for its population and a key source of foreign currency. Jamaican officials presumed (reasonably) that the United States would take up the slack, since independent nations in the Western Hemisphere were not subject to US immigration quotas. But US officials delayed lifting Jamaica's 100-person quota, fearing a flood of poor black migrants to the United States. Jamaican leaders' hopes were buoyed in 1965 by news of the Hart-Cellar immigration reform bill, which promised to remove the United States' old discriminatory quota system and create equal quotas for all countries. But although Hart-Cellar passed, raising Jamaica's annual immigration quota from 105 to 20,000, the US Congress delayed its implementation for three years, while Jamaica's urban poor rioted over unemployment (Lindsey 1995).

The H-2 program came under attack in the United States just as Jamaica was losing its UK outlet. US farmworker unions had been lobbying against growers' access to guestworkers since World War II, but by the early sixties, they had finally gained strength and powerful allies. In 1964, the Mexican bracero program ended, and Willard Wirtz, the secretary of labor under Lyndon B. Johnson, was seriously considering refusing to authorize the importation of H-2 workers as well. While deciding, he restricted the program to the sugar and apple industries, raised guestworkers' wages, and demanded that growers pay workers' airfare to the United States and the cost of their housing. Domestic farmworkers took up the labor slack, proving to Wirtz that guestworkers had not been necessary.

He was not so sure that this was true in sugarcane, however. Calling it "the worst job in the world" (Hahamovitch 2011:147), he doubted that even the most desperate Americans would take work cutting cane. Florida's sugar industry, which had still not succeeded in mechanizing the harvest process, was more desperate for labor than ever. Because relations between the Fidel Castro regime and the United States had reached a head in early 1960, the United States had embargoed all Cuban exports, including sugar. But Cuba had been supplying half of all the sugar Americans consumed. Lifting restrictions on domestic sugar production that had been in place since the Great Depression, Congress frantically urged Floridian growers to turn over their acreage to cane. US Sugar immediately doubled its productive capacity, building a second mill equal to its first (Salley 1984:23–24, 27). Cuban exiles snapped up Florida farms, and vegetable growers and cattle ranchers transformed themselves into sugar planters almost overnight. The total acreage of cane in Florida grew nearly eightfold, from less than 36,000 acres in 1955 to more than 276,000 in 1973 (Hollander 2008:180–186; McCoy and Wood 1982:3; Salley 1984:47–78). Yet, Secretary Wirtz was considering cutting off the sugar industry's only source of cane cutters.

Ultimately, the Cold War saved the H-2 program. Jamaica's acting prime minister, Donald Sangster, had little leverage in negotiations with Florida's growers over the terms of the H-2 program, but he could play Jamaica's "Cuba card" to save it. He insisted repeatedly that if the farmworker program ended, his government would fall and the socialist PNP would come to power. The PNP, he warned, would bring Jamaica into Castro's orbit. Although that was not a very likely prospect, Jamaica was certainly unstable in the early 1960s. Riots in 1965 were followed by a massive strike wave, then more riots (Hahamovitch 2011:147–150; Lindsey 1995:195).[47] Under intense pressure at home, Jamaica's acting prime minister made his case in angry conversations with the US consul. Unless Jamaica's farmworker program was retained, Sangster insisted, its infinitesimal share of the US sugar quota enlarged, and its immigration quota expanded, potentially "explosive" problems could "seriously jeopardize U.S. interest[s]."[48]

Sangster's threat might have been overblown, but it effectively undercut Secretary Wirtz's reform effort. In the heyday of the Cold War, Jamaica had a measure of power as a bulwark against communism in the region. When the US Labor Department was "too tough on the program," John R. Kanline, the US State Department's chief of Jamaican affairs explained, the Jamaican ambassador would call the State Department, and the State Department would call the Department of Labor to set up a meeting between the ambassador, Secretary Wirtz, and perhaps the chief liaison officer. Wirtz would be warned to call off his dogs (Kramer 1966:81).[49] Wirtz ultimately let the H-2 program live, though he kept his new regulations in place.

RISK THE TRUCK

Although Wirtz had raised wages and required employers to pay for housing and transportation, his reforms had little effect. Wage hikes rarely translated into bigger paychecks. Because growers paid cane cutters by the row, not the hour, it was easy for unscrupulous employers to circumvent wage hikes by simply dropping their row prices. Growers were supposed to pay "build-up pay" if men paid by the row made less than the hourly minimum, but cane companies got around that requirement, according to liaison officer Walter Comrie, by training the "ticket writers" who recorded what the men accomplished each day to record fewer hours than the men actually worked. The result was that men appeared to earn more per hour than they actually did.[50] All sugar producers shaved hours from workers' timecards to greater and lesser degrees, Comrie reported in his records (Kramer 1966:41–51).[51]

The cane companies looked for other ways to cut their costs as well. According to Comrie, US Sugar responded to a 1963 wage hike by increasing the amount it deducted for meals from each man's pay. Comrie protested this deduction in a letter to the chief liaison, Harold Edwards, noting that "the increase of the hourly wage...as handed down by the Department of Labor was intended to be borne by the sugar producing employers from their profits," but Edwards ignored him.[52] "Sugar cane used to be one of our best crops," the chief liaison from the Bahamas recalled. "I can remember when our men at Fellsmere made $16 a day and knocked off at 2 p.m. But when the U.S. Agricultural Department...raised the minimum hourly wage for cane harvesting to $1.15, production demands on the men went up far more than wages as cane growers tried to get more work out of the men." The Bahamas withdrew its men. "It isn't worthwhile working for nothing," the liaison noted (Kramer 1966:10, 14).

Lacking support from their home governments and from the chief liaison, guestworkers took matters into their own hands, requesting higher row prices and striking when they did not get them. The consequences were dire. In the 1965–1966 season, according to a liaison officer, 600 of the 5,200 offshore workers imported by just one of the two recruiting associations were "breached" and repatriated, most as a result of wage disputes.[53]

Ironically, when Jamaica's conservative Labour Party fell from power in the early 1970s, the triumphant PNP was just as inclined to defend the program against US reform efforts. Although for years his party had criticized the Labour Party's use of the H-2 program as a source of patronage, Jamaican prime minister Michael Manley admitted that under his government, the distribution of farmworker tickets remained a patronage system: "Local members of parliament within a region find it convenient to recommend different people from year to year, all as a rather superficial way of... scoring some political points." The program retained its economic importance, Marley noted. The sending governments could just "walk away from it," but "so far all Jamaican governments, looking at the level of poverty... have felt that on balance it was in the interests of people to take advantage of this program." However, he admitted "[they] have frankly faced the bargaining in...a completely unequal situation."[54] He did not mention that his government collected guestworkers' mandatory savings in US dollars, kept the interest, and paid workers in Jamaican dollars at unfavorable exchange rates. The men would have done better exchanging the money on the street themselves, remarked *Palm Beach Post* reporter Beth McLeod.[55]

In early 1974, two tragic accidents seemed to underline Jamaica's gross inferiority in its negotiations with US employers. In the first incident, a Gulf & Western truck overturned in Florida, injuring thirty-six guestworkers. The cane cutters had been standing in the truck bed and carrying their razor-sharp cane knives, even though two weeks earlier, the US Labor Department had ordered the cane companies to use trucks with fixed seating. Jamaica's government responded to the accident with silence. Three weeks later, another G&W truck rolled over, this time injuring all eighty-six passengers, one fatally. The US Department of Labor fined G&W a total of $1,800. Unable to remain silent a second time, Manley sent Jamaica's ambassador to Florida's sugar region. There, he was asked by a reporter about the problem of growers' lack of compliance with the Labor Department's regulations regarding trucks. His response was telling: if a man came to him with a choice between not working or being transported standing upright in the back of a grower's truck and asked his personal opinion of what the man should do, he would have to tell him, "Risk the truck."[56]

THE GLOBAL RACE TO THE BOTTOM

The Jamaican example reveals the many reasons that sending nations' efforts to manage migration have been so feeble. The magnetic pull of remittance dollars, the prospect of foreign exchange, and poor people's desperate need for jobs all made Jamaican officials willing to ignore violations of workers' contracts. Jobs almost always trumped justice. On the one occasion in 1946 when Jamaica tried to put its foot down, its protest was undercut by Barbados, which was equally desperate to secure jobs for its people. Because receiving countries could pick from among the world's poor, they could pit one poor country against another in a race to the bottom.

One might sensibly counter that, as a small and new republic, Jamaica was particularly incapable of acting forcefully in its negotiations with the United States. Yet, what is remarkable is how typical Jamaica's experience was of other guestworker-sending countries. Mexico was much bigger and a far more important US trading partner, but its efforts to bargain on behalf of Mexican braceros usually failed too. Mexico wanted US growers to recruit from deep within the Mexican state so that the benefits of the program would be spread around and so that prospective migrants would not create shantytowns near the US border. US growers found it cheaper, however, to drive to the border and contract labor there or simply to hire undocumented workers they found in the United States. US officials backed US growers, dealing with the nation's illegal immigration by legalizing apprehended, unauthorized migrants as guestworkers. It called this policy, which completely undercut Mexico's efforts to set the terms of the bracero program, "drying out the wetbacks." By 1950, the number of braceros who had been legalized and "paroled"—without Mexico's consent—

outnumbered those recruited in Mexico five to one (Calavita 1992:2; Galarza 1964:63).[57] On two occasions, US officials undercut Mexico's negotiating power much more dramatically. In 1949 and 1954, negotiations between US and Mexican officials failed and the bilateral agreement lapsed when US employers would not agree to wage hikes and a written minimum wage. On both occasions, US officials simply opened the border to Mexican migrants, signing them up as guestworkers on the growers' terms against the Mexican government's express opposition (Craig 1971:69–70; Galarza 1964:49–51; Garcia 1980:75–77; Rochester 1940:151).[58]

The problem of inequality between nations was not particular to North America either. By the 1980s, there were far more guestworkers per capita in the Middle East and Asia than there were in North America, but there, too, sending governments exerted little authority over their migrants' conditions. The scale of the programs exacerbated the problem. In 1993, for example, the Philippines' Overseas Workers Welfare Administration had just thirty-one labor attachés, twenty welfare officers, and twenty coordinators to deal with the complaints of 4.2 million migrant workers in 120 countries (Castles and Miller 1998:149).

Competition among labor-exporting nations for the same jobs undermined standards everywhere. Just as Jamaica tried to boycott Florida in 1946, only to capitulate when Barbadians stepped in to take the jobs, Bangladesh and Pakistan tried to ban the outmigration of female servants in 1983 in response to reports of abusive employers in Persian Gulf states. Indonesian women took up the slack with the encouragement of their government, forcing the Bangladeshi and Pakistani governments to capitulate. In 1986, both recommended *lowering* the wages of their nationals in the Middle East to keep them competitive (Chin 1986:102; Gardezi 1997).

As long as no one scratches too hard at the surface, guestworker programs appear to be a sensible and legitimate way to manage migration. But guestworkers' contracts and the presence of consuls, liaisons, and worker welfare offices only add a patina of legality to what are, in essence, employer-dominated labor recruitment schemes. Guestworker programs cannot be managed by sending nations because those nations have too much to lose if they push too hard. Faced with losing access to foreign work programs or workers having to get in the back of an employer's truck as part of an international shape-up, poor nations have little choice: they will risk the truck.

Notes

1. This chapter is based on Hahamovitch 2011.

2. Public Records Office (hereafter, PRO), Colonial Office (hereafter, CO) 859/95/11; Bahamas, no. 52, Message from His Royal Highness the Governor to the Speaker and Members of the Honourable the House of Assembly [*sic*], PRO, WO 166/522.

3. *Waterbury Republican* (June 27, 1943):14.

4. *Daily Gleaner* (May 26, June 4–7, August 16, 1943).

5. Leaford Williams, interview by author, November 18, 2002.

6. Sir A. Richard, Jamaica, to Secretary of State for the Colonies, June 29, 1943, and Anglo-American Caribbean Commission to Secretary of State for the Colonies, July 7, 1943, PRO, CO 318, 448/11, Recruitment of Labour for U.S.; Report to Mr. Middleton, July 1, 1944, PRO, CO 318/460/1; *Public Opinion* (September 25, 1943):1; *Chicago Bee* (July 11, 1943):2.

7. *Public Opinion* (May 17, 1943):1; *Daily Gleaner* (May 17 and 19, 1943).

8. *Public Opinion* (January 24, 1942).

9. *Amsterdam News* (June 5, 1943):13; James W. Vann, August 1942, general correspondence, box 16, file RP-M-85-183, monthly reports, RG 96, National Archives and Records Administration (hereafter, NARA); Correspondence, 1943–1944, box 75, file 4-FLT-R57, RG 224, NARA.

10. Parliamentary debates (Hansard), Great Britain, Parliament, House of Lords, 166:475.

11. PRO, CO 859, 46/16, 12251/1, Minutes of Meetings, 1943.

12. *Daily Gleaner* (September 22, 1943):4.

13. *Daily Gleaner* (September 21, 1943):1.

14. *Amsterdam News* (November 6, 1943):7B.

15. Ibid.; *Pittsburgh Courier* (October 30, 1943).

16. *Daily Gleaner* (May 26, 1943).

17. *Public Opinion* (June 20, 1944):1.

18. *Daily Gleaner* (November 6, 1943):15; *Palm Beach Post* (October 9 and 15–16, 1943):12; Herbert G. McDonald [*sic*] to Labour Adviser, Labour Department, Kingston, Jamaica, Office of Censorship, USA, October 21, 1943, PRO, CO 318/460/1.

19. *Pittsburg Courier* (October 26, 1943).

20. Nathaniel Allen, Staystonville, Delaware, to Alice Eldemire, Montego Bay, July 10, 1944, PRO, CO 318/460/1.

21. *Washington Bee* (July 22, 1944):2.

22. Pahokee Farm Labor Center, April 1944 report by George E. Winston, Manager, file: C2-R36—Florida, box 51, RG 224, Office of Labor (War Food Administration, hereafter WFA), General Correspondence, 1943–1944, NARA.

23. General Correspondence, 1943–1944, box 51, RG 224, Office of Labor (WFA), NARA.

24. *Palm Beach Post* (August 29, 1945):2.

25. The remaining five seats went to independents. *Public Opinion* (December 16, 1944; May 2, 1945), PRO, CO 318/460/2.

26. *Norfolk Journal and Guide* (May 25, 1946).

27. *Glades County Democrat* (December 26, 1947).

28. Farm Labor Supply Program, Hearings before the Committee on Agriculture, House of Representatives, 80th Cong., 1st sess., on H.R. 1388 to Provide for the Continuance of the Farm Labor Supply Program up to and including June 30, 1947 (Washington, DC: GPO, 1947), 82–83.

29. *U.S. Statutes at Large* (Washington, DC: GPO, 1917), vol. 39, pt. 1, 878.

30. Morrison interview, West Palm Beach, Florida, April 20, 2000; Immigration Act of 1917, *U.S. Statutes at Large* (Washington, DC: GPO, 1917), vol. 39, pt. 1, 877.

31. *Union Labor News* (August 15, 1947):3; Report of the Executive Council, National Farm Labor Union, December 12, 1947, Little Rock, Arkansas, Workers Defense League Papers, box 166, folder 5; K. A. Butler, Assistant Director of Labor, to Chief of Operations, South East Division, August 30, 1945, file: Welfare 2: Recreation and Child Care, box 95, WNRC, RG 224, Office of Labor, general correspondence, 1945, NARA.

32. Report on the Function of the BWICLO, April 13, 1951, CO 1042/189, PRO, Kew Garden, England. It is not clear whether the interest went into government coffers or particular officials' pockets.

33. George E. Winston, November 1947, file: Camps 12-1 Florida, Clewiston, Narrative Report, box 110, WNRC, RG 224, general correspondence, 1947, NARA.

34. According to the 1960 Census, 6,000 Jamaican men were in the United States working as farmworkers on temporary contracts in 1960. That year, there were 258,941 men between the ages of fifteen and thirty-four in Jamaica, many of whom were too young to have participated in the program. Conservatively deducting 20,000 to account for teenagers too young to participate, there was a pool of 240,000 men of recruitment age in Jamaica. Half of them were listed as agricultural workers. See tables 1.7 and 2.24 in Francis 1963:1–23, 2–36.

35. Undated correspondence, Stephanie Black files, in author's possession.

36. The East Coast Migrant Conference of 1954 estimated the number of migrant farmworkers in Florida at 60,000, of whom 50,000 were registered with the US Employment Service. Of those, there were approximately 6,000 Puerto Ricans, 2,700 whites, 4,000 Bahamians, 6,000 British West Indians, and 41,000 African Americans, most of whom traveled in family groups. *Migrant Farm Labor in Florida* (State of Florida, Legislative Council and Legislative Reference Bureau, January 1963), 5.

37. Ibid.:6.

38. The president of the United Brewery Workers complained that foreign contract workers were being deployed to undermine the nineteen union locals the CIO had established among citrus workers. "Reports are pouring into the state headquarters in Florida from all over the citrus belt," he noted, "of our people working from two to four days per week, while Bahamians are working six and seven days per week." When 5,000 out of an estimated 125,000 citrus workers joined the United Brewery Workers, he reported, growers successfully appealed to have Bahamians supplement the West Indians in the orchards. Like the NFLU before them, the brewery workers gave up, and no union attempted to organize citrus workers again until the 1960s. Karl Feller, president of the union, claimed to have blocked a proposed 250 percent increase in the number of foreign farmworkers imported into Florida the previous winter. Statement of Karl Feller (president of the International Union of United Brewery, Flour, Cereal, Soft Drink, and Distillery Workers of America–CIO) before the Senate Subcommittee on Labor and Management Relations, February 27, 1952, folder 2, box 156, Workers Defense League Papers; *Palm Beach Post* (October 17, 1950), in folder 7, box 154, Workers Defense League Papers, Walter Reuther Library, Wayne State University, Detroit, MI.

39. A. G. H. Gardner-Brown, Colonial Secretary's Office, Bahamas, to F. C. Catchpole, comptroller, Development & Welfare in the West Indies, Barbados, February 1953, PRO, CO 1042/204.

40. Reports of the BWICLO in the United States, PRO, CO 1031/614/240/83/01.

41. Randall resigned from the Public Service of the Bahamas the same year, though it is not clear whether his resignation was related to these events. Herbert MacDonald, chief liaison officer, to chairman, Regional Labour Board, Barbados, BWI, December 16, 1952, PRO, CO 1042/204; Labour Office Report, 1952, PRO, CO 1042/204.

42. Charles A. Browne, "Cotton Harvest: Arkansas," October 18, 1952, PRO, CO 1031/614.

43. David's letter is transcribed in a report written by Herbert G. MacDonald, chief liaison officer, WICLO, December 15, 1952, CO 1030/614.

44. George Porter, interview by author, July 10, 2006.

45. *U.S. Statutes at Large* (1952), 82nd Cong., 66:163–282.

46. Foreign Service Despatch, June 13, 1961, NARA, RG 59, CDF, 1960–1963, box 2479, 841F.00/3-2860.

47. American Embassy, Kingston, to Department of State, October 10, 1965, RG 59, Central Foreign Policy, files 1964–1966, Economic Labor and Manpower, box 1305, file: Lab-Labor and Manpower J.; Foreign Service Despatch, June 13, 1961, NARA, RG 59, CDF, 1960–1963, box 2479, 841F.00/3-2860; Despatch A238, American Embassy, Kingston, to Department of State, April 22, 1966, RG 59, Central Foreign Policy, files 1964–1966, Economic Labor and Manpower, box 1305; Despatch A-30, RG 59, Central

Foreign Policy, files 1967–1969, Politics and Defense, box 2241, file: Political Affairs and Relations, Jamaica.

48. March 13, 1965, Despatch A-235 and May 5, 1965, Despatch A-278, NARA, RG 59, Central Foreign Policy files, 1964–1966, POL 2 General Reports and Stats, box 2372, file: POL 2–3 Politico-Economic Jamaica.

49. March 11, 1966, RG Central Foreign Policy, files 1964–1966, POL 2 General Reports and States, box 1305, file: Lab-Labor and Manpower; Despatch A-190, file: POL 2–3, Politico-Economic Jamaica, box 2372, RG 59, Central Foreign Policy, files 1964–1966, POL 2, General Reports and Stats.

50. Comrie's assertions were confirmed a few years later by a wage-and-hour study, whose publication was squelched under pressure from the sugar industry. Its publication was eventually made mandatory by a federal judge. US Department of Labor, "Wage Survey for 1973–74 South Florida Sugar Harvest," reprinted in appendix IV, Department of Labor, Employment Standards Administration (Washington, DC: US GPO, 1974).

51. Comrie, interview by author, July 31, 2002; Walter Comrie to Harold Edwards, chief liaison, May 4, 1964, copy in author's possession; US Department of Labor, "Wage Survey for 1973–74," 97.

52. Fred C. Sikes to Harold F. Edwards, November 15, 1963, and Walter Comrie to Harold Edwards, November 20, 1963, Walter Comrie's files, both in author's possession.

53. Comrie said that the companies would not tolerate contradiction and would send home any worker who complained. He attended a number of grievance hearings for individual workers, at which the company would always present evidence that a complaining worker was either a troublemaker or unproductive (i.e., requiring build-up pay). The best the liaison officer might do was to get the worker transferred to another company. Summary of interview with Walter Comrie, memorandum from Sarah Cleveland to Bruce Goldstein et al., September 19, 1996. Files of Edward Tuddenham, in author's possession.

54. Manley interview by Stephanie Black, n.d., 4.

55. Beth McLeod, "Jamaican Poverty Helps US Growers Prosper," *Palm Beach Post* (December 28, 1986).

56. The ambassador was Douglas V. Fletcher. See "I Would Live Here," *Palm Beach Post* (January 24, 1974):C1.

57. By 1950, over 96,000 out of the approximately 116,000 braceros in the United States were legalized unauthorized immigrants, and the majority of braceros in the United States spent their days on cotton plantations in Texas.

58. "Labor Dearth and Cotton Production," *New York Times* (September 27, 1909):6.

2

The H-2A Program

Evolution, Impacts, and Outlook

Philip Martin

The H-2A program and its predecessors have been admitting foreign farmworkers to fill seasonal US farm jobs primarily in the eastern United States for more than a half-century; in 2009, more than 8,000 US farm employers were certified to fill a record 100,000 farm jobs with foreign workers. The H-2A program is widely criticized by farm employers and by farmworker advocates, albeit for opposite reasons: farmers think that the process to be certified to recruit and employ foreign workers is too cumbersome, whereas worker advocates charge that the program fails to protect US and H-2A workers. Most H-2A workers filled sugarcane jobs in the 1970s and 1980s and tobacco jobs in the 1990s, but in the twenty-first century, there has been diversification. Tobacco jobs were only a quarter of H-2A jobs in 2010, and their share is likely to shrink if the H-2A program expands as envisioned in the pending AgJOBS bill.

OVERVIEW

The H-2A program allows US farm employers to request certification from the US Department of Labor (DOL) to have foreign workers admitted "temporarily to the United States to perform agricultural labor...of a temporary or seasonal nature." DOL certification involves, inter alia, ensuring that two conditions are satisfied: (1) "there are not sufficient workers who are able, willing, and qualified, and who will be available at the time and place needed, to perform the labor or services involved in the employer petition and, (2) the employment of the alien in such labor or services will not adversely affect the wages and working conditions of workers in the United States similarly employed."[1]

US farms in 2007 created around 3 million jobs, according to the Census of Agriculture, and farmers reported hiring 2.6 million workers directly (the same worker employed on two farms is counted twice), with a third, or 911,000, of these jobs lasting at least 150 days.[2] Since most H-2A workers are employed at least 150 days, legal foreign workers with H-2A visas fill about 10 percent of the 150-day-or-more jobs on US farms. Yet, most farm jobs and farmworkers are seasonal: jobs usually last less than 150 days on one farm, and workers are employed less than six months in agriculture. Seasonal farmworkers earned about half of the average $19 an hour of private sector non-farmworkers in 2009 and worked about half as many hours as non-farmworkers, giving them one-quarter of the average $38,000 annual income of non-farmworkers.

The seasonal farm labor market resembles a revolving door—new-comers enter, but most remain seasonal farmworkers for less than a decade before moving to non-farm jobs. Definitions of socioeconomic problems suggest solutions, so defining the seasonal farm labor problem in minimizing-cost terms, as farm employers often do, suggests that the optimal way to minimize seasonal farm labor costs is to open the border gates to newcomers willing to accept the current wages and conditions. However, defining the farm labor problem in terms of labor market outcomes, such as low wages and earnings, as worker advocates do, suggests government intervention to raise farmworker incomes or to provide poor farmworkers and their children with services to mitigate their poverty.

The federal government has had contradictory responses to these different definitions of and solutions to the seasonal farm labor problems. On the one hand, it generally accedes to employer requests for foreign workers, even if their presence lowers the rate of increase in wages and slows the productivity-increasing investments that could keep US agriculture competitive in a globalizing world. On the other hand, the federal government supports programs that spend over $1 billion a year providing services to migrant and seasonal farmworkers (MSFW) and their children, in part to compensate for low farm wages.

The federal government is likely to continue both to admit or tolerate foreign farmworkers and to fund programs that help poor MSFWs and their children. Funding for MSFW programs has increased even as the number of farmworkers, especially migrant workers who follow the crops around the United States, has decreased. Under the Agricultural Job Opportunities, Benefits and Security Act (AgJOBS) bill, unauthorized farmworkers and their families could receive blue cards immediately and eventually become legal immigrants by continuing to do farmwork, and farm employers would gain easier access to H-2A workers. The net effect of AgJOBS would likely be an increase in the supply of workers tied to agriculture, including blue card holders and additional H-2A workers.

This chapter has three major sections. The first summarizes the history of guestworkers in US agriculture, emphasizing that determining whether foreign farmworkers are truly needed has been a public policy issue for more than a century. The second section examines the employment of guestworkers in the Florida sugarcane industry, which mechanized within five years after workers sued for underpayment of wages. The third section outlines the AgJOBS proposal, which would grant legalization to currently unauthorized workers, the goal of worker advocates, and give farm employers easier access to H-2A workers. The conclusion emphasizes that the comprehensive immigration reform embodied in AgJOBS is likely to benefit individuals who are currently unauthorized at the cost of more H-2A workers, who may be harder to protect.

FROM BRACERO TO H-2A

Seeing the United States as a nation of immigrants, the US government has generally favored the admission of immigrants over temporary workers. Green card holders are foreign nationals with visas that allow them to live in the United States and work in most US jobs not requiring citizenship. After five years, most immigrants may become naturalized US citizens. Green card holders, who may work in most private sector jobs, change US employers, and be jobless without losing the right to be in the country, are generally considered intending to become Americans.[3]

Braceros I: 1917–1921

There was no statutory basis for the admission of temporary foreign workers between 1885 and 1952, but exceptions to immigration laws were made several times to admit foreign farmworkers. The Immigration Act of 1917 imposed a literacy test on foreigners aged sixteen and older and doubled the head tax to $8. Western US farmers asked the US Department of Labor, which included the Bureau of Immigration, "to admit temporarily otherwise inadmissible aliens" who could not pass the literacy test or pay the tax to fill farm and railroad jobs.[4] The DOL on May 23, 1917, waived the head tax and literacy test for aliens from Mexico and Canada entering the United States temporarily to do farmwork (and railroad work in 1917–1918), despite the skepticism of some DOL officials about the claims of labor shortages. For example, the assistant secretary of labor at the time, Louis Post, said, "The farm labor shortage is two-thirds imaginary and one-third remedial."[5]

DOL regulations laid out detailed procedures for determining whether to admit Mexican and Canadian farmworkers. An employer had to provide proof to the local US Employment Service office that there were not sufficient US workers, and the local ES office could deny or certify the employer's request for foreign workers. If an employer's request was certified, the employer recruited the foreign workers and provided them with contracts spelling out their wages and benefits. Scruggs (1960:324) concluded that the "basic weakness of the program was the lack of adequate enforcement machinery," so neither workers nor employers felt that they had to abide by the contracts they signed. Some 80,000 Mexican workers were admitted, primarily for "employment in the sugar beet fields of California, Colorado, Utah, and Idaho, and in the cotton fields of Texas, Arizona, and California" (Scruggs 1960:322).[6] The then Bureau of Immigration reported that, assured of ample supplies of workers, "large acreages were planted and record crops harvested throughout the Southwest" in 1917 (qtd. in Congressional Research Service 1980:7).

The Mexican government was ambivalent about this first bracero program. The 1910–1917 Mexican revolution damaged the haciendas on which many peasants lived and worked, leaving many Mexicans with neither land nor jobs and eager to migrate to the United States for work. However, the Mexican government was concerned about the treatment of its citizens in the United States, especially in Texas, where "No Dogs or Mexicans" signs were common. Some braceros returned to Mexico with few savings or in debt because of charges they incurred at the farmer-owned stores and labor camps (Fuller 1942:19853).

Legal and illegal Mexican immigration surged in the 1920s after the first bracero program ended, with considerable seasonal movements of Mexicans into and out of the United States. With few US border-entry stations and Border Patrol agents, illegal entry from Mexico usually meant entering the United States without paying the head tax at one of the border stations.[7]

The 1930s were marked by farm labor surpluses, especially in California. The state had 5.7 million residents in 1930, and Dust Bowl migration brought 1.3 million displaced people from Oklahoma and

Arkansas over the next decade, increasing the population by 25 percent. Steeped in the Jeffersonian family farm ideal, some Dust Bowl migrants drove up to California farmhouses and asked for work, expecting to be treated as hired hands who would live and work alongside large fruit and vegetable farmers and later become fruit and vegetable farmers themselves. Dust Bowl migrants soon learned that California's commercial farms hired crews of seasonal workers when they were needed, not year-round hired hands. Decades of yawning social gaps between white farmers and generally minority farmworkers meant that there was a relatively sparse on-farm infrastructure to accommodate hired workers. Many Dust Bowl migrants wound up in tent camps known as Hoovervilles, where union organizers were active. Since Dust Bowl migrants were US citizens, there was concern that these Hoovervilles could become a fertile breeding ground for communists and others who wanted major changes in the socioeconomic system, prompting the creation of federally funded farmworker housing centers, one of which served as a backdrop for John Steinbeck's 1939 novel, *The Grapes of Wrath*.[8]

Braceros II: 1942–1964

In 1940, the secretary of agriculture testified before a Senate subcommittee that the number of farmworkers far exceeded the number who could expect to make a decent living from agriculture (Rasmussen 1951:14). California farmers nonetheless requested supplemental foreign workers in 1941, but their request was rejected by the DOL at the behest of the state's governor (ibid.:200).[9] However, after the United States declared war on the Axis powers in December 1941, a federal interagency committee in May 1942 concluded that supplemental foreign farmworkers would be needed for the fall harvest. Despite protests from US unions and Mexican American groups,[10] the interagency committee drafted a guestworker agreement and sent it to Mexico, which modified it slightly before approving it.[11] The first of what would become a series of Mexico-US bracero agreements was signed on July 23, 1942, via an exchange of diplomatic notes.[12]

These new Mexican braceros entered the United States at El Paso on September 27, 1942, and headed to sugar beet fields near Stockton, California. Only 4,189 braceros were admitted in 1942 (Congressional Research Service 1980:16), in part because the bracero agreement called for a minimum wage of $0.30 an hour at a time when US farmworkers were not subject to the federal minimum wage.[13] Some farmers refused to hire braceros because they feared that the minimum wage required for braceros could be extended to the US farmworkers they employed (Congressional

Research Service 1980:22). East Coast farmers recruited workers from the British West Indies under separate memorandums of understanding (MOU) between the War Food Administration and the Bahamas (MOU signed March 16, 1943), Jamaica (April 2, 1943), and Barbados (May 24, 1944).

Some 310,000 foreign farmworkers were admitted between 1942 and 1947, including 220,000 Mexicans (71 percent). Admissions peaked in 1944, when 84,340 foreign farmworkers were admitted, 74 percent Mexicans and 19 percent Jamaicans. Foreign workers were employed in twenty-four states; half were in California, and they were about 2 percent of US farmworkers during World War II. The major crops in which braceros worked were cotton, sugar beets, fruits, and vegetables (Scruggs 1961:163).

The labor agreements with Mexico and the Caribbean islands had similar provisions. They exempted foreign farmworkers from the usual immigration admissions tests and from the US military draft, guaranteed round-trip transportation and the same wages and housing as similar US workers, and allowed the sending governments to determine who could leave Mexico and the Caribbean for US farm jobs (Congressional Research Service 1980:17).

The wartime farm labor program was codified by Congress with the enactment of Public Law 45 on April 29, 1943. PL 45, the first of what came to be known as the farm labor supply appropriations acts, appropriated federal funds for the recruitment, transportation, and placement of farmworkers and explicitly stated that funds could not be used to "fix, regulate, or impose minimum wages or housing standards...except with respect to workers imported into the US from a foreign country, and then only to the extent required to comply with agreements." That is, the minimum wages and housing standards guaranteed to braceros were not to be extended to US farmworkers (qtd. in Congressional Research Service 1980:18). PL 45 was followed by PL 229 (1944) and PL 80 (1947), which had similar provisions.

The US laws providing the funding to recruit and admit foreign farmworkers lapsed in 1947, but the international agreements remained valid. Many of the Mexican workers employed in US fields between 1948 and 1951 arrived illegally. These workers, known as "wetbacks" even in official documents, were returned to the border if detected inside the United States, were issued documents, and then were transported back to the US farm where they had been employed.

The President's Commission on Migratory Labor (1951) reviewed farm labor issues and, noting that 74,600 Mexican workers were admitted legally between 1947 and 1949 while 142,000 "wetbacks already in the US were legalized by being put under contract" (1951:53), recommended that no more braceros be admitted. The commission concluded that the presence of braceros depressed wages in the crops where they were concentrated, especially cotton: "Alien labor has depressed farm wages and, therefore, has been detrimental to domestic labor" (1951:59).

Growers opposed the commission's recommendation to end the bracero program, and the outbreak of the Korean War persuaded Congress to enact PL 78, the Migratory Labor Agreement of 1951, as an amendment to the Agricultural Act of 1949. PL 78 was signed into law on July 12, 1951, by President Harry Truman despite a DOL recommendation that it be vetoed because it did not offer the same wages and protections to US farmworkers that had to be offered to braceros (Congressional Research Service 1980:32).[14]

PL 78 gave the DOL a central role in determining the need for foreign farmworkers. Section 503 prohibited the admission of braceros unless the secretary of labor had determined and certified the following: (1) "Sufficient domestic workers who are able, willing, and qualified are not available at the time and place needed to perform the work,... (2) the employment of such workers will not adversely affect the wages and working conditions of domestic agricultural workers similarly employed, and (3) reasonable efforts have been made to attract domestic workers for such employment at wages...comparable to those offered to foreign workers." State employment service agencies were enlisted to "assist the [DOL] Secretary in recruiting domestic farm workers and determining if they [were] available" (Congressional Research Service 1980:34).

Several issues arose as bracero admissions climbed from 192,000 in 1951 to a peak of 445,000 in 1956. The first was protections for US workers. The DOL argued that US workers should receive the same wages and benefits that were guaranteed to Mexican braceros. However, Representative W. R. Poage (D-TX) successfully opposed the DOL, asserting that the lack of a minimum wage was "one of the greatest safeguards that you can provide for American labor. If it, in fact, costs the employer more to bring in foreign labor," employers will prefer US workers (Congressional Research Service 1980:35). Thus, braceros, but not US workers, had contracts with wage and work guarantees.

The second issue was illegal migration. The number of unauthorized foreigners apprehended, almost all Mexicans, rose from less than 12,000 a year in the early 1940s to more than 500,000 a year in the early 1950s, peaking at 1.1 million in 1954 (table 2.1). On July 13, 1951, the day after PL 78 was signed into law, President Truman asked Congress to approve, inter

Table 2.1
Bracero Admissions and Apprehensions, 1942–1964

	Admissions	Apprehensions
1942	4,203	11,784
1943	52,098	11,175
1944	62,170	31,174
1945	49,454	69,164
1946	32,043	99,591
1947	19,632	193,657
1948	35,345	192,779
1949	107,000	288,253
1950	67,500	468,339
1951	192,000	509,040
1952	197,100	528,815
1953	201,380	885,587
1954	309,033	1,089,583
1955	398,650	254,096
1956	445,197	87,696
1957	436,049	59,918
1958	432,857	53,474
1959	437,643	45,336
1960	315,846	70,684
1961	291,420	88,823
1962	194,978	92,758
1963	186,865	88,712
1964	177,736	86,597
Totals	4,646,199	5,307,035

Source: Congressional Research Service 1980:36–37. Note: bracero admissions and apprehensions are events, not unique individuals.

alia, sanctions on employers who hired illegal workers and to provide more funds for the INS to enforce immigration laws. Sections 274 and 287(a)(3) of the Immigration and Nationality Act of 1952 did include the so-called Texas proviso, which made harboring illegal aliens subject to a $2,000 fine and up to five years' imprisonment, but the act exempted employment from the definition of harboring.[15]

With illegal migration surging, Attorney General Herbert Brownell visited the Mexico-US border in August 1953 and pronounced the lawlessness of unauthorized Mexicans entering the United States "shocking." Brownell expanded the Border Patrol from 1,079 to 1,479 agents in fiscal year 1954–1955 and appointed General Joseph Swing to lead Operation Wetback, which involved Border Patrol agents, in cooperation with state and local police, checking areas with large numbers of Mexicans (Congressional Research Service 1980:40). The 1955 INS Annual Report noted that the sweeps encouraged tens of thousands of Mexicans to leave "on their own accord." Growers cooperated with Operation Wetback because Swing promised to help them to secure domestic and legal foreign workers (Congressional Research Service 1980:42). The INS's review emphasized that "border control" might be costly and difficult, but it was, "in the long run, more economical and more humane than the expulsion process" (Immigration and Naturalization Service 1955:15).

The DOL secretary, James Mitchell, considered the bracero program "of minor importance" in the mid-1950s but began to actively oppose it in the late 1950s. Mitchell appointed four consultants to study the bracero program, and they issued a report in October 1959 concluding that the DOL had failed to achieve the goal of preventing braceros from adversely affecting similar US workers. The consultants concluded that some employers preferred to hire Mexican rather than US workers because the braceros had to satisfy their employers in order to remain legal US workers. They concluded that the presence of braceros depressed US farm wages despite requirements that braceros be paid the minimum wage, and they urged the DOL to more carefully study the relationship between the share of braceros in a particular farm labor market and farm wage trends in that market.

The consultants recommended changes to bracero recruitment requirements, urging the DOL to make clear in its regulations that the "primary responsibility for the recruitment of domestic workers [should rest] with the employer himself," not local ES offices.[16] The DOL should not certify the need for bracero workers, according to the report, unless the employer has "undertaken positive and direct recruitment efforts" to attract US workers, offering conditions "equivalent" to those of employers who have successfully recruited US workers and offering wages and benefits to US workers equivalent to those that had to be offered to braceros (Mexican Farm Labor Consultants Report 1960[1959]:282–283). The report noted that 20,000 braceros were employed in year-round jobs, in apparent violation of regulations limiting them to filling seasonal jobs, and that more than 60 percent of braceros worked in crops that were in surplus supply, such as cotton and sugar. The consultants questioned the wisdom of admitting foreign workers to pick crops whose excess production was subsidized with tax dollars (ibid.:272–273).

Mitchell implemented many of the consultants' recommendations in regulations issued on November 20, 1959, prompting a failed effort in Congress to divide the jurisdiction of the bracero program between the DOL and the Department of Agriculture. The national elections in 1960 made Arthur Goldberg the DOL secretary, and he reported in 1961 that, in eighty bracero-dominated labor markets, prevailing wages had not increased during the previous decade whereas the wages of US farmworkers in areas with few braceros had risen. In an effort to overcome this wage depression, Goldberg tried but failed to get PL 78 amended to require that the wages offered to braceros be at least 90 percent of the national or state average farmworker wage (Congressional Research Service 1980:52).

President John Kennedy announced plans to end the bracero program in 1961.[17] Hearings in Congress featured testimony arguing that, without braceros, the production of many commodities would be sharply reduced. Congress voted to extend the bracero program for two years, until the end of 1963, and then for a final year, until the end of 1964. After the bracero program ended, illegal Mexico-US migration remained relatively low but then was on a rising trajectory, with 110,000 apprehensions in 1965 and 284,000 in 1969. The Congressional Research Service concluded, "The Bracero program only seemed to reduce illegal migration when it was combined with both a massive law enforcement [Operation Wetback] and an expansion of the farm labor program to the point where it almost certainly had an adverse impact on the wages and working conditions of domestic workers [as in the mid-1950s]" (1980:58). In other words, the Congressional Research Service suggested that there was a trade-off: a smaller bracero program and more illegal migration or a larger bracero program and more depression of US farm wages.

THE H-2 VISA PROGRAM

The H-2 program was created by the omnibus Immigration and Nationality Act (McCarran-Walter Act) of 1952, which was enacted by Congress over President Truman's veto.[18] Section 101(a)(15)(H) outlined procedures to admit three types of temporary workers: persons of distinguished merit and ability, other temporary workers, and trainees.[19] The H-2 designation specifies that "other temporary workers" must have "a residence in a foreign country" that they have "no intention of abandoning" and be "coming temporarily to the US to perform other temporary services or labor, if unemployed persons capable of performing such services or labor cannot be found in this country." Section 214(c) gave the attorney general the final authority to deal with petitions from employers for H-2 visas for foreign workers "after consultation with the appropriate agencies of the government." The attorney general normally denies employer petitions unless they are accompanied by a certification from the DOL that US workers are not available and that the presence of H-2 foreign workers will not adversely affect US workers.

Unlike the bracero program, which was begun to deal with specific wartime labor shortages, the H-2 program is a permanent part of US law. Technically, it is not a program, but a visa classification, in that unlike the bracero and British West Indies (BWI) programs, it does not operate under agreements negotiated by the United States and foreign governments. Instead, the H-2 program is unilateral; when the attorney general (now, the Department of Homeland Security) accepts their petitions for foreign workers, employers can recruit in any country they wish and in any manner allowed by that country's laws.

After the bracero program ended on December 31, 1964, many farmers expected to employ Mexican workers under the H-2 program. However, the DOL on December 19, 1964, had issued regulations requiring employers of H-2 workers to offer and pay any US workers they employed the "adverse effect wage rate" (AEWR) and to provide US workers housing and transportation, effectively extending the wage and benefit guarantees afforded to H-2 workers to US workers at a time when US farmworkers were exempt from many labor laws (Congressional Research Service 1980:65). During the January 15–16, 1965, hearings before the Senate Committee on Agriculture, the DOL secretary, Willard Wirtz, asserted that the purpose of the regulations was to reduce the employment of foreign workers in order to reduce unemployment among US farmworkers.

The December 19, 1964, regulations guided the administration of the H-2 program until they were modified by the Immigration Reform and Control Act of 1986. Most H-2 workers between the mid-1960s and the mid-1980s cut sugarcane in Florida and picked apples along the eastern seaboard. Most H-2 workers incurred costs in order to be selected in their country of origin, and most had the cost of their return transportation deducted from their pay if they did not finish their contract, making them less likely than US workers to complain.[20]

Several important court cases involved the H-2 program in the 1970s. In *Elton Orchards Inc. v. Brennan* (508 F.2d 493), a New Hampshire apple grower challenged a DOL requirement that inexperienced Louisiana workers who responded to his required ads be hired, rather than experienced Jamaicans. A US district court ruled that Elton could hire the experienced Jamaicans he preferred, based on the business justification that apples are perishable and have to be harvested quickly.[21] However, a US court of appeals ruled on December 19, 1974, that US employers must give preference to US workers, concluding that there is no "legal right to use alien workers upon a showing of business justification" that the foreign workers are more productive.

PHILIP MARTIN

The DOL issued regulations on March 10, 1978, reaffirming the requirement that US workers receive the same wages and benefits as H-2 workers and that an AEWR was needed to offset past wage depression due to the presence of foreign farmworkers (Congressional Research Service 1980:77–78). These regulations were modified by the Immigration Reform and Control Act of 1986 (PL 99-603, Title III, pt. A, secs. 301–305).

H-2 IMPACTS: FLORIDA SUGAR

Between the 1950s and 1980s, most H-2 workers were employed in Florida, the major farm state on the eastern seaboard. About 80 percent of Florida's farm sales of almost $8 billion a year was from the sale of crops, most of which required seasonal workers to harvest. Three crops dominated the discussions of seasonal farm labor issues in Florida: sugarcane, oranges, and tomatoes. Between the 1940s and 1990s, sugarcane was in the spotlight because of its reliance on guestworkers from sugar-producing Caribbean islands. Oranges have long been Florida's most important fruit, but urbanization, freezes, and trade are shrinking the groves, and these factors plus rising wages may spur the mechanization of the harvesting of oranges processed into juice. Florida produces most of the fresh tomatoes grown in the United States during the winter months, and the Coalition of Immokalee Workers has pursued a strategy of pressuring the buyers of Florida tomatoes, such as fast food chains, to raise the prices they pay growers for tomatoes so that growers can raise pickers' piece rates (Griffith 2009a).

Sugarcane and Guestworkers

Sugarcane production began in the 1930s in south-central Florida when a few large landowners realized that they could grow the perennial grass in the area's subtropical climate. Obtaining harvest workers was a problem, in part because local workers knew of the debt peonage that sometimes occurred on sugar plantations.[22] In 1942, the US Sugar Corporation and four of its managers, as well as the sheriff of Hendry County, were indicted by a federal grand jury for violating federal peonage statutes by holding workers by force until they repaid their debts.[23]

Sugar mill owners wanted a labor force that could not leave the fields for other jobs. They found such workers in sugar-producing Caribbean islands such as Jamaica and imported them as guestworkers so that they would have to stay with the mills or leave the United States (Griffith 2006; Hahamovitch 2011). Caribbean cane cutters were admitted, first, under exceptions in US immigration law and later with H-2 and then H-2A visas. In 1942, the US War Food Administration negotiated MOUs with governments in the British West Indies to recruit farmworkers for Florida and other eastern states. At peak, 16,000 Jamaicans were admitted in 1944.

After World War II ended, the guestworker program continued, with the British West Indies Central Labour Organization (WICLO) representing the island governments. The WICLO controlled the list of workers from which US employers could make their selections, and it required workers selected by US employers to sign supplemental agreements allowing US employers to deduct some of their earnings and forward these deductions to government-controlled banks in their home countries.

Jamaicans with H-2 visas were admitted to harvest Florida's sugar crop. Since sugarcane harvesting was mechanized in Louisiana and in Australia and other countries, there were calls to mechanize the Florida harvest, but the mill owners argued that the muck soil could not support the weight of harvesting machines. After class action suits were filed in the early 1990s alleging that the mills underpaid cane cutters, a state court initially agreed that the cutters were owed over $100 million in back wages. The Florida sugarcane harvest was mechanized within five years.

Big Sugar in Florida

Florida's sugar production was limited until trade with Cuba was halted by the US government in July 1960 in retaliation for Fidel Castro's confiscation of the assets of US firms there. The Cuba embargo encouraged Florida's cane acreage to quadruple within five years and to double again between the mid-1960s and mid-1980s.[24] In 2005–2006, Florida harvested 13 million tons of cane worth $30 a ton, or $390 million, from 402,000 acres. Most of the cane was from large corporate farms. Flo-Sun, controlled by the Fanjul family of Palm Beach, had 150,000 acres of sugarcane in the early 1990s, followed by the US Sugar Corporation with 140,000 acres; Talisman Sugar, a subsidiary of the St. Joe Paper Company, 48,000 acres; and Texas-based King Ranch, 20,000 acres. The sugar industry is vertically integrated. The mills own farmland and grow at least some of the cane they grind, called "administration cane," and harvest their own cane, as well as that of independent growers.[25]

A 1992 USDA review of Florida sugarcane cited four major problems facing the industry: soil subsidence, yields, labor, and environmental issues (Buzzanell, Lord, and Brown 1992). Soil subsidence is the biological oxidation process that results in an average of 1.2 inches of soil in the Everglades area being lost each year as bacteria turn the organic residue soil into particles that are blown away. By keeping water levels higher, soil subsidence is reduced, so some growers plant rice in the summer fallow months and flood the fields to minimize subsidence. Cane yields were about 32 tons an acre from the 1960s through the 1980s and rose to 35–36 tons an acre in 1990–1991. New varieties have increased yields, with three mainstay varieties falling from more than 80 percent of Florida cane in the mid-1980s to less than 60 percent a decade later.[26]

Environmental issues remain problematic. The Florida sugar industry is mostly in the Everglades Agricultural Area, created in the 1930s and the 1940s by draining swamplands. After back-to-back hurricanes flooded most of southern Florida in 1947, the Army Corps of Engineers was ordered to create the EAA and the Everglades National Park. The organic or muck soils in the EAA were ideal for growing cane, as were the wet and warm summers and the dry and freeze-free winters, but cane farming slowed the flow of fresh water entering the Everglades National Park during the summer months and added phosphates to the water supply, enabling cattails to replace native saw grasses.

The federal and state governments in the 1990s debated how to protect the Everglades "river of grass." The result was an $8 billion, twenty-year project that has involved government purchases of 250,000 acres of land surrounding the Everglades park, including 60,000 acres of farmland, with cane growers making a small contribution.[27] The sugar industry's major concern was to avoid paying for the cleanup of the Everglades park. A 1996 state ballot initiative, Amendment 4, would have required sugar companies to pay a one-cent-per-pound tax on the sugar they produce to raise $700 million to filter phosphate-laden water before it enters the Everglades. It was defeated with the help of $25 million from the sugar companies.[28]

Labor Issues

Labor was the final challenge facing the sugar industry. Almost all Florida cane was cut by about 10,000 guestworkers in the early 1990s. Employers were required to recruit US workers first, which they did by completing DOL form ETA 790, the "job clearance" order that spells out the wages and working conditions offered. These job orders were circulated, or cleared, throughout the United States so that workers seeking farm jobs could learn about them and respond.[29] The job order became a contract between the mills and any US or H-2/H-2A workers hired to cut cane.

US sugar prices are kept higher than world sugar prices by a complex policy that limits sugar imports; US sugar policy also includes a higher-than-usual minimum wage. Like all H-2A jobs, sugar job orders in the late 1980s offered a government-mandated minimum wage, the adverse effect wage rate, of at least $5.30 an hour at a time when the federal minimum wage was $3.35 an hour. However, cane cutters earned a piece rate wage, which the mills called a task rate, and workers who could not cut fast enough to earn at least $5.30 an hour at this piece or task rate could be terminated. If the mills retained slower cutters, they had to "make up" their piece rate earnings so that all workers earned at least $5.30 an hour. To give workers who had not previously cut cane an idea of how much cane they would have to cut in order to avoid termination, the mills' job orders included the statement "A worker would be expected to cut an average of eight (8) tons of harvest cane per day throughout the season." Mills reserved the right to test a worker's productivity any time after a seven-day training and break-in period. If a worker failed on three days to cut fast enough to earn $5.30 an hour at the mill-specified piece or task rate, the worker could be terminated and sent home.

The combination of the government-set minimum wage of $5.30 an hour and the mill-set productivity standard of a ton an hour, or eight tons a day, created an iron triangle that should have made the piece or task rate for cutting cane $5.30 a ton. If we use a different crop as an example, it becomes clearer. If the minimum wage is $10 an hour and the piece rate $10 for a bin of apples, then the productivity standard is a bin an hour. A worker who picks only three-quarters of a bin in one hour would earn $7.50 at the piece rate wage, but, because of the $10 minimum wage, the employer would have to "make up" $2.50 to bring his wage to the $10 minimum. Most employers fire workers who cannot work fast enough at the piece rate employers set to earn the minimum wage.

Most job orders specified all three parameters of the iron triangle: the minimum wage, the piece rate, and the productivity standard. The sugar mills' job orders were unusual because they specified a "task rate" rather than a piece rate, which was explained on a handout given to cutters as follows: "The task, set for each day in terms of the number of feet of cane the worker is expected to cut in one hour, is based on the experience of the company over many years.... Over 95 percent of the cutters have made the task in the past, and it is considered a reasonable task and work standard by the company." To have "made the task" meant cutting cane fast enough to earn the minimum wage.

The mills used the task rate to save money. The mill owners, but not the workers, knew how many tons of cane were in 100 or 150 feet of cane because they could estimate cane yields accurately. The mill owners kept meticulous records and set task rates that required workers to cut 1.3–1.7 tons of cane an hour. Supervisors, who were ex-cutters with H-2/H-2A visas, carried tape measures and "checked out" cutters who did not cut cane fast enough, ordering them to stop working and sit on the bus until the end of the workday. After three check-outs, a cutter could be terminated, which usually meant a quick return trip to Jamaica.

The key to understanding how the mills but not the cutters knew how many tons of cane were in the 100- or 150-foot task assigned to a worker lies in the fact that cane is planted in rows five feet apart and workers are assigned to cut two adjoining rows of cane, known as a cut row.[30] Since there are 43,560 square feet in an acre, the mill owners knew that a field with 43.56 tons an acre had a ton of cane in every 100 feet of a cut row.[31] If the task rate required workers to cut 150 feet in one hour, then the productivity standard was 1.5 tons an hour. The mills did not have to weigh the cane cut by each worker, because the owners became very good at estimating yields. Since feet equal tons, mill owners knew how many tons of cane the workers cut, because they knew how many feet of cane were cut.

The US Department of Labor defines a piece rate wage as one that measures the work done by individuals. The mill owners argued that the task rate was not a piece rate because the work done by individuals was not measured, and the DOL agreed. In 1982, migrant advocates sued the DOL because it failed to order employers to raise their piece rates when the government raised the minimum wage (AEWR). The advocates argued that if the DOL did not require employers to raise their piece rates in lockstep with the minimum wage, workers would have to work harder to earn the higher wage.[32]

The US Department of Labor accepted this logic and in 1985 ordered farm employers to raise their piece rates as the minimum wage rose.[33] However, under pressure from the sugar mills, the DOL concluded again that the task rate in sugarcane was not a piece rate, which exempted sugar from the link between the minimum wage and task rates. Migrant advocates again sued the DOL, and a federal judge ordered the department to determine whether the task rate system was in fact a piece rate system. The draft DOL study concluded that sugar had a piece rate wage system and the eight-ton statement was a productivity standard. But the political clout of sugar mills was evident in the final report, which concluded again that the task rate system was not a piece rate system.[34]

Suits, Mechanization, and Lessons

In 1989, class action suits were filed by cane cutters asserting that the eight-ton productivity standard and the $5.30 an hour minimum wage created a contract that promised cutters a piece rate of $5.30 per ton. The suit used the iron triangle argument: if the minimum wage was $5.30 an hour and workers had to cut an average of 8 tons of cane in an eight-hour day to be considered satisfactory,[35] then the piece rate for cutting cane must be $5.30 a ton.[36] The mills paid workers much less, about $3.75 a ton, and the lawsuits asked for back wages of $1.55 a ton, or about $100 million with interest.

A Florida state judge in August 1992 found the iron triangle argument convincing and ordered the mills to pay each cutter $1,000 to $1,500 in back wages for the several years of harvesting that were not excluded by the statute of limitations.[37] This decision prompted US Sugar to reverse course and adopt a "labor peace" program that included the settlement of suits alleging that US Sugar underpaid its H-2A workers.[38] US Sugar acknowledged that its task rate was a piece rate, offered cutters $5.10 per net ton (after trash was removed from the stalk), required workers to cut at least one gross ton of cane an hour, and paid $5.6 million to settle the workers' suit in July 1998.[39]

The other mills appealed the judge's decision, and a state appeals court agreed that there should be a trial to determine whether the contract was "clear and unambiguous" about the $5.30-a-ton piece rate. The first case involved Atlantic Sugar, one of the mills controlled by the Fanjul family.[40] A jury was asked to answer "should" and "could" questions: *should* the mills have paid cane cutters an average of $5.30 per ton, and *could* the companies have paid cutters $5.30 a ton without weighing the cane cut by each worker? Workers' attorneys used the iron triangle argument to make the "should" argument and companies' yield data to make the "could" argument. The mill owners countered that they never promised to pay cutters $5.30 a ton, and they bolstered their case by citing the DOL conclusion that the task rate was not a piece rate. Some cutters, testifying in Jamaican patois, said that their work assignment was to cut a certain number of feet, not a certain number of tons. The mills showed that they did not pay exactly $3.75 a ton. They paid slightly more in fields with recumbent or flattened cane and slightly less when the cane was straight and easier to cut.[41]

The jury decided that Atlantic did not promise cutters $5.30 a ton, but it also concluded, "Atlantic Sugar consistently misrepresented to the cutters the incentive features of their task system of payment. It was shameful." Juries reached similar verdicts absolving Okeelanta and the Sugar Cane Growers Cooperative, agreeing with the mills that, since the DOL found that the task rate was not a piece rate, workers could not expect to be paid $5.30 a ton. Instead, workers could expect to earn $5.30 an hour if they worked fast enough to complete their assigned task.

The cutters did not get back wages, but the mills began to mechanize when they realized that successful cutter suits could raise their labor costs by 40 percent. Talisman Sugar, a mill not involved in the lawsuits, mechanized cane harvesting in the early 1980s. Citing "unfounded legal hassles" associated with the H-2A program, the Sugar Cane Growers Cooperative of Florida mechanized harvesting after the 1991–1992 season. US Sugar was the last mill to mechanize, after the 1995–1996 season. In Louisiana, where African Americans rather than H-2A workers cut sugarcane, the harvest had been mechanized in the 1950s and 1960s.

Sugar is widely acknowledged to be the poster child for US farm policies that slow economic development abroad and increase immigration to the United States. The sugarcane industry exists in southern Florida because trade barriers keep lower-cost sugar out of the United States. For years, cane growers argued that they could not find US workers to cut cane and could not mechanize because of the area's unique soil conditions. Migration instead of trade continued for five decades, from the 1940s until the 1990s, when worker lawsuits alleging wage underpayments spurred mechanization.

One lesson from the sugar experience is skepticism about growers' claims that there are no alternatives to imported farmworkers. The speedy mechanization of the harvest when the owners were faced with higher wages, from $3.75 a ton to $5.30 a ton, belied the assertions that there were no alternatives to human harvesters. A second lesson concerns cumulative causation in the H-2A program. Once employers become accustomed to guestworkers, it is very hard to revert to US workers. Decades of recruitment in the British West Indies meant that supervision, housing, and work had all adjusted to facilitate the employment of BWI workers. The few US workers who applied for cane-cutting jobs felt out of place and soon quit.

Third, as is the case with most industries using guestworkers, the H-2 program gave sugar employers great control over workers, since losing a job meant removal from the United States. Some of the mills fired a few slower cutters early in the season to inspire the remaining cutters to work faster. The mill owners reasoned that even if they had to pay return transportation for the fired workers, the fact that the remaining cutters would work faster to keep their jobs would reduce the total number of cane cutters needed. Workers who were fired did not know how much cane they cut, but company records show that some of those terminated early in the season cut more than a ton an hour, but not the 1.5 tons an hour required by the task rate.

H-2A TODAY AND AgJOBS PROPOSALS

The humiliating end to the H-2A program in Florida sugar, which revealed institutionalized wage theft and other injustices against guestworkers, occurred as the H-2A program was beginning to expand to other crops and regions and diversify its labor source countries, with the major source of workers shifting from Jamaica to Mexico. Between 1952 and 1992, most H-2A workers were from Jamaica, and most were employed in the United States to harvest sugarcane in Florida and to pick apples along the eastern seaboard (Griffith 2006). With the Florida sugarcane harvest mechanized in the mid-1990s, most H-2A workers came from Mexico and were employed to tend tobacco and vegetables such as cucumbers and onions in the southeastern states, although Jamaicans still worked in apples (Bump, Goździak, and Lowell, chapter 8, this volume).

The number of jobs certified by the DOL to be filled with H-2A workers reached a low of 30,000 in the mid-1990s. The number then began to rise as more farm employers in more states requested certification to employ H-2A workers. The DOL stopped publishing an annual report on its H-2A activities but makes raw employer requests and DOL decision data available online (www.flcdatacenter.com/CaseData.aspx). In fiscal year 2010, 7,025 employers were certified by the DOL to fill 94,200 jobs with H-2A workers; almost 99 percent of these employer requests were approved (259 employer requests were denied and 136 employer requests were withdrawn).[42]

It is hard to extract information by job title because some employers simply request "farmworkers" whereas others request "Vidalia onion workers" (eight employers were certified to fill 823 jobs in Vidalia onions with H-2A workers in fiscal year 2010). The most common job certified was tobacco worker; almost 2,000 farms were certified to fill 21,800 tobacco jobs with H-2A workers in 2010. The second largest request was from 1,000 farm employers certified to fill 16,700 "farm labor" or "farmworker" jobs. Some 200 nursery employers were certified to fill almost 3,100 jobs with H-2A workers (there were also horticulture and greenhouse jobs certified). The largest single certification was for the Washington Farm Labor Association, which was certified for 900 "farmworker" jobs between May and November 2010. Washington's Zirkle Fruit was certified to employ 750 H-2A farmworkers between August and November 2010, and Arizona's S&H Farms was certified to fill almost 700 cantaloupe jobs in October 2009 and another 650 in June–July 2010. The North Carolina Growers Association filed multiple requests, including one for 716 tobacco workers between May and November 2010 and another for 799 tobacco workers between March and November 2011.

Employers specify start and stop dates and must provide work for at least three-fourths of the work period that they specify, for example, at least three forty-hour weeks in a four-week, forty-hours-a-week job order. The average number of workdays in employer requests in fiscal year 2010 was 178, that is, from April 2010 through November 2010. The maximum number of workdays reported by DOL is 260 a year, which was the number assigned to sheepherders, who generally work 365 days a year. Typical tobacco workdays were 135; that is, employers requested certification from May through November.

The H-2A program's expansion and diversification, combined with continued cases of wage theft and other abuses in the employment of guestworkers, have raised the possibility for a revamping of the program. This prospect has been bolstered by continued political unwillingness in Congress to push for comprehensive immigration reform and by heightened anti-immigrant sentiments across the United States since 2007. Although comprehensive immigration reform has proven politically unpopular, one compromise piece of legislation, crafted by labor advocates and agribusiness representatives, demonstrates the enduring interest in guestworkers as a solution to domestic labor scarcities—real or perceived—and the trend toward appeasing private interests with public support: AgJOBS.

AgJOBS Legalization

The H-2A program could be changed by the Agricultural Job Opportunities, Benefits and Security Act (AgJOBS), which would legalize unauthorized farmworkers (sought by labor advocates) and make employer-friendly changes in the H-2A program (sought by agribusiness). AgJOBS includes a legalization program that would allow up to 1.35 million unauthorized farmworkers who have done at least 150 days or 863 hours of farmwork in a twenty-four-month period to apply for blue cards that would make them probationary immigrants.[43] Unauthorized farmworkers would apply for blue cards via government-approved, designated entities or licensed attorneys by presenting evidence of their qualifying farmwork, such as employer-issued payroll records, time cards, and other work-related documents, or affidavits from contractors or fellow workers that "by a preponderance of the evidence" demonstrate that they have done sufficient qualifying farmwork.

Blue card holders could work and travel freely within the United States and enter and leave the country. The unauthorized family members of blue card holders who are in the United States could obtain a "derivative," probationary legal status that would allow them to obtain work permits. Unlike blue card holders, family members would not have to do farmwork, but like blue card holders, they could travel into and out of the United States with their derivative legal status. Blue card holders could earn immigrant status for themselves and their families by continuing to do farmwork under one of three options: (1) performing at least 150 days (a day is at least 5.75 hours) of farmwork a year during each of the first three years after the enactment of AgJOBS; (2) doing at least 100 days of farmwork a year during the first five years after enactment; or (3) working at least 150 days in any three years, plus 100 days in a fourth year (for workers who do not work 150 days in the first three years). Employers of blue card holders must provide blue card employees with written records of their farmwork and submit a copy to the Department of Homeland Security (employers may be fined up to $1,000 for not providing employment records to DHS).

To become legal immigrants within seven years of first receiving blue cards, currently unauthorized foreigners would have to document their continued farmwork, show that they filed income tax returns, and pay an application fee and a $500 fine; their family members would become legal immigrants at the same time. Blue card holders could receive up to twelve months' credit for farmwork not done due to pregnancy or injury to themselves or a minor child, severe weather conditions that reduced farm jobs, or being fired without "just cause" by a farm employer and unable to find another farm job after a "reasonable job search." Administrative mechanisms would be established so that injured and unjustly fired blue card workers could receive appropriate work credit.

AgJOBS and H-2A Changes

In return for concessions involving a path toward citizenship, something employers generally oppose, AgJOBS would make it easier for US farm employers to employ H-2A guestworkers, with most of the changes to the H-2A program beginning a year after enactment. The three major changes to the H-2A program involve attestation, housing, and wages. First, attestation would replace certification, effectively shifting control of the border gate from the US Department of Labor to employers. Employers would attest to the DOL that they have vacant farm jobs, are paying at least the minimum or prevailing wage, and will comply with other H-2A requirements. Employer job offers, to be filed at least twenty-eight days before workers are needed (down from the current forty-five days), would be posted on the Internet and no longer circulated via the interstate clearance system. Not more than fourteen days before the employer-specified starting date, the employer would have to advertise for US workers.

The DOL would review employer assurances for "completeness and obvious inaccuracies" and approve them within seven days of receipt. Foreign H-2A workers would arrive and go to work, and DOL enforcement of employer assurances would involve responding to complaints of violations of H-2A regulations, such as the three-fourths guarantee (the employer would have to offer work for at least three-quarters of the work period specified by the employer). Employers would have to hire local workers (including blue card holders) who respond to recruitment ads until 50 percent of the work period is completed. Finally, employers would have to reimburse 100 percent of the transportation costs of workers who complete the job.

Second, rather than the current requirement to provide free housing to H-2A and out-of-area US workers, AgJOBS would allow farm employers to pay a housing allowance of $1 to $2 an hour, depending on local costs to rent two-bedroom units (which are assumed to house four workers).[44] State governors would have to certify that there is sufficient rental housing for the guestworkers in the area of employment before employers could pay the housing allowance rather than provide free housing. Although this is not as beneficial to workers as receiving housing, it is better than the housing regulations under H-2B visa provisions, in which workers have to pay for employer-provided housing and the rents charged often constitute a form of wage theft.

Third, the adverse effect wage rate, the minimum wage that must be paid to legal guestworkers and any US workers employed alongside them, would be frozen and studied (see www.foreignlaborcert.doleta.gov/adverse .cfm). If Congress failed to enact a new AEWR within three years, the AEWR would be adjusted on the basis of the three-year change in the Consumer Price Index and eventually rise with the CPI by up to 4 percent a year.

The H-2A program currently allows only employers offering seasonal farm jobs to participate, although for decades, H-2A sheep and goat herders have been allowed to work in the United States continuously for up to three years as an exception to this seasonal rule. Under AgJOBS, dairy workers would be added to the sheep and goat exception, so dairies could employ H-2A workers for three years. Dairy farms accounted for 13 percent of direct-hire labor expenses in 2007 and reported hiring 207,000 workers, 55 percent for more than 150 days of work. Allowing dairy farmers to hire H-2A workers is a significant step toward securing support for AgJOBS, given that dairy farms are in every state and that dairy products are often portrayed as critical to the growth of children.

Employer job orders become contracts that H-2A and US workers can sue to enforce. Currently, H-2A workers can sue to enforce these contracts in state courts; under AgJOBS, they could sue employers in federal courts. If workers file suit to enforce their contracts, growers can request mediation from the Federal Mediation and Conciliation Service, and the parties must attempt to resolve their dispute for at least ninety days before the suit can proceed.

Under AgJOBS, H-2A workers would be offered protections comparable to those contained in the Migrant and Seasonal Agricultural Worker Protection Act (MSPA) of 1983 (www.dol.gov/esa/whd/regs/statutes/0001. mspa.htm), including assurances that the vehicles used to transport them are safe. Even though many of those who recruit H-2A workers are or should be licensed as farm labor contractors, AgJOBS, unlike MSPA, would not require the disclosure of wages and working conditions to workers at the time and place of recruitment. Many requirements of the H-2A program would continue under AgJOBS, including having employers reimburse H-2A workers (and US workers from beyond commuting distance) for their transportation and subsistence costs if they complete their work contracts, requiring employers to continue to hire US workers until half of the work contract period is completed, and guaranteeing work to H-2A and US workers for at least three-quarters of the contract period.

CONCLUSIONS

The H-2A program is expanding and may expand faster if comprehensive immigration reforms are enacted. There are several reasons for this expansion, including a short-lived attempt by the outgoing George W. Bush administration to allow employers to attest to their need for H-2A workers rather than undergo certification, effectively streamlining the paperwork that so many employers find burdensome. Under the Bush regulations, the AEWR was reduced by about $1 an hour by switching its basis from the USDA's farm labor survey to the DOL's Occupational Employment Statistics (OES) wage survey.[45] The Barack Obama administration reverted to the previous H-2A regulations in 2010 and made some additional changes, including more disclosure of farm employers' job offers.

Second, stepped-up border and interior enforcement, combined with the spread of Arizona-type anti-immigrant laws to other states, may be slowing the influx of unauthorized workers and encouraging some farm employers to invest in recruitment and housing for H-2A workers. Up to 20 percent of US crop workers in the twenty-first century have been newcomers, meaning that they were in the United States less than a year. If tighter border enforcement reduces the arrival of newcomers, employers worried about the availability of workers may prefer the certainty of H-2A workers to the uncertainty of unauthorized workers, especially if I-9 audits require some employers to terminate large numbers of workers.[46]

Third, some farm employers are turning to H-2A workers because of their "loyalty," that is, the requirement that they stay with the employer with whom they have a contract or else become unauthorized. During the construction boom of 2004–2007, there were complaints from farmers that US workers cherry-picked farm jobs, seeking those that offered easy work or enabled them to earn high piece rate wages and then quitting when harder work or lower earnings loomed. H-2A workers are loyal in the sense that they cannot change employers and that they lose their right to be in the United States if they are fired. Labor reliability such as this is particularly important to producers of perishable products with narrow harvesting windows.

With its much expanded H-2A program, AgJOBS could usher in a new era for farm labor. Farm employers and worker advocates agreed in December 2000 to help currently unauthorized farmworkers to earn legal immigrant status in exchange for a more employer-friendly H-2A program. In 2012, it is easy to assert that the US farmworkers of tomorrow are growing up today somewhere outside the United States, but it is hard to predict whether they will be employed in the United States as unauthorized workers, guestworkers, or legal immigrants or in some other status.

Notes

1. Public Law 82-414, sections 214(c) and 101(a)(15)(H)(2), created the H-2 program in 1952, and Public Law 99-603 (IRCA) modified it in 1986, renaming it the H-2A program. Regulations issued on June 1, 1987, implemented the DOL's handling of the H-2A program; these regulations have been modified several times since.

2. Table 7, Census of Agriculture (US Department of Agriculture 2007), reported that 2.6 million workers were hired by 482,000 farms and direct-hire labor expenditures were almost $22 billion. These direct hires included 911,000 workers hired 150 or more days on the responding farm and 1.7 million employed for less than 150 days on the responding farm.

3. There have been several exceptions to this immigrant-with-freedom-in-the-labor-market concept, including slavery and contract workers. Until the American Revolution in 1776, bound labor (a worker who was tied to an employer in the colonies upon arrival) was the rule (Briggs 1992).

4. Reisler (1976:25–26) reports that many Mexicans in the United States returned to Mexico in the spring of 1917 because of rumors that all men in the United States, including foreigners, could be drafted into the US Army.

5. Quoted on pages 10–11, RG 83, Records of the Bureau of Agricultural Economics, Department of Agriculture, 1923–1946, folder: Farm Labor (1941–1946), box 239: Entry 19, Reports on Farm Labor Shortages and the Works Project Administration,

prepared by the War Production Agency for the House Committee Investigating National Defense Migration, July 3, 1941.

6. A small number of workers from Canada and the Bahamas were also admitted.

7. Scruggs 1960 noted that before the Border Patrol was created in 1924, sixty mounted men patrolled the entire Mexico-US border.

8. The Weedpatch migrant camp in Arvin (today, the Sunset Migrant Center) provided the backdrop for *The Grapes of Wrath*. After its publication, farmers accused Steinbeck of having communist sympathies, Steinbeck received death threats, and the FBI investigated the author.

9. The USDA and DOL Interbureau Coordinating Committee reported that during 1941, "there was some confusion in the use of the term 'shortage'" as well as a tendency in some cases "to identify increases in wages, irrespective of the number of workers available, as a shortage." Quoted in Hahamovitch 1997 from Report of the Interbureau Planning Committee on Farm Labor, "Review of the Farm Labor Situation in 1941," 12/31/41, RG 16, Records of the Office of the Secretary of Agriculture, no. 17, General Correspondence of the Office of the Secretary, 1906–1970, Subject: Employment, file: 1. Labor.

10. The Congressional Research Service (1980:20) says that US unions were mollified by promises that the Mexican farmworkers would leave the United States when their seasonal jobs ended. Mexican Americans were more ambivalent, fearing that the importation of Mexicans would have an adverse effect on their wages.

11. The Mexican Labor Law of 1931 required foreign employers to pay round-trip transportation for workers taken out of the country and required Mexicans going abroad to work to have contracts approved by the Mexican government.

12. Mexico, which declared war on Germany, Italy, and Japan on June 1, 1942, considered its workers in the United States to be a contribution to the Allied war effort.

13. The US minimum wage was set at $0.25 an hour on October 24, 1938, and raised to $0.30 an hour a year later (www.dol.gov/esa/minwage/chart.htm). Employer-set piece rates had to enable the average worker to earn $0.30 an hour or the prevailing wage, whichever was higher (Congressional Research Service 1980:23). In 1946, the minimum wage was raised to $0.37 an hour.

14. As introduced, PL 78 would have covered all farmworkers from the Western Hemisphere, but in the end, it covered only Mexicans because East Coast farmers argued that their private arrangements with Caribbean governments were satisfactory (Congressional Research Service 1980:32).

15. Senator Paul Douglas on February 5, 1952, offered an amendment to impose penalties on employers who had "reasonable grounds to believe a worker was not legally in the US." It was defeated on a 69–12 vote.

16. In many cases, if an employer requested 200 workers from an ES office and the ES office could refer only 100 workers, the ES office would certify the employer's need for 100 braceros. In such cases, the employer's only recruitment was that of calling the local ES office.

17. In signing a two-year extension of PL 78 in 1961, President Kennedy said, "The adverse effects of the Mexican farm labor program as it has operated in recent years on the wages and employment conditions of domestic workers is clear and cumulative in its impact.... Therefore, I sign this bill with the assurance that the Secretary of Labor will, by every means at his disposal, use the authority vested in him under the law to prescribe the standards and to make the determinations essential for the protection of the wages and working conditions of domestic agricultural workers" (qtd. in Congressional Research Service 1980:52–53).

18. PL 82-414 was vetoed by President Truman on June 25, 1952, because it retained the national origins selection system that gave preference to Western Europeans: 70 percent of the 270,000 immigrant visas a year were allotted to natives of the United Kingdom, Ireland, and Germany (most went unused). The veto was overridden on June 27, 1952, and the law went into effect on December 24, 1952.

19. PL 82-414, section 212, states the negative: that is, aliens are ineligible for visas unless "(14) the secretary of labor has determined and certified to the secretary of state and to the attorney general that (A) sufficient workers in the United States who are able, willing, and qualified are available at the time (of application for a visa and for admission to the United States) and place (to which the alien is destined) to perform such skilled or unskilled labor, or (B) the employment of such aliens will adversely affect the wages and working conditions of the workers in the United States similarly employed." See http://tucnak.fsv.cuni.cz/~calda/Documents/1950s/McCarran_52.html.

20. In a November 22, 2005, interview, Hahamovitch said, "We've never had a guest-worker program that was not rife with abuse, and I think the key to that is that employers hold the deportation card. That deportation card has become the new whip." See www.wm.edu/news/?id=5397.

21. DOL secretary Ray Marshall in 1977 told apple growers that foreign workers could not be imported "just because they [could] do a better job than available domestic workers" (qtd. in Congressional Research Service 1980:71).

22. Allison T. French, supervisor of the US Employment Service in West Palm Beach, in the early 1940s noted, "Negro labor in Florida will not work for the Sugar Corporation." He admitted, "It was true that Negroes were occasionally beaten for attempting to leave the job when they owed debts at the company's commissary, and others were sometimes required to work as many as 18 hours a day at cane cutting" (qtd. in Williams 1991).

23. These indictments were later dismissed because of improper jury selection.

24. Florida's sugarcane acreage rose from 49,000 in 1960–1961 to 220,000 in 1964–1965 and has been about 400,000 since the mid-1980s (Buzzanell, Lord, and Brown 1992).

25. The average mill capacity in the early 1990s was 16,400 tons a day, meaning that the industry could grind about 115,000 tons of harvested cane a day. US Sugar is the largest cane miller, with two mills that can grind 22,000 and 16,000 tons of cane a day. In the early 1990s, the cooperative's mill could grind 21,000 tons a day; Flo-Sun subsidiaries Okeelanta and Osceola, 21,000 and 12,000 tons a day; Atlantic, 12,000 tons a day; and Talisman, 11,000 tons a day (Buzzanell, Lord, and Brown 1992).

26. In 2006, sugar variety CP 89-2143 was planted on 27 percent of Florida cane acreage, CP 80-1743 on 23 percent, CP 88-1762 on 18 percent, and CP 78-1628 on 13 percent. (*CP* stands for Canal Point, the location of a public-private facility.)

27. The federal and state governments would share the cost of the cleanup, with sugar companies contributing $230 million. James McKinley, "Sugar Companies Play a Pivotal Role in Effort to Restore Everglades," *New York Times* (April 16, 1999).

28. The sixteen-county South Florida Water Management District is in charge of Everglades restoration, but it does not have the estimated $12 billion needed to implement the cleanup. The *New York Times* reported that after US Sugar's debts climbed sharply, US Sugar approached the state to sell its land, and the state agreed to a relatively high price. Don Van Natta Jr. and Damien Cave, "Deal to Save Everglades May Help Sugar Firm," *New York Times* [March 7, 2010].

29. Most of the sugar mills relied on the Florida Fruit and Vegetable Association to handle worker recruitment, including filing forms with the DOL, arranging for the recruitment and transport of workers, and returning migrants to their countries of origin when they were terminated or the harvest ended.

30. Workers cut two rows of cane at a time: worker A takes rows one and two and throws his cut cane between rows two and three and his trash between one and two; worker B takes rows three and four and throws his cane between rows two and three with A's, putting his trash between rows three and four. A continuous loader picks up the cut cane from the pile rows, cuts it into smaller than 8-foot-long pieces, and loads it into cane wagons pulled by tractors. One tractor typically can pull four cane wagons, each of which holds 3 to 5 tons of cane. The wagons take the cane to a transfer station, where it is transferred to trucks or rail cars, taken to the mill, and weighed before being ground and processed. By weighing the cane coming from each field, companies know the actual yields.

31. A field with 43.56 estimated tons of cane per acre (ET-acre) has 1 ton of cane in each 1,000 square feet or in 100 cut-row feet (two rows planted 5 feet apart). If the task rate or row price is $3.75 in such a field, then the cutter is being paid $3.75 for cutting

100 feet, or \$3.75 a ton; if the task rate is \$4, then the piece rate is \$4 a ton, and so on. The formula to convert the task rate per 100 feet (PR-100) into the price per estimated ton (P/ET) is P/ET = PR-100//ET-acre/43.56. If the estimated yield per acre is 43.56 tons, then the price per 100 feet, PR-100, equals the price per estimated ton, P/ET. As the yield falls below 43.56, the price per estimated ton exceeds the price per 100 feet; for example, if the yield is 22 tons an acre, then the price per estimated ton is twice the price per 100 feet (there are 0.5 tons each 100 feet). If the yield exceeds 44 tons, then the price per estimated ton is less than the price per 100 feet; for example, if the yield is 50 tons per acre and the price per 100 feet is \$4, then the P/ET = 4//(50/43.56) = \$3.49.

32. *NAACP, Jefferson County Branch et al., Plaintiffs, v. US Secretary of Labor et al., Defendants, and US Sugar Corporation et al., Defendant-Intervenors*, September 22, 1994, US District Court for the District of Columbia, 865 F. Supp. 903.

33. The DOL regulations at 20 C.F.R. § 655.207(c) state, "In any year in which the applicable adverse effect rate is increased, employers shall adjust their piece rates upward to avoid requiring a worker to increase his or her productivity over the previous year in order to earn an amount equal to what the worker would earn if the worker were paid at the adverse effect wage rate." Some grower experts opposed linking hourly and piece rate increases, arguing that forcing piece rate wages to increase in lockstep with the AEWR might discourage innovation, since the grower could not reap the productivity increases that might result from, for example, lighter ladders or lighter bags into which to pick apples.

34. US Department of Labor, Final Report Regarding Methods of Payment in Sugar Cane, November 12, 1993, mimeograph in possession of author. The DOL wrote that the task rate system utilized by the sugarcane industry was "incapable of the type of mathematical adjustment required" by the requirement to link AEWR and piece rate increases.

35. The sugar companies cannot raise the productivity standard from, say, eight to twelve tons a day during the season as workers get more proficient and the cane gets heavier. Such a "moving the goalposts" change would require cutters to do more work to earn the same pay and would hurt any US workers who joined crews during the harvest. Under the H-2/H-2A programs, employers must hire US workers who show up to work until the harvest is at least 50 percent completed.

36. The precise relationship is minimum hourly earnings (\$/hour)/productivity standard (units/hour) = task or piece rate (\$/unit). The more usual expression is PS x TR or PR = task or piece earnings, which must be at least the minimum hourly earnings or the employer must provide makeup pay. Employers are not required to retain workers who cannot achieve the minimum hourly earnings, and most such workers are fired.

37. Most workers earned $5,000–$7,000 during the five-month harvest.

38. US Sugar had earlier been a staunch defender of the task rate system. In an August 4, 1992, letter to the *Washington Post*, James Terrill of US Sugar wrote, "Cane cutters work an average of six to 6½ hours per day and cut about 1.2 to 1.5 tons per hour. Their typical wage is close to $7 per hour and is monitored by electronic time-keepers. Housing and medical care are free. Food is subsidized. At home they would earn $3 per day."

39. US Sugar reported in April 1993 that under the new piece rate system, the average cutter earned $48 a day in 1992–1993, up from $42 in 1991–1992, and average hourly earnings rose to $7.24 from $6.54; the fastest cutters earned $11 per hour when the AEWR was $5.91.

40. Four Fanjul brothers, Alfonso, or "Alfie," José, or "Pepe," Alexander, and Andres, control Flo-Sun, Inc., which has sugarcane and mills in Florida and the Dominican Republic. They are major contributors to both Democratic and Republican politicians. Jeffrey Birnbaum, "Cuban-American Contributors Open Checkbooks after Torricelli Exhibits an Anti-Castro Fervor," *Wall Street Journal* (August 3, 1992).

41. However, an analysis of the task rates across the thousands of fields harvested by the mills found that 91 percent of the variation in task rates between fields could be explained by estimated yields.

42. In some cases, the H-2A data sheet says that the employer's request was certified in full, but there is no entry in the "workers certified" column.

43. Under the House version of AgJOBS, unauthorized workers earning at least $7,500 from farmwork during the qualifying period would also qualify for blue cards.

44. The housing allowance would be based on the 40th percentile of fair-market rents (FMRs) established by the US Department of Housing and Urban Develop-ment (www.huduser.org/portal/datasets/fmr.html). For two-bedroom apartments in Fresno County in 2011, for example, the FMR was $855 a month, so four workers each employed 160 hours per month, or 640 hours in total, would receive a housing allow-ance of $1.33 an hour. In Salinas that year, the FMR was $1,092, making the housing allowance for four full-time workers $1.70 an hour.

45. Stan Eury of the North Carolina Growers Association, the largest single H-2A user, complained in an interview with the *Packer* on February 26, 2010, that reverting to the old H-2A regulations would raise the wages of H-2A workers in North Carolina by an average of $1.75 an hour. If 100,000 US and H-2A workers averaged 1,500 hours each on farms that used the OES data to determine the AEWR, employers saved about $150 million ($1,500 x 100,000) with the H-2A regulation in effect in 2009.

46. Gebbers Farms, a 5,000-acre apple and cherry operation north of Wenatchee in Brewster, Washington, had its employment records audited by ICE late in 2009.

Gebbers fired 550 workers and gave the fired workers until April 1, 2010, to vacate company housing. In 2010, Gebbers was approved to hire 1,200 H-2A workers for six months. They began arriving in June 2010 and included 300 Jamaicans. "H-2A, ICE, RICO," Rural Migration News 16, no. 3 (July 2010). http://migration.ucdavis.edu/rmn/more.php?id=1550_0_4_0.

3

Temporary Foreign Workers in Canada

Flexible Labor in the Twenty-First Century

Josephine Smart

Temporary migrant workers, or guestworkers, have been coming to Canada for almost as long as the country has been in existence. These workers have come from around the world in a pattern that corresponds closely to what we today call transnational flow or globalized mobility, yet their presence in the labor market precedes contemporary understandings of transnationalism by more than a century. Early temporary migrant workers included the European and Chinese workers on the Canadian Railway project in the late nineteenth century, Chinese "houseboys" in western Canada at the turn of the twentieth century (Trumper and Wong 2007:152), black women from Guadeloupe who worked as domestic servants in Montreal and Quebec City in the late 1800s and early 1900s (Mackenzie 1988), post–World War II displaced persons and veterans of Polish origin who were deployed mostly in farmwork throughout the prairie provinces of western Canada (Trumper and Wong 2007:153), and the seasonal agricultural workers from the Caribbean countries of Jamaica, Trinidad and Tobago, Dominican Republic, and Barbados since 1966 (Mexico was added to this program in 1973). Over time, the flow of temporary foreign workers (TFWs) into Canada has expanded significantly, with the number of TFWs nearly doubling, from 109,000 to 192,000 from 1999 to 2008 (Citizenship and Immigration Canada 2008:66). Over the years, it has become ever more formalized through legislative and administrative interventions (see Fudge and MacPhail 2009), although, following state investment in establishing temporary worker programs, it has been gradually transferred to more private control.

The Non-Immigrant Employment Authorization Program (NIEAP) was created in 1973. At that time, the program catered only to highly skilled workers such as academics, business executives, and engineers (Fudge and MacPhail 2009:7; Nakache and Kinoshita 2010:4). It was restructured and expanded in 2002 under the Immigration and Refugee Protection Act to include low-skilled and unskilled workers and, after the implementation of the National Occupations Code (NOC), was renamed the NOC C&D Pilot (hereafter, the Pilot). The Pilot is administered jointly by two federal departments: Citizenship and Immigration Canada (CIC) and Human Resources and Skills Development Canada (HRSDC) (Elgersma 2007:1). Enforcement and control of the Pilot was moved from CIC to the Canada Border Services Agency when the latter was created in 2003 (Auditor General of Canada 2009:9).

Until the twenty-first century, the traditional top sources for temporary foreign workers in Canada were the United States, Jamaica, Mexico, the United Kingdom, and the eastern Caribbean. In 2008, the Philippines became the top source country for foreign workers in Canada for the second year in a row, followed by the United States, Mexico, the United Kingdom, Australia, France, India, Japan, and the People's Republic of China (Citizenship and Immigration Canada 2008:60). The number of foreign workers from Asian countries—India, China, South Korea, Taiwan, Singapore, and Thailand—showed some of the highest rates of increase between 1999 and 2008 (ibid.), a trend that is likely to continue. The proportion of women among the temporary foreign workers has increased steadily: it was over 40 percent in 2008 (ibid.:67). These two trends—increasing numbers of countries and increasing numbers of women involved in temporary worker programs—indicate that the Canadian state, under the influence of Canadian employers and employers' associations (see Preibisch, chapter 4, this volume), have been actively shopping global labor markets to contract labor forces that conform to specific workplace needs. It is likely, too, that cultural and gender stereotypes influence these trends, with employers seeking workers they view as predisposed to performing specific tasks. Preibisch suggests that the gradual increase of women in Canadian greenhouses, as well as workers from Guatemala and El Salvador, may be due to employer perceptions that women and workers from politically unstable, fragile states are more vulnerable and easier to control.

The economic significance of the Pilot in Canada was clearly articulated in a 2007 parliamentary report, which states, "Canada is becoming increasingly reliant on temporary foreign workers to meet labour market shortages.... The Canadian government benefits not only from the sustained economic growth fostered by the Temporary Foreign Worker Program but also from the tax revenue generated by the program" (Elgersma 2007:1, 5). This chapter examines the future direction of growth of the Pilot in Canada and highlights lessons learned about the management and mismanagement of the Pilot since its inception. The first part of the chapter provides a descriptive analysis of the structure and scale of the Pilot in Canada and follows with a brief survey of the Pilot's impact on the Canadian economy and sending communities. The last section discusses the future growth of the Pilot and the strengths and weaknesses of managed labor migration in Canada.

STRUCTURE AND SCALE OF THE NOC C&D PILOT

The Pilot is a highly segmented program that reflects the historical legacy of preexisting temporary foreign worker programs such as the Seasonal Agricultural Worker Program (SAWP), the Live-In Caregiver Program, and the NIEAP. The expressed goal of the program is to channel temporary workers into a wide array of occupations with different skill types and skill-level requirements in order to meet short-term labor shortages. With the exception of the most highly qualified temporary workers, who may receive permission to remain in Canada permanently, the majority of temporary foreign workers are not allowed to stay as permanent residents (Nakache and Kinoshita 2010). The Canadian government's approach to immigration leans heavily toward favoring "designer" immigrants whose economic and sociocultural attributes are deemed by the state to be favorable to the economic and social development of Canada and toward refusing permanent residence to workers considered low-skill, disposable, and easily replaceable from a growing number of foreign sources (Ley 2010; Simmons 2010). A new immigration category known as the "independent" class was created in 1967 to select for new immigrants who are educated, bilingual (English and French), and skilled. In the early 1980s, the independent class was expanded to include those with money and business experience, and this drew many voices of dissent from the public that does not share the government's notion of what constituted a "desirable" or worthy immigrant (Smart 1994).

Despite these objections, the government continues to take as its prerogative the management of its immigrant population in light of political-economic developments, further legitimating itself in the eyes of select economic sectors. The Pilot strengthens the Canadian government's power to regulate the types of immigrants it receives by creating an administrative platform that allows low-skilled workers (undesirable candidates for Canadian immigration) into the country without any avenue toward permanent residency. At the same time, the segmented structure of the Pilot enables the government to offer permanent residency to selected individuals with high skills or other desirable attributes. This bureaucratic mechanism creates different classes of immigrants and non-immigrants, whose roles in the Canadian economy are highly defined.

The Pilot was created in 2002 to replace the NIEAP, but the SAWP and the Live-In Caregiver Program continue to exist as parallel and separate guestworker programs (for the distinctive features of TFWPs in Canada, see the appendix). It should be noted that Pilot applicants can be hired in agricultural and live-in caregiving employment under the specific administrative structure and requirements of the Pilot; as long as employers can make an argument to the HRSDC that a labor shortage exists, the Pilot offers employers an alternative that is less closely monitored than the other two foreign worker programs (Preibisch, chapter 4, this volume).

As Preibisch (this volume) notes, government involvement in the Pilot is significantly less than in the Seasonal Agricultural Worker Program. It is an employer-driven program, reflecting the increasing privatization of immigration policy across North America. In practice, employers first initiate the offer of employment to a potential temporary worker, with clearly stated terms including location of the work, job description, length of employment, wages, and working conditions. Second, employers are required to provide housing and health care coverage for the temporary foreign worker and to cover all worker travel expenses and recruitment charges if a broker or recruitment agency is used (see information under *Pilot* at the Government of Alberta's website, http://www.albertacanada. com, and see http://www.hrsdc.gc.ca/eng/workplaceskills/foreign_workers). In short, with the exception of often illegal recruitment fees paid to labor contractors in their home countries, TFWs coming to Canada do not have to pay up-front to cover travel, broker's fees, and living expenses before securing employment (Basok 2000). They also know ahead of time the terms and conditions of their employment, the length of their employment, and the geographical location of their employment in Canada (Smart 1998).

In theory at least, according to the government of Canada, "foreign workers, including temporary foreign workers, have the same rights and protections as all Canadian workers" (HRSDC website, http://www.hrsdc

.gc.ca/eng/workplaceskills/foreign_workers). In reality, violations of the rights of temporary foreign workers and failure to comply with the terms of employment are the main reasons for some of the harshest criticisms leveled at the Pilot and the government by nongovernmental organizations like the Agriculture Workers Alliance (http://awa-ata.ca/en) and the United Food and Commercial Workers (UFCW) of Canada (http://www.ufcw.ca), which Preibisch (chapter 4, this volume) discusses at some length. Hence, as with many guestworker programs, there exists a disjuncture between the legal protections and expectations and the real, on-the-ground functioning of the program—a fact that officials from the home countries of immigrants, including their embassies and liaison service offices, often have great difficulty coming to terms with. It is important to emphasize that the program's structure, particularly the reduced role of the state, has created an administrative context in which worker abuse without significant legal repercussion is possible. Employers from different economic sectors, in other words, can combine state policy with their individualized approaches to labor relations to achieve production and productivity goals, whether or not those labor relations are primarily coercive or benign.

Temporary foreign workers in Canada are employed in a myriad of occupations ranging from management executive positions to entertainment positions in exotic dancing and other performing arts to on-the-job training in meat and processing plants. Equally telling, TFWs come from an increasing number of countries. Chinese workers are hired in large numbers at the Maple Leaf meatpacking plant in Brandon (Manitoba), and many work at the oil sand projects in Fort McMurray (Alberta). Spanish-speaking agricultural workers from Mexico, Guatemala, Ecuador, and other Central and South American countries can be found in British Columbia, Alberta, Ontario, and Quebec (Hughes, chapter 7, this volume; Preibisch, chapter 4, this volume). The use of temporary foreign workers in fast-food chain outlets in both urban and rural Canada is becoming increasingly common. Filipino workers are hired in large numbers in fast-food outlets for their high level of English proficiency, although many temporary foreign workers are not proficient in English or French. An accidental death of a worker in 2010 revealed the little-known fact that non-English-speaking temporary workers from Thailand were working as electricians in the city of Calgary.

A growing economic sector incorporating temporary foreign workers has been construction. According to the Construction Sector Council (Canada), TFWs accounted for less than half a percent of Canada's construction workers in 2005. Of the more than 1 million people working in construction that year, only 3,000 were temporary foreign workers, yet these came from twenty countries. The top source countries were the United States, the United Kingdom, the Philippines, Germany, Mexico, and Poland, with the number rising with demand during special construction events, such as the 2010 Olympic building projects in Vancouver.

Today, temporary foreign workers in Canada come from more than 120 countries (table 3.1). Three Asian countries—the Philippines, India, and China—are rapidly becoming a major source of TFWs, whereas the dominance of the United States as the top source country of TFWs for Canada has diminished since 2007. National diversity has been matched by gender and ethnic diversity. More women are now among the TFWs, increasing from just over 26,000 to nearly 106,000 from 1999 to 2008, or from just over 24 percent to nearly 55 percent of the total TFWs (Citizenship and Immigration Canada 2008:67). A significant percentage of the workers from the United States (64 percent), Europe (53 percent), and Africa and the Middle East (61 percent) were ranked as skilled and highly skilled. In contrast, most workers from Asia and the Pacific (59 percent) and Central and South America (85 percent) were in low-skill positions in 2006 (Trumper and Wong 2007:157). This shift in demographics by gender, skill level, and source country leads Trumper and Wong to conclude that, first, temporary workers have been racialized by skill level, with skilled and highly skilled workers tending to come from the United States and Europe and lower-skilled workers tending to come from Asia, the Pacific, and the Americas (excluding the United States). Second, there is a gendered occupational pattern, with men more likely to be in highly skilled or skilled occupations (the exception being farmworkers from Central and South America) and women of color more likely to be in lower-skilled occupations (with the exception of Filipina nurses who come as live-in caregivers). Both Hughes (chapter 7) and Preibisch (chapter 4) discuss the relations between gender and occupation in Canadian agriculture, where women are becoming a preferred workforce in greenhouses. These national, gender, and ethnic differences dovetail with the segmented structure of Canada's TFWPs by separating the Canadian labor force in ways that undermine its ability to engage in collective action or to marshal an effective social movement aimed at increasing worker and human rights. The uneven distribution of TFWs across economic sectors and Canadian geography enhances this.

Within Canada, the geographic distribution of TFWs is uneven. The provinces of British Columbia and Alberta have experienced the highest increases of TFWs (table 3.2), but Ontario remains the top destination of TFWs by number, largely due to its legacy of seasonal workers in greenhouses

TABLE 3.1
Foreign Workers Present in Canada on December 1 by Selected Source Country

Source Country	1999	2000	2001	2002	2003	2004	2005	2006	2007	2008
Philippines	6,002	6,338	8,268	10,785	12,504	15,307	17,687	21,566	33,882	45,006
US	20,267	21,354	21,041	20,205	21,012	21,043	23,658	25,278	26,779	28,754
Mexico	8,120	9,995	11,172	11,606	11,641	11,950	13,306	15,185	18,154	22,579
UK	5,720	6,526	7,031	7,041	7,482	9,433	10,713	11,138	12,623	14,530
Australia	4,031	4,577	5,441	6,254	6,897	8,269	8,606	9,063	9,842	13,222
France	2,888	3,368	3,778	4,033	4,400	5,968	7,481	9,085	10,023	11,788
India	1,536	1,879	1,898	2,174	2,689	3,710	5,087	6,344	8,671	11,114
Japan	7,155	6,568	6,493	7,828	8,281	8,608	8,841	8,428	7,871	9,316
China (PRC)	1,231	1,338	1,588	1,824	1,950	2,427	3,080	4,206	6,632	8,534
Germany	1,658	1,993	2,267	2,068	2,257	3,119	3,639	5,430	6,908	8,239
Jamaica	5,511	5,255	5,670	5,357	5,832	5,890	6,083	6,375	6,667	7,316
S. Korea	992	1,175	1,355	1,504	1,931	2,394	3,033	3,734	4,835	7,275
Taiwan	210	186	238	261	277	329	522	918	1,525	2,816
United Arab Emirates	44	75	128	190	225	264	324	473	1,046	1,740
Guatemala	13	15	15	13	238	353	276	396	780	1,438
Trinidad and Tobago	1,666	1,786	1,755	1,614	1,599	1,657	1,628	1,472	1,407	1,351
Singapore	90	99	103	92	194	335	521	708	1,187	1,259
Thailand	117	153	126	192	214	262	326	879	1,257	1,123
Totals	82,111	89,793	96,525	101,259	109,860	125,367	141,032	161,295	199,942	251,235

Source: adapted from Citizenship and Immigration Canada 2008:60–61

TABLE 3.2
Foreign Workers Present in Canada on December 1 by Province or Territory

Province or Territory	1999	2000	2001	2002	2003	2004	2005	2006	2007	2008
Newfoundland and Labrador	763	989	882	1,030	925	874	941	917	882	1,065
Prince Edward Island	138	127	135	138	146	152	140	212	295	459
Nova Scotia	1,234	1,012	1,275	1,400	1,292	1,674	1,520	1,715	2,027	2,539
New Brunswick	535	584	602	510	623	793	907	1,127	1,414	2,031
Quebec	10,401	12,591	13,649	13,865	15,379	18,036	20,160	21,630	23,360	25,970
Ontario	42,445	46,491	49,548	50,537	53,458	58,973	64,775	72,012	82,474	91,276
Manitoba	1,619	1,711	1,790	1,954	2,064	2,415	2,667	3,315	4,557	5,357
Saskatchewan	1,220	1,320	1,339	1,465	1,527	1,722	2,006	2,182	2,978	4,350
Alberta	8,730	9,465	10,385	10,757	11,391	13,167	15,747	22,020	37,128	57,707
British Columbia	14,714	15,196	16,575	19,301	22,231	26,795	31,425	35,157	43,355	58,307
Yukon	69	56	49	54	76	97	95	106	157	245
Northwest Territories	149	196	237	199	248	269	284	270	306	302
Nunavut	16	16	14	25	33	33	44	47	53	31
Not stated	78	51	45	24	467	367	321	585	956	1,596
Totals	82,111	89,793	96,525	101,259	109,860	125,367	141,032	161,295	199,942	25,123

Source: adapted from Citizenship and Immigration Canada 2008:64

and other agricultural industries (Basok 2000; Hughes, chapter 7, this volume; Preibisch, chapter 4, this volume). By rough estimate, about 40 percent of TFWs in Canada in 2008 were located in rural areas. Newfoundland and Labrador (75.7 percent), Prince Edward Island (62 percent), and the Northwest Territories (75 percent) had the highest rate of TFWs in non-urban locations in 2008, whereas Quebec showed the lowest in non-urban locations (24 percent). Rural-based TFWs are likely to work in agriculture, natural resources (oil and gas, forestry), food processing and manufacturing, and hospitality.

The year 2008 marked a milestone in Canadian immigration history, when the total number of temporary foreign workers (251,235 persons) outnumbered the total number of new permanent residents or landed immigrants (247,243). This signals a major shift in the dynamics of the labor market in Canada in the twenty-first century: Canada's deployment of temporary foreign workers is no longer a "temporary" solution to labor shortages but has become a pervasive feature of the Canadian labor market (Nakache and Kinoshita 2010; Preibisch 2007b; Sharma 2006). As in other guestworker-dominated industries, such as sugar in southern Florida (Martin, chapter 2, this volume) and apples in Virginia's Shenandoah Valley (Bump, Goździak, and Lowell, chapter 3, this volume), TFWs have become an institutionalized part of Canadian political economies, deepening the nation's global connections and making more complex its globalized and racialized labor force. Recognizing this, labor unions and other labor rights advocates have been targeting Pilot occupations as potential areas for new organizing and human rights campaigns.

IMPACT OF THE PILOT ON CANADA AND SENDING COUNTRIES

On June 20, 2010 (Father's Day), the UFCW Canada hosted an international migrant workers forum at the University of Toronto campus. The forum, titled "No Rights, No Rules," was described as follows: "This event shall highlight the devastating effects of family separation and human displacement that [have] resulted from the migrant and guest worker programs, such as the Canadian Temporary Foreign Workers [sic] Program.... to map out the steps forward to work with those fathers and mothers, brothers and sisters, who leave their homes only to be disappointed, neglected and abused through the Canadian Temporary Foreign Workers Program. This event shall reinforce our commitment towards migrant and immigrant worker dignity, respect and justice in Canada" (http://www .ufcw.ca/index.php?option=com_multicategories&view=article&id=203 8:e-news-vol3-issue-15&Itemid=0&lang=en).

TABLE 3.3

Management Incidents and Episodes in Program Administration

Ref. Pp.	Problem	Recommendation
30–31	Human Resources and Skills Development Canada's practice[s] do not ensure quality and consistency of decisions when issuing labour market opinions.	HRSDC should • provide clear directives, tools, and training to officers engaged in issuing labour market opinions (LMO) and • implement a qualityassurance framework to ensure the quality and consistency of opinions across Canada.
32–33	The genuineness of job offers is not systematically verified.	CIC and HRSDC should verify their respective roles and responsibilities and put mechanisms in place to ensure that the genuineness of job offers is systematically verified.
33–35	Concerns remain about the integrity of the program and the protection of temporary foreign workers. 2.108: Lower-skilled foreign workers entering Canada may be vulnerable to exploitation or poor working conditions, usually because of their economic conditions, linguistic isolation, and limited understanding of their rights. 2.112: Lack of follow-up on job offers can have implications not only for the integrity of the programs but also for the well-being of foreign workers.... CIC and HRSDC officials told us that neither the IRPA nor the regulations give them authority to conduct compliance reviews of employers who have not consented.	CIC and HRSDC should implement mechanism[s] that would better enable them to ensure the integrity of the Pilot and the protection of individuals.
37	A quality assurance framework has not yet been implemented. 2.127: In our 2000 report, we also raised concerns about the quality of visa officers' decisions on applications to immigrate to Canada. We stressed the need for a quality assurance framework to ensure that decisions are consistent and fair. 2.128: The Dept subsequently developed a quality assurance framework that is available to all missions, but there is no requirement for immigration program managers to implement it or to report on quality assurance. Consequently, although some quality assurance is performed in some missions when time permits, it is not comprehensive, is not necessarily consistent with the framework, and does not ensure the overall quality and consistency of decisions. Of the eight missions we visited, only one had recently implemented the framework.	Citizenship and Immigration Canada should ensure that its quality assurance framework is implemented fully and consistently in all missions.

Department Action

- In March 2009, an electronic mailbox was created for regional staff to seek direction and exchange information on issues related to policy and operations.
- In June 2009, a new team was created to develop and implement a quality assurance framework that will strengthen the responsiveness, consistency, speed, and quality of decision-making when issuing LMOs.
- In July 2009, a new monthly teleconference was launched specific to integrity issues
- The Dept. continues to hold annual meetings and monthly teleconference[s] to discuss operational and procedural issue[s].

- A new information-sharing agreement between CIC and HRSDC will enable a more active exchange of information pertinent to the assessment of the genuineness of job offers.

- HRSDC has introduced new compliance review initiatives to better detect and address instances of non-compliance with conditions specified on LMOs.
- Information-sharing agreements with a number of provinces are either signed or forthcoming to support enforcement of federal and provincial laws and standards.
- New policies were introduced that limit LMO validity to six months and enable revocation of LMO when the conditions that supported that opinion are found to be no longer valid.
- In June 2009, an electronic mailbox was created at HRSDC for CID [*sic*] and Canada Border Services Agency staff to seek direction on specific labour market opinions issued by HRSDC, as well as providing a mechanism for reporting possible fraud.

Source: Auditor General of Canada 2009

The sentiments expressed by the organizer (UFCW) and sponsors (Workers Action Centre, Migrante Canada, Barrio Nuevo, Agriculture Workers Alliance, Students Against Migrant Exploitation Canada, Ontario Federation of Labour, and others) are typical of the "Capitalism is evil" and "Migrant workers are victims of exploitation" styles of discourse. They rightly direct public attention to a multitude of social and economic problems common to migrant labor worldwide (see Fudge and MacPhail 2009:30–42; Nakache and Kinoshita 2010:31–35; Smart and Smart 2001; Smart 1998), including non-enforcement of employment contracts, being "squeezed" by recruitment agencies or corrupt government officials for payments to obtain employment or work permits, unpaid or underpaid wages, substandard living conditions, and all sorts of violations of established labor laws regarding working conditions, maximum number of working hours per day, paid holidays, and other entitlements.

Yet, not only the labor organizations have spoken out against Canada's guestworker programs. Some of the harshest criticism of the Pilot has come from the Office of the Auditor General of Canada. In a 2009 report to the Canadian House of Commons, the auditor general identified a series of mismanagement incidents and episodes in program administration, coordination, and regulation that seriously affected the integrity of the Pilot (Auditor General of Canada 2009:ch. 2; table 3.3).

The impacts of TFWs on the economy and society are as complex and contentious in Canada as they are in the United States, Europe, Australia, and other areas where the guestworker presence is growing, with the same issues raised again and again. A positive view may point to the fact that the expansion of KFC, A&W, Tim Hortons, McDonald's, and other fast-food chains in rural Canada, for instance, cannot be sustained without the large-scale utilization of TFWs. Labor shortages in rural and northern regions are often due to the emigration of young people to urban centers, and the offer of higher wages alone is not sufficient to attract or retain workers in the food-processing, service, and hospitality sectors. Similarly, in the absence of mechanization, the fruit and greenhouse agriculture sector in Canada would be greatly reduced without guestworkers. Large projects like the 2010 Olympic construction in Vancouver and the oil sand explorations in northern Alberta would be difficult to achieve without the Pilot.

Yet, opponents of TFWPs cite an equal number and range of negative impacts from TFWs on Canadian society (Basok 2000; Preibisch, chapter 4, this volume). Again, these are similar to objections raised elsewhere: it is said that guestworkers depress wages, take jobs from native workers, and frustrate union campaigns. Although the opposition to TFWs is likely to persist, if one considers the low fertility rate in Canada, the highly controlled numbers of new permanent immigrants each year (under 250,000), and the steady decline of rural populations throughout Canada, it is difficult to dismiss the significance and potential utility of the Pilot in sustaining and fueling the growth of the Canadian economy in selected sectors.

By the same token, the supply of international labor seems inexhaustible. Despite the many problems with the TFWPs, foreign nationals are eager to come as temporary workers to Canada. Bump, Goździak, and Lowell (chapter 8, this volume) describe a worker who continued coming to pick Virginia apples for two decades even though he complained of substandard housing. This desire has underwritten the development of recruitment schemes in sending countries, many handled by private contractors who engage in unscrupulous practices. Even so, along with labor demand, at least two other factors attract international labor migrants to Canada:

1. Some temporary workers hope to obtain permanent resident status in Canada by using the Pilot as a stepping-stone (Nakache and Kinoshita 2010:30).
2. The wages earned in Canada are substantially higher than what guest-workers can earn in their home countries. This is particularly the case where domestic livelihoods have been eroded due to neoliberal reforms, the withdrawal of state support, and weak commodity prices for domestic products (Griffith and Contreras, chapter 6, this volume; Hughes, chapter 7, this volume).

In a comprehensive study of Mexican seasonal agricultural labor in southern Ontario, Basok (2000:80–81) finds that these workers have worked in Canada for an average of six and a half years and their income from the eight months of employment (the maximum period allowed under the SAWP) is equivalent to five years of income in their home regions in Mexico. The seasonal employment in Canada enables the Mexican workers to improve the standard of living for their families and supports greater access to education for their children (Basok 2000). Some productive investments (in land, equipment, technology) are also supported by the Canadian earnings, and there is some potential for technology and knowledge transfer arising from their Canadian work experience to enhance future development in sending countries (Griffith and Contreras, chapter 6, this volume; Smart 1998). Yet, there are trade-offs. Time spent in Canada entails extended separation from family and social networks at home. The stress on marital relationships, intergenerational interactions, and knowledge transfer can be substantial and disruptive. Finally, if a guestworker should opt for illegal settlement in the host country, she is likely to become

highly vulnerable to all sorts of employment abuse, social isolation, instability, and prolonged separation from family in the home country (Griffith
and Contreras, chapter 6, this volume).

DISCUSSION: THE FUTURE OF THE TFWP IN CANADA

Currently, the global mobility of labor is growing in scale and scope
from year to year, but international labor flows are by no means a new
phenomenon and mobility has fluctuated over time. Although distinct in
many ways from current flows, precedents exist in the historical context
of the slave trade created during the colonial expansion of Europe beginning in the sixteenth century and the Chinese coolie deployment in North
America, the Caribbean, and Australasia in the nineteenth century. What
was new with the international mobility of labor in the twentieth century
was the role that bilateral and multilateral politics played in channeling the
flow of labor migrants from specific sending countries to specific receiving countries. Much of labor mobility in the twenty-first century continues
to be shaped by bilateral and multilateral agreements, with a noticeable
emphasis on temporary and fixed-term employment contracts for low- and
semi-skilled workers. Italy and Spain, according to Ruhs (2006:7), support
their guestworker programs under the framework of bilateral agreements
with migrant-sending countries in northern Africa and Latin America. In
the United States, the bracero program (1942–1964) involved a bilateral
agreement with Mexico, but H-2A and H-2B visas are issued in the absence
of such agreements. Germany had the Gastarbeiter program (1955–1973),
and the Canadian SAWP (1966–present) is an example of a multilateral
agreement.

Canada is not alone in following a multiple-track approach to foreign
labor migrants, segmenting its temporary foreign labor force by mode of
government oversight, skill level, potential for permanent residence, gender, nationality, and other factors. As a general rule, the highly skilled are
enticed to stay with offers of citizenship or permanent residence, whereas
the low-skilled are welcome to work but not to stay permanently. The use
of temporary foreign workers to sustain national economic growth is fast
becoming a normative mode of labor deployment flexibility in many countries, both developed and developing, involving workers of all skill levels,
genders, and nationalities from both the North and the South. Critics call
this particular form of temporary labor deployment an "extreme form of
flexible labour" (Fudge and MacPhail 2009), which is characterized as being
intense on labor utilization but short on granting full rights and benefits to
those who are deployed (http://www.ufcw.ca; Nakache and Kinoshita 2010;

Ruhs and Martin 2008). In other words, it is a form of labor exploitation in the classic Marxian sense. The state and the capitalist are working hand in hand, the former largely an instrument of the latter even as the state strengthens its legitimacy vis-à-vis the prevailing political economy and, in the process, becomes an indispensable actor in the nation's labor relations.

Ruhs and Martin (2008:260) offer a different perspective by arguing that the TFWP may be seen as "the best compromise between the extremes of no borders and no migrants" for high-income countries facing strong public opposition to labor immigration. Large numbers of low-skilled temporary workers can be hired to support economic growth cheaply. In spite of all the well-documented problems of the Pilot, its failure to meet program objectives, and the many associated, unintended consequences, such as nonreturn (Ruhs 2006:7), some view TFWPs as win-win for all stakeholders (Bump, Goździak, and Lowell, chapter 8, this volume; Ruhs and Martin 2008:249–250). Guestworker-receiving countries benefit from the labor input to economic growth, sending countries welcome remittances and skill and technology transfers, and guestworkers are happy to earn higher wages and receive skill training in the host country.

Moving away from the rhetoric of rights and numbers, extreme labor flexibility, and liberal democracy, there are practical issues and implications to consider within the context of temporary foreign worker deployment. Many aspects of the program design and management deserve further debate and improvement to ensure adequate worker rights protection, full compliance with the terms of employment by both employers and employees, the possibility of collective bargaining, and the effective harmonization of costs and benefits for all key stakeholders. In the long run, Canada must assess critically whether the growing reliance on temporary foreign workers is the best means to enhance the national economy and global competitiveness. In the short term, the TFWP will continue to grow at a fast pace and very likely will increase the geographic scope of temporary worker recruitment.

POSTSCRIPT: CHINA'S ROLE IN CANADIAN LABOR MIGRATION

A final point of particular interest concerns Canada's deepening relationship with China, a growing force in world economics and one that is by no means neutral or benign in circles of international competition, with direct consequences for the flow of international labor (Bump, Goździak, and Lowell, chapter 8, this volume). The conclusion of several major bilateral agreements between Canada and China is likely to contribute to a stronger flow of TFWs between the two countries in the near future, likely involving low-skilled temporary workers from China to Canada and high-skilled temporary workers or professionals from Canada to China. China agreed in June 2011 to buy more wheat from Canada and to reopen its market to Canadian beef after a ban was imposed in May 2003. Furthermore, Canada was named an "approved tourist destination" by the Chinese government for its citizens. In return, the Canadian government fast-tracked a major Chinese government investment in an oil sand project in Alberta soon after this announcement. Chinese overseas direct investments, coming from both the state and independent entrepreneurs, have been quite aggressive in the twenty-first century in their global reach into natural resources, mining, oil and gas, construction, manufacturing, and agricultural production. The Chinese government and independent investors have been buying and leasing agricultural land in Africa, Latin America, and Southeast Asia for export production. It is rumored that as many as a million Chinese agricultural workers now work in Africa. Canada is a country of tremendous agricultural output with a surplus that is the envy of countries like China, which is highly concerned about food security. It can be expected that China will not overlook Canada as a possible investment target in agricultural production. The number of temporary workers from China can be expected to rise in correspondence with the rise in Chinese overseas direct investment in Canada, and their deployment will widen in scope as Chinese overseas direct investments diversify to include the primary agricultural sector in Canada in addition to current interests in the oil and gas sector.

In the aftermath of the 2008 economic crisis, when many countries are still struggling to cope with its adverse impacts, China stands out in its resilience and its ability to maintain an annual growth rate at just over 8 percent. A stronger relationship with China in trade and investment is considered by many to be both desirable and inevitable. Canada is not alone in its efforts to foster closer links with China under the rubric of globalization and economic integration. As mentioned above, greater economic integration and improving bilateral relationships are likely to foster a greater scope for migration in both permanent and temporary forms. The Canadian government announced in April 2012 new changes to the temporary foreign workers program, and two issues stand out in their central relevance to this chapter. First, the TFW applications will now be fast-tracked so that employers who submit an application can expect to receive an answer from the appropriate government office within ten days, instead of the usual twelve to fourteen weeks. Second, temporary foreign workers can now be paid up to 15 percent less than the going rates for Canadians (for details, see http://www.immigration.ca/news-all.asp?id=334). These changes in the TFWP regulations clearly favor the employers at the economic expense of the temporary foreign workers. The institutionalized exploitation of temporary foreign workers in their pay as compared with the going wages for Canadian workers for the same jobs is bound to exacerbate any existing hostility toward TFWs as aliens who take jobs away from Canadians. In light of the expected growing number of future temporary workers from China and other Asian countries, these regulation changes may spark a highly racialized hostility toward Asians, with possibly terrible outcomes. Canada is a country respected for its strong multiculturalism, yet its history speaks of its capacity for racist outbursts. The Chinese Exclusion Act in 1923 is just one example.

Greater economic integration, like globalization, is a two-edged sword. Inequality and exploitation are inherent features of the current TFWP in Canada, and these flaws, with their tremendous social and political implications, must not be ignored.

PART II

Fluctuations in Guestworker Programs in the Twenty-First Century

4

Managed Migration and Changing Workplace Regimes in Canadian Agriculture

Kerry Preibisch

In the Canadian province of Ontario, the small rural town of Leamington is known both as the country's tomato capital, for its production of the field crop essential to large processing companies such as Heinz, and more recently as the greenhouse capital of North America, for hosting the continent's largest concentration of glass houses. A travel blog about the club scene in Canada's southernmost municipality includes the following:

> If it is nightlife you seek in this Tomato Town, head on down to The Basement, also known to some residents as its Spanish equivalent "El Sotano," a bar located just behind the Royal Bank. Around midnight the ambience of this subterranean, Tropical Chic–style den comes alive with the contemporary beats of Latin pop and reggaeton. The demographic is overwhelmingly young, male, and Guatemalan, although there are enough women— mostly Thai or White Canadian—to keep the dance floor pumping. Pool tables are available, but from 12 pm on, you may have to negotiate in Thai to get your hands on a cue.
>
> A second Leamington club, La Molisana, is more suited to those preferring the Cowboy–"border town" scene. Don't be fooled by the Italian name, this café/pool hall/sports bar is one hundred percent Latin, cantina-style. The crowd here is

largely Mexican, over forty, and the DJ has his dial set on the U.S.-Mexican border with cumbia and norteña beats. While the gender ratio is heavily weighted toward the Y chromosome, with only a small group of Mexican and Canadian women and one or two Asians, unaccompanied male patrons may practice their salsa moves with one of the club's weekend taxi dancers.

This portrait of these similarly masculinized yet very distinct spaces, as witnessed in Leamington at the start of the second decade of the millennium—one young, Guatemalan, and contemporary, the other older, Mexican, and traditional—reflects broader transformations in the social relations of labor-intensive agriculture in Canada. During the twenty-first century, the migrant workforce serving the Canadian agriculture and food system has grown in size, extended into new regions, and become increasingly diversified along a number of social relations of power, including race, ethnicity, state nationality, and gender. In this chapter, I explore changes to Canada's temporary migration programs (TMPs) and their implications for agricultural labor markets and the social relations of production. I argue that employers' greater access to migrant workers across industries and regions and from a wider range of global sources, within a regulatory context void of any meaningful parameters or sanctions, has resulted in the growing precariousness of farmwork as experienced by migrants and Canadian citizens alike. Attempts to weaken and cheapen farm labor, however, have not gone uncontested. In the second part of the chapter, I examine how the labor movement and civil society organizations attempt to influence workplace regimes in agriculture in favor of migrant farmworkers. These struggles have transcended labor rights to focus on issues of human mobility and migrant rights, including reconceptualizing some of labor's traditional goals to include elements that are more attuned to the concerns of an increasingly globally mobile proletariat. Thus, despite the growing precariousness within farmwork, achieved in part through the highly exploitable sources of labor provided by TMPs, this chapter highlights spaces in which labor can shape workplace regimes more favorably for workers.

MIGRANT WORKERS AND FLEXIBLE ACCUMULATION IN AGRICULTURE

Since the 1980s, the restructuring of agriculture on a global scale has resulted in significant transformations in rural labor markets throughout the world. In high-income countries, a striking trend has been the rising employment of international migrants. In Europe, even former countries of emigration, such as Italy, Greece, and Spain, now employ large numbers of migrant agricultural workers (Kasimis et al. 2010; Labrianidis and Sykas 2009; Reigada Olaizola 2009). The 2004 enlargement of the European Union had dramatic results for countries such as the United Kingdom, with international migrants becoming the dominant workforce in labor-intensive horticulture (Frances et al. 2005). Labor market deregulation has accelerated these trends elsewhere. Norway, a country that formerly employed few migrants in agriculture, today hosts a large migrant labor force (Rye and Andrzejewska 2010). In the United States, where migrant workers have been structurally embedded in agriculture for a century, researchers have traced the dispersal of the migrant workforce from labor-intensive agriculture into a number of agrifood industries (Friedland et al. 1981; Griffith 2006; Martin 1988, 2002; Mitchell 1996).

States use multiple mechanisms, often simultaneously, to regulate the entry of migrants into their national territory to fill jobs in agriculture and other low-skilled economic sectors. These mechanisms include weak controls over undocumented workers, the liberalization of the labor move-ment within regional blocs with uneven development, and, increasingly, the "managed migrations" of workers with temporary visas. Guestworker policies that went into decline in the 1960s and 1970s, including the high-profile American bracero (1942–1964) and German Gastarbeiter (1955–1973) programs, are currently experiencing a revival. Since the 1990s, several high-income countries—including Belgium, Germany, Greece, Ireland, Italy, the Netherlands, Norway, Spain, Sweden, and the United Kingdom—have established schemes for the temporary or seasonal entry of limited numbers of workers (Castles 2006; Organisation for Economic Co-operation and Development 2003; Plewa 2007; Plewa and Miller 2005). Over the same time period, new and existing guestworker programs in the United States and Canada (as will be shown later) were expanded (Basok 2002; Griffith 2006; Preibisch 2007b). In 2007 and 2008, New Zealand and Australia also established seasonal worker schemes for agriculture (Gibson et al. 2008; Maclellan 2008). By 2008, the International Organization for Migration (IOM) reported that the world was on the threshold of a new era in temporary labor migration programs (International Organization for Migration 2008a). Indeed, Stephen Castles, who signed the obituary for guestworker programs in Europe in 1986, has acknowledged a general return to such policies (Castles 2006).

TMPs deliver extremely flexible labor to agriculture, a sector for which the benefits of flexible labor strategies have long been recognized (Selwyn

2009). Moreover, the current environment facing agrifood firms has bolstered the search for flexible labor, due to increasing pressures on profit margins resulting from greater retailer consolidation, a wider and shifting range of retailer and consumer demands, rising energy costs, and highly competitive, globalized markets. In general, TMPs deliver a workforce that can be assembled and disbanded with relative ease, that physically separates productive from reproductive labor, and that is often legally bound to a designated worksite (Burawoy 1976; Ruhs and Martin 2008). Indeed, because renewing managed migrants' contracts is contingent on the ongoing approval of a single employer or labor broker, some scholars view managed migrants as more vulnerable than undocumented workers (Holley 2001). Unsurprising, the extreme subordination of temporary migrant workers to employers has led unions to generally view them as a neither feasible nor desirable group to organize (Hill 2008).

A political-economic approach to understanding labor-capital relations in contemporary agriculture and the role of TMPs exposes both the social relations of the labor process and the politics in which the social organization of production is embedded (Burawoy 1985). Burawoy's concept of workplace regimes considers the set of labor arrangements that compose the productive process, the negotiations that shape them, and the range of actors involved (1985; see also Rogaly 2008; Rutherford 2004). This approach draws attention to the various levels of governance (largely, a national state) that regulate labor relations (Burawoy 1985; Rutherford 2004), including using immigration policy to enforce workplace discipline in national labor markets by encouraging competition between migrant and citizen workers (Sharma 2006). Further, a focus on workplace regimes also illuminates their historical and cultural contexts (Burawoy 1985; Rogaly 2008; Rutherford 2004). Research on waged labor in export horticulture calls for attention to the combination of local, regional, and global factors influencing the nature of labor systems, including how globally embedded labor regimes are mediated by local actors such as trade unions (Selwyn 2009). Thus, while parts of the state apparatus may collaborate with organized capital to weaken workers' bargaining power, including drawing on politically subjugated sources of labor and despotic labor control, workers also struggle to position themselves more advantageously within the accumulation process (Selwyn 2012).

In the following section, I explore Canada's TMPs available to farm and food industries and their implications for workplace regimes, in particular the introduction in 2002 of a new, sector-wide guestworker program available to employers in any industry seeking temporary workers to fill jobs designated as low-skill—a policy change resulting in greater precariousness in farm and food industry jobs. Next, I look at how the labor movement and other actors in civil society have resisted capital's attempts to remain competitive in Canada's increasingly globalized food system and how these influence strategies of struggle for labor rights. My analysis draws on secondary documents and extensive primary studies carried out within a program of research focused on the social relations of labor-intensive agriculture in Canada. I rely principally on in-depth interviews conducted between 2002 and 2010 with a diverse set of stakeholder participants in Ontario and British Columbia, including 39 civil servants in Canada and migrant-sending countries, 39 employers and industry representatives, 122 migrant workers, and 27 members of outreach or advocacy organizations. Finally, my analysis is informed by ethnographic insights from field research and my participation in various multi-stakeholder forums on migrant labor issues.

CANADA'S MANAGED MIGRATION PROGRAMS FOR AGRICULTURE AND FOOD WORKERS

Labor migration to Canada has changed significantly since the country's adoption of a new immigration framework in 1967 and the entrenchment of neoliberalism since the 1970s. Chief among these trends is the entry of growing numbers of workers on temporary visas compared with landed immigrants on the path to eventual citizenship. In 2008, the number of foreign workers entering Canada surpassed 192,000, a historic high (Citizenship and Immigration Canada 2010c). In 2006, the western province of Alberta received more temporary workers than permanent residents; British Columbia followed in 2008 (Citizenship and Immigration Canada 2010c). These figures are noteworthy for a country that used to pride itself on welcoming more immigrants per capita than any other high-income state (Dolin and Young 2004). The annual number of temporary workers entering Canada began outpacing that of workers granted settlement in 1980 and was particularly pronounced in the second half of the 2000s, after the government facilitated the ability of employers to import temporary visa workers during economic expansion, particularly in the oil, gas, and construction industries (Fudge and MacPhail 2009; Sharma 2006). Temporary workers for farm and food industry jobs in Canada enter under one of three initiatives: the Seasonal Agricultural Worker Program (SAWP); the Pilot Project for Occupations Requiring Lower Levels of Formal Training, National Occupations classification C&D (hereafter, the Pilot); or the Agricultural Stream of the Pilot.

THE SEASONAL AGRICULTURAL WORKER PROGRAM

Implemented in 1966, the SAWP is Canada's longest-standing TMP for low-skilled workers; under it, bilateral agreements signed between Canada and participating migrant-sending countries establish and operate agricultural guestworker programs. The first, the Commonwealth Caribbean Agreement, was signed in 1966 with Jamaica and subsequently included Trinidad and Tobago, Barbados, and members of the Organization of Eastern Caribbean States. In 1974, a similar agreement was signed with Mexico. From a program that initially involved just over 250 guestworkers, the SAWP now moves some 25,000 migrants annually from the partner countries into Canada and, following the completion of their six-week to eight-month contracts, returns an estimated 98 percent of them home. This high degree of "circularity"—cyclical labor migration that does not result in permanent settlement—is one of the main reasons that the SAWP has earned an international reputation as a model TMP (Hennebry and Preibisch 2010). The SAWP's structure, its modification over the years, and its ongoing administration are largely responsible for ensuring that its migrating participants remain temporary (i.e., refrain from seeking permanent settlement) and a valuable investment for their employers. Although this has been analyzed in great detail elsewhere (Basok 2002; Binford 2004; Hennebry and Preibisch 2010; Preibisch 2004, 2007b), I will briefly describe the structure and operation of the program.

The policy aim of the SAWP is to use temporary migration to ease seasonal labor shortages in primary agriculture. The Canadian government thus issues visas that are valid only between January 1 and December 15, with employment authorizations lasting a maximum of eight months (table 4.1). The SAWP program has no pathway to eventual citizenship, and the visas contain no entry provisions for dependents. Migrants residing in Canada without their families are a particularly flexible workforce, more likely to agree to work overtime, on weekends, and during particularly busy production periods yet also to remain on the farm when work is slow rather than seek work elsewhere. Ironically, unlike other flexible workers, much of these guestworkers' flexibility is tied to their *lack* of mobility: migrants are issued work permits that are valid only with a specified employer, binding them to a single worksite. Since 1986 it has not been subject to any quotas as a program driven by employer demand. Employers submit requests for migrants to the labor ministry of the Canadian federal government, Human Resources and Skills Development Canada (HRSDC), which issues approval in the form of a labor market opinion (LMO). Eligible employers must produce a commodity deemed "primary agriculture"

TABLE 4.1

Comparison of Canada's Temporary Migration Programs for Agriculture

	SAWP	NOC C&D Pilot	Agricultural Stream of Pilot
Year implemented	1966	2002	2011
Confirmed positions in 2010	27,359	9,748 in agrifood industries	709
Work permit type	Employer-specific	Employer-specific	Employer-specific
Work permit length	≤ 8 months	≤ 24 months	≤ 24 months
Forced rotation	Migrants must return home by December 15, can return by January 1.	After 24 months, migrants must return home for ≥ 4 years.	After 24 months, migrants must return home for ≥ 4 years.
Employment contract	Standard contracts; Canada, sending country, employer, and worker are parties.	Employers write contracts according to guidelines; employer and worker are parties.	Standard contracts: employer and worker are parties.
Program structure	Federal program resting on bilateral agreements signed between Canada and sending countries, formalized in memoranda of understanding	Federal program that approves employers to hire workers from abroad	Federal program that approves employers to hire workers from abroad
Countries eligible	Mexico, Jamaica, Trinidad and Tobago, Barbados, and the Organisation of Eastern Caribbean States (nine members)	Any country	Any country
Employers eligible	A specific list of commodities considered primary agriculture	Any employer requiring workers in occupations designated as low-skilled, when Canadians cannot be found	A specific list of commodities considered primary agriculture
Worker recruitment	Government responsibility: sending countries fill grower requests communicated by authorized private sector organizations.	Employer responsibility: employers contact workers independently (often through brokers).	Employer responsibility: employers contact workers independently (often through brokers).
Program costs employers can recover from wages	Portion of return airfare (except British Columbia); rent for housing (British Columbia only)	——	Rent for housing ($30 per month)

Source: Human Resources and Skills Development Canada 2010

with seasonal labor needs and must attempt to recruit Canadian citizens or permanent residents. Two employers associations manage much of the program: Foreign Agricultural Resource Management Services (FARMS, Ontario) and Fondation des Entreprises en Recrutement de la Main-D'œuvre Agricole Étrangère (FERME, Quebec). These two private organizations, financed on a user-fee basis, process most employer applications, arrange transportation, communicate information to employers, and manage public relations. Through these agents, employers request the nationality, gender, skills, and other characteristics of workers they seek to hire, information subsequently communicated to migrant-sending countries for worker recruitment, selection, and job matching.

Migrant-sending countries generally recruit workers according to pro-poor criteria; rural location, low education levels, and family status (dependents) determine applicants' eligibility.[1] Ensuring circularity thus involves selecting participants whose economic need creates a sharply defined, dual frame of reference (Waldinger and Lichter 2003), whereby migrants' comparisons between their Canadian wages and their earning opportunities at home induce them to conform to employers' demands so that they will be called back. Sending countries implement additional mechanisms to ensure that migrants meet employer and bilateral agreement expectations. Most SAWP partners implement forced rotation, insisting that workers return home annually to be eligible for subsequent seasons; those who fail to comply are blacklisted. Mexico also requires employers to evaluate workers annually; negative assessments affect future placements, as can a migrant's request to change employers. Countries in the Caribbean operate a forced savings scheme, whereby migrants must return home to recoup a portion of their wages.

Moreover, all sending countries post government agents in Canada to mediate employer-worker relationships, ensure that migrants return, and win over potential employers. The Caribbean countries run liaison services (financed in part by mandatory deductions from worker wages), and Mexico deploys officials through its consulates and embassies. Although these government agencies supposedly advocate for their citizens, sending states' economic interest in retaining and expanding foreign employment opportunities compromise effective representation; to foster harmonious diplomacy with Canada, further, they work to ensure that temporary migration remains circular. Not surprising, migrants are highly critical of their government representation. Further, a few government agents often oppose workers' interests; some, for example, have blacklisted union organizers and arranged to deport workers requiring extended medical treatment (McLaughlin 2009; United Food and Commercial Workers of Canada 2011a).

Distinguishing the SAWP from other guestworker programs in North America is its high degree of state management at both ends of the migrant corridor. Along with posting staff in Canada, migrant-sending countries participate in annual intergovernmental negotiations, renewing the standard contract to which the employer, the sending-country government, the government of Canada, and the worker are parties. The contract includes various aspects of the worker's working and living conditions in Canada, including wage rates, and commits employers to provide free worker housing and to cover the cost of workers' visa and return airfare (most of which can be recovered later), among other commitments.[2]

THE PILOT PROJECT AND ITS NEW AGRICULTURAL STREAM

The second main initiative by which temporary workers take up farm and food industry jobs in Canada is the Pilot.[3] Formerly the Low-Skill Pilot Project, this initiative was implemented in 2002 as a general TMP to fill purported gaps in the labor market in jobs requiring lower levels of formal training (Fudge and MacPhail 2009). Since the Pilot is not limited to one industry but covers low-skilled occupations in general, it gave those agrifood businesses formerly excluded from the SAWP due to year-round production (e.g., mushrooms, poultry, and bait worms) access to the global labor market. The SAWP and the Pilot have notable similarities and differences. Like the SAWP, Pilot visas are temporary, but unlike the SAWP's mid-December cutoff, Pilot visas can be issued for any time of the year, thus creating more flexibility for year-round farm and food businesses. Holding a Pilot visa does not include a pathway to citizenship, although Pilot migrants—like SAWP migrants—can be nominated as candidates for provincial immigration programs. Workers who enter under the Pilot can bring spouses or children to Canada but must convince an immigration officer that they can financially support them (Fudge and MacPhail 2009). Migrants under the Pilot receive work permits that are valid only with a named employer, can work up to twenty-four months, and can have their time extended by their employer. After workers under the Pilot accumulate four years of employment, however, they must return to their home country for four years. Conversely, the SAWP does not specify a maximum tenure; some migrants have accumulated thirty years of experience. Although the so-called 4/4 Rule is unpopular with both employers and migrant rights groups—with the former referring to the problem it poses for "turnover" and the latter complaining that it "creates a disposable workforce"—the policy keeps in place the ideological and highly political component of the guestworker program as temporary (Hahamovitch 2003).

In comparison with the SAWP, the Pilot is much less regulated, with the government's role significantly reduced: whereas in the bilateral model of the SAWP, Canada and the migrant-sending countries jointly manage migration, the Pilot functions as a unilateral mechanism allowing eligible employers to hire workers from abroad. Similar to workers recruited with US H-2A and H-2B visas, Canada does not sign or negotiate agreements with migrant-sending states, which consequently are not accorded a formal role in negotiating their migrants' working and living conditions, nor in administering the movement of workers. These fundamental changes in the architecture of the new TMP presume an expanded role for market institutions in activities such as recruitment. Significantly, in the absence of bilateral agreements, the Pilot allows employers to recruit workers from around the world, effectively expanding their global labor pool.[4]

As a sector-wide TMP, the Pilot has no standard contract. Rather, in employers' applications, they submit a sample employment contract outlining wages, duties, and conditions related to the transportation, accommodation, and health and occupational safety of workers. The wage rate paid to migrant workers is expected to be equal to or higher than the prevailing wage rate paid to Canadians in the same occupation and region or, in a unionized environment, equal to the rate established under the respective collective bargaining agreement. Employers are also expected to provide medical coverage until the worker is eligible for provincial health insurance coverage and to register all workers under the appropriate provincial workers compensation/workplace safety insurance plans. Costs have also been streamlined: employers under the Pilot must cover the round-trip transportation costs for their migrant workers to travel from their countries of permanent residence to the Canadian worksite, but employers need not provide accommodation. This element of the new initiative has made the program relatively more expensive, as those agrifood employers who desire on-site housing cannot recover any costs for providing accommodation by charging migrants for a portion of their airfare, as is possible in the SAWP.

For the first eight years of the Pilot, employers of agricultural workers had the option to hire migrants under the SAWP, under the new guest-worker initiative, or both. Beginning in 2011, however, employers seeking to hire farmworkers in those commodities eligible for the SAWP have been obliged to follow new requirements tailored to the farm and food industry, referred to as the new Agricultural Stream under the Pilot. As noted in table 4.1, the new Agricultural Stream retains most of the elements of the Pilot with some aspects of the SAWP. The global labor pool remains open, leaving employers free to hire outside the SAWP's bilateral partner countries, and employers must still pay for the entire cost of migrants' return transportation. Aligning with the SAWP, however, employers must abide by SAWP-negotiated rates and provide worker housing, for which they can charge rent. Indeed, the creation of the Agricultural Stream sought to equalize the two programs' costs, a complaint that had been raised by employers.[5] The Agricultural Stream also seeks to equalize wage structures and worker protections; in addition to employers being obliged to pay SAWP rates, they must follow a standard contract and enroll the migrants they hire in workers compensation schemes in those provinces where farmworkers remain excluded from them.

Changes to the Migrant Labor Force Serving Farm and Food Industry Jobs

The Pilot and the new Agricultural Stream are part of a policy shift to facilitate access to temporary migrant workers for Canada's food and farm industries. Although the SAWP is almost five decades old, its growth has occurred principally since the late 1990s. Of particular importance was the government's lifting of the quota restricting the SAWP's size and the transfer of its administration to the private sector (FARMS and FERME) in 1987, which resulted in more than doubling the number of migrant agricultural workers by 1989, in part due to FARMS and FERME efforts to market the program (Alberta Federation of Labour 2003). Increased access to migrant workers contributed to phenomenal growth in Canada's greenhouse industry and kept less competitive commodities viable as agricultural and food markets globalized. In 2008, the SAWP approved 28,231 positions, a historic high (Human Resources and Skills Development Canada 2010). Meanwhile, the Pilot has increased the migrant component of the agricultural workforce. Within five years of the Pilot's implementation, Canada was approving an additional 10,000 temporary positions in agriculture annually. In 2009, as the global economic crisis deepened and the government tightened restrictions on LMO approvals, the SAWP and the Pilot declined 2 and 3 percent, respectively (figure 4.1). Despite this overall decline, however, the Pilot continued to grow across the top three occupations in agriculture and food (general farmworkers, nursery and greenhouse workers, and harvesting laborers) (Human Resources and Skills Development Canada 2011a).

Since the late 1990s, the migrant workforce in Canada's agriculture and food industries has also increased its geographical scope. By 2004, the SAWP had extended beyond eastern Canada to operate in nine of the country's thirteen provinces and territories. The extension of the SAWP

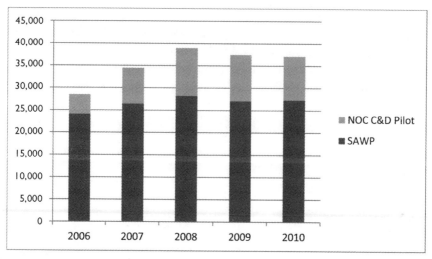

FIGURE 4.1

Number of confirmed temporary foreign worker positions on labor market opinions (LMOs) in agriculture, 2006–2010. Source: Human Resources and Skills Development Canada 2011a. Data include the following occupations: farmers and farm managers; agricultural and related service contractors and managers; farm supervisors and specialized livestock workers; nursery and greenhouse operators and managers; landscaping and grounds maintenance contractors and managers; supervisors, landscape and horticulture; aquaculture operators and managers; general farmworkers; nursery and greenhouse workers; harvesting laborers; landscaping and grounds maintenance laborers; aquaculture and marine harvest laborers; and laborers in food, beverage, and tobacco processing.

that year to British Columbia, a province that contributes the fourth largest share of Canadian agriculture and food-processing employment, was particularly significant, adding some 3,500 Mexican workers to the farm labor force within four years (Otero and Preibisch 2010). Combined with the Pilot, this expansion has rebalanced the geographical concentration of migrant farm and food industry workers, who were formerly concentrated in Ontario and Quebec. These two provinces accounted for 96 percent of SAWP employment in 2003; by 2009, this had dropped to 79 percent. If migrant workers in both programs are considered together, Ontario and Quebec account for an even smaller proportion of Canada's migrant workers (figure 4.2).

The migrant workforce serving the Canadian agriculture and food system has also diversified along a number of social relations of power, including race, ethnicity, nationality, and gender. With the Pilot extending the breadth of the labor pool available to employers beyond the SAWP's

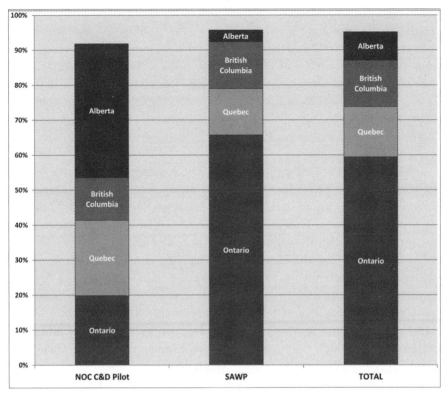

FIGURE 4.2

Provincial share of approved migrant agricultural worker positions, 2008. Source: Human Resources and Skills Development Canada 2011c, 2011d.

handful of bilateral partners in Mexico and the English-speaking Caribbean to the entire world, there occurred a rapid diversification of the nationalities of the migrant labor force in agriculture and food processing (Smart, chapter 3, this volume). Apart from diversifying nationalities— and, by extension, race and ethnicity—there is evidence of the replacement of predominantly Mexican workers by Central Americans. Within five years of the Pilot's implementation, Guatemala was sending the highest number of migrant farmworkers—the majority being indigenous Mayans—to Canada after Mexico and Jamaica. Much of this employment has taken place in Quebec, where Guatemalans have replaced Mexicans as the preferred labor force, increasing their numbers sixteen times between 2003 and 2011 while the number of Mexican and Caribbean workers remained stable (Dolin and Young 2011; F. Borja, personal communication, October 18, 2009).

There is also evidence of a shift toward the feminization of the agricultural workforce, with women's share increasing from 33 percent to 40.5 percent between 2002 and 2007 (Fudge and MacPhail 2009). Although the data tracking of actual entries of migrant workers into agriculture-related jobs under the Pilot by gender is incomplete, there are indications that the new initiative is more feminized than the SAWP. In 2008, migrant women's share of total entries in agriculture-related jobs under the SAWP and the Pilot was 3.2 and 15.4 percent, respectively (Citizenship and Immigration Canada 2009a, 2009b).

Rising numbers of migrant workers and the incorporation of new social groups influence the work experience in the agrifood sector. Research in British Columbia and Ontario has found that both migrant and domestic farmworkers perceive that they are experiencing heightened competition for their jobs. In British Columbia, employers and supervisors have threatened landed immigrant farmworkers with improving their productivity or risking replacement with migrant Mexican workers under the SAWP; conversely, Mexican migrants are threatened that the employer will return to hiring domestic workers (Otero and Preibisch 2010). In Ontario, some businesses split their workforces between both programs and hire different nationalities through each. Albeit the threat of labor replacement can be used effectively against both resident and migrant workforces, the broadening of the international labor market beyond the SAWP bilateral partners has introduced new groups of vulnerable workers into the agricultural labor force. New groups may be positioned more precariously in relation to their migratory livelihoods in Canada due to the situations in their home countries, such as greater economic deprivation, incidence of political violence, or access to migratory alternatives (e.g., Mexico's northern border with the United States), altering dual frames of reference such that some workers appreciate Canadian employment more than others. For example, whereas Mexico ranks 57 on the United Nations Development Programme's Human Development Index, Guatemala ranks 131; in Mexico, 3.4 percent of the population earns less than US$1.25 a day, whereas in Guatemala, the share is 13.1 percent (United Nations Development Programme 2011a, 2011b). Although both countries are experiencing growing violence, Guatemala's political past has more recently involved state-sponsored terror. In addition, Mexican workers have only one border to cross to access the US labor market. In interviews, both Mexican and Guatemalan migrants agree that Guatemalans are a more vulnerable group of workers, making statements such as "[Employers] humiliate the Guatemalans more" or "Guatemalans and Salvadoreans work harder than Mexicans for less pay."

The broadening of the global labor pool to countries that are positioned lower on the "global hierarchy of states" (Stasiulis and Bakan 2003) is but one process increasing the vulnerability of agricultural labor migrants. The Canadian government's failure to regulate the recruitment and employment of migrant workers has been another. In addition to the fact that the very architecture of the Pilot transferred recruitment to the private sector, the Canadian government does not adequately regulate recruiters and employers. This regulatory void has subjected migrants to a range of exploitative practices documented by researchers, the press, and activists (Auditor General of Canada 2009; Preibisch and Hennebry 2012; Standing Committee on Citizenship and Immigration 2009; United Food and Commercial Workers of Canada and Agriculture Workers Alliance 2011).[6] Similar to the case of Indian workers that Austin (chapter 5, this volume) discusses, chief among abuses by recruiters have been the charging of excessive recruitment fees or fees for nonexistent jobs and misinformation regarding migrants' prospects for permanent immigration, the nature of their jobs, and their expected earnings (Auditor General of Canada 2009; Standing Committee on Citizenship and Immigration 2009). Migrants' struggle to repay usurious recruitment fees—at times totaling more than two-thirds of their expected annual earnings—constitute examples of contemporary debt bondage.[7] Employers have also engaged in exploitative practices, including a failure to provide the hours promised to migrants, withholding pay during periods deemed to be training, and other unscrupulous practices. These developments have led defrauded migrants to join the undocumented workforce in a bid to finance the outstanding costs of their migration, obtain the hours they expected, or escape despotic workplaces (Preibisch and Hennebry 2012).

Shifting Workplace Regimes to Benefit Migrants

As the changes described above result in growing precariousness for workers, they also give rise to organized efforts both to expand labor rights for farmworkers and to address transnational migrants' needs. The struggle for farmworker rights in Canada is not new; since at least the 1970s, attempts have been made to organize farmworkers, although with mixed results (Bush and Canadian Farmworkers Union 1995). The 2000s, however, have led to new advancements in farmworker organizing and the migrant rights movement. In 2001, the Global Justice Care Van Project, which sought to document and expose migrants' working and living conditions, launched a new chapter of organizing around migrant farmworkers that can now be considered a broad-based social movement.

The origins of this movement and its characteristics have been described and analyzed as a form of "globalization from below," and migrants have experienced an expanded enjoyment of social citizenship in Canada (Gabriel and Macdonald 2011; Preibisch 2004, 2007a). The 2001 Care Van, organized by labor activists and funded by several unions, put in motion several distinct but overlapping initiatives. Most high profile has been the multi-pronged campaign focused on migrant agricultural workers by Canada's largest private-sector union, the United Food and Commercial Workers of Canada (UFCW). Around the same time, other labor activists formed Justicia for Migrant Workers (J4MW), and faith-based initiatives and other not-for-profit organizations expanded their work with migrants (Gabriel and Macdonald 2011; Preibisch 2004). Since the early 2000s, heightened public awareness of migrant farmworkers and increased media coverage have accompanied the proliferation and growth of migrant support and advocacy organizations. The movement around migrant farmworker issues is multifaceted, involving a range of social justice and faith-based organizations.[8] Here, I examine the UFCW Canada's campaign as an illustration of organized labor's efforts to influence workplace regimes in workers' favor.

The UFCW Canada's recent strategy to organize farmworkers operates on different scales, ranging from the local to the transnational, and focuses on various levels of migrant workers' structural vulnerability. This includes defending and extending legal rights and protections for farmworkers and migrants; providing direct support and outreach; organizing farmworkers into collective bargaining units in Canada and as transnational migrant activists in their sending countries; and conducting a lobbying campaign that combines public awareness with pressure on political leaders. In the twenty-first century, the emphasis on each of these strategies has altered in response to the changing political climate in Canada, which has shifted to the right under consecutive Conservative Party administrations since 2006. The UFCW Canada has also responded to the changing social composition of the workforce, with the rising incorporation of more vulnerable groups, such as indigenous Central Americans, challenging its organizational strategies.

Advancing the legal rights of farmworkers became a central plank of the union's campaign in the 2000s. Working through the courts to advance farmworker rights was a recognition of the agricultural lobby's influence in government. The then national coordinator of the migrant agricultural worker support centers stated, "Basically people who are interested in establishing and securing human rights and the basic rights for the agricultural sector had to launch legal challenges and force governments to govern" (Raper and Preibisch 2007). Accordingly, the union lodged legal challenges regarding migrant workers' contributions to the federal benefit scheme for employment insurance (2003), the exclusion of Ontario farmworkers from the provincial Occupational Health and Safety Act (2003), and Quebec employers' overcharging of rent to Guatemalan workers in the Pilot (2010), among others (United Food and Commercial Workers of Canada 2011b; United Food and Commercial Workers of Canada and Agriculture Workers Alliance 2011).

The most prominent legal challenge was the protracted bid to secure trade union and collective bargaining rights in the province of Ontario, a case that spanned sixteen years. The challenge was initially lodged in 1995 when the UFCW Canada took the Ontario government to court, charging that the province's legislative prohibition of farm unions was a violation of workers' rights under Canada's Charter of Rights and Freedoms. In 2001, siding with the union, the Supreme Court of Canada ordered the Ontario government to draft new legislation. The resulting Agricultural Employees Protection Act (AEPA), which allows farmworkers to form associations, but not collectively bargain, was rejected by the union, which subsequently challenged it in the Ontario Superior Court. Although the challenge was dismissed in 2006, the Ontario Court of Appeal ruled in favor of the union in 2008, leading the Ontario government to appeal to the Supreme Court of Canada (United Food and Commercial Workers of Canada 2011b). In 2011, the country's highest court dealt a stinging blow to the union. Eight of nine judges ruled against extending trade union rights and collective bargaining to farmworkers, on the basis that, although the Charter grants workers the right to form associations and to discuss work conditions with employers, it does not prescribe a particular model of collective bargaining or outcome.[9] The 2011 defeat kicked the bottom out of the UFCW's strategy of pursuing farmworker rights through the courts and will likely lead its organizers to focus on other elements of their campaign.

One of these other elements is the UFCW Canada's outreach activities. Ten agriculture worker support centers operate in association with the union's Agriculture Workers Alliance (AWA), which bills itself as the largest national organization for agriculture workers (United Food and Commercial Workers of Canada and Agriculture Workers Alliance 2011). The centers are located where farmworkers concentrate.[10] Services were initially targeted at the numerically dominant, Mexican SAWP population, with the hiring of Spanish-speaking staff and the opening of the first center in 2002 in Leamington, Ontario, where over 4,000 Mexicans worked. However, emphasis in recent years has been placed more on providing services to a broader population, with the latest catering to a largely Punjabi landed immigrant clientele. At the centers, frontline staff assist farmworkers in claiming insurance and benefits (workers compensation, parental benefits leave, pension), provide translation services, host education and training activities (language classes, workplace health and safety, rights awareness, bicycle safety), and engage in direct advocacy (defending workers in cases of premature repatriation). Catering to a mobile population, the AWA offers a national database that workers can access to track the development of their files, such as benefit claims or investigation of workplace incidents (United Food and Commercial Workers of Canada and Agriculture Workers Alliance 2011). The organization also hosts a website and an e-newsletter service that is available in English, French, Spanish, Thai, and Punjabi. The AWA and the UFCW claim that their outreach campaign received some 35,000 worker inquiries in 2010 through center visits, via phone calls, or during outreach events (United Food and Commercial Workers of Canada and Agriculture Workers Alliance 2011). Indeed, the support centers have been highly successful at gaining access to the Mexican migrant workforce and, increasingly, other groups. In 2007, the Abbotsford center in British Columbia had case files for about half of the 2,000 Mexican workers in the province that season (Otero and Preibisch 2009). Part of the centers' appeal is undoubtedly their filling of the void in services that neither the Canadian government nor migrant-sending countries provide. From 2004 to 2009, the AWA/UFCW Canada staff helped file more than $23 million in accumulated parental benefit claims on behalf of SAWP workers (United Food and Commercial Workers of Canada 2009).

The centers act as hubs, organizing workers into collective bargaining unions. Between 2006 and 2011, the AWA/UFCW Canada, with the support of UFCW Canada local unions, filed eleven certification applications before provincial labor boards, resulting in collective bargaining agreements at several farm enterprises in British Columbia and Quebec (United Food and Commercial Workers of Canada and Agriculture Workers Alliance 2011). Of particular note are the contracts at worksites employing both domestic and migrant farmworkers. These agreements represent the first opportunity for migrant workers to be involved in negotiating their terms of employment, which, for the vast majority of temporary visa workers, are drawn up between governments (SAWP), employers (NOC C&D Pilot), and/or Canadian civil servants (Agricultural Stream). Remarkably, the collective agreements contain provisions that take into account the vulnerability imposed by TMPs, including grievance procedures to address migrants' risk of repatriation and recall and seniority rights to challenge their disposability. Such negotiations have forced the UFCW Canada to reassess some components of collective agreements usually held sacred to trade unions. During one set of negotiations, for example, migrants rejected mandatory overtime pay, suspecting employers would simply hire additional migrants to avoid paying overtime and thus compromise their ability to maximize their time-limited contracts.[11] In the end, the contract allowed farmworkers the right to choose overtime paid at their regular wage rates. Further, a number of UFCW local unions with large numbers of temporary visa employees have addressed the disposability inherent in managed migration schemes by requiring employers to restrict the hiring of migrant workers to those who qualify for provincial immigration programs (Provincial and Territorial Nominee Programs)12 and to process migrants' applications for permanent residency under such initiatives within six months. Through such actions, the labor movement has been able to secure residency rights and a path to citizenship for migrants in programs designed precisely to avoid permanent immigration.

Most recently, the UFCW Canada has extended its organizing transnationally. Within migrant-sending communities, this has involved formal negotiations and also grassroots organizing. In Mexico, the union has engaged in dialogue with government officials, political leaders, leaders of trade unions, and public interest groups. This has resulted in the signing of pacts between the UFCW Canada and state-level governments in Mexico (Michoacán, the Federal District, and Tlaxcala), committing both sides to ensuring the human rights of migrant agricultural workers from these states while they are in Canada (United Food and Commercial Workers of Canada and Agriculture Workers Alliance 2011). It has also resulted in groups within Mexico lobbying political leaders for greater protections for migrant workers in Canada. For example, when the UFCW exposed the complicity of the Mexican consulate in Vancouver in the blacklisting of union supporters, the largest political organization representing rural Mexicans—the National Peasant Confederation (Confederación Nacional Campesina)[13]—demanded answers from the minister of labor in the Senate and questioned the absence of union representation in the SAWP annual negotiations (El Proceso 2011). The AWA/UFCW Canada also engages in direct organizing and has staff posted in Mexico City. In 2010, the union participated in two demonstrations outside the Canadian embassies in both Mexico and Guatemala that were organized by migrant workers to protest injustices in Canada's managed migration programs (Agriculture Workers Alliance 2010).[14] The UFCW Canada has also appealed to international institutions to bring transnational labor regulations to bear on farmworker rights in Canada. In response to a complaint lodged by the union, the International Labour Organization (ILO) ruled in 2010 that the exclusion of collective bargaining rights in Ontario's AEPA is a violation of human rights under two United Nations conventions.[15]

The ILO ruling feeds into broader strategies of political lobbying and a media campaign to promote social justice for migrant and domestic agriculture workers. The UFCW Canada has allied with a number of other social justice organizations to pressure the federal and provincial governments, with successes such as the 2006 extension of provincial health and safety legislation to farmworkers in Ontario (United Food and Commercial Workers of Canada and Agriculture Workers Alliance 2011). More recently, a multimedia public awareness campaign exposed the IOM's Guatemala office as forcing Pilot workers to post a $400 bond in order to work in Canada (ibid.). The union's communication strategy also involves active use of the Internet and social networking sites alongside more traditional press releases and media interviews.

Despite the advances of the AWA/UFCW Canada and groups in the broader social movement in increasing public awareness of the working and living conditions of migrant and domestic workers in Canada's food system and promoting their rights, these should not overshadow the structural weakness of migrant farmworkers in TMPs as laid out earlier in this chapter and argued extensively in the literature (Basok 2002; Binford 2004; Preibisch 2004; Verma 2003). Furthermore, modifications to Canada's TMPs have introduced new groups of even more vulnerable migrants, whose incorporation into the labor force has only exacerbated the precarious status of farmwork for both migrant and domestic workers. Moreover, the success of the AWA/UFCW Canada support centers has resulted in zealous employer efforts to prevent workers from visiting the centers. Employers have tried to stop the AWA/UFCW from setting up centers in rural locations; have threatened workers by saying that their jobs are at risk if they associate with outsiders, particularly the union; and, most recently, have begun to provide some of the same services as the centers do, such as filing income tax returns and helping with parental benefits and pensions, to discourage their migrant employees from visiting the AWA/UFCW centers. Repressive tactics have also been directed at the liaison officers and consular staff of SAWP bilateral partners, who continue to receive threats that any complaints regarding migrants' working or living conditions will result in employers switching to another supply country. As the displacement of Mexicans by Guatemalans in Quebec shows, such threats are real.

It is not surprising that it is nearly impossible to set up a union meeting with migrant farmworkers, let alone sign an AWA membership card. Within this context, the successful negotiation of collective bargaining rights at some agrifood operations is remarkable. But these successes can be short-lived. The first farm contract for both domestic and migrant workers lasted only a year, and then the workers voted unanimously to decertify the local union (Rural Migration News 2009). Although workers had complaints about the contract, migrant advocates claim that the Mexican consul held a closed-door meeting with workers prior to the vote and threatened to blacklist them if they did not endorse decertification (ibid.).

CONCLUSION

The global restructuring of agriculture has had critical repercussions in the social relations of labor-intensive agriculture in Canada. The migrant workforce employed in the country's agriculture and food system has become increasingly diversified by race, ethnicity, nationality, gender, and other social relations that influence workplace power, at the same time expanding in size and geographical reach. These changes have been enabled by the expansion and restructuring of Canada's TMPs. The federal government has facilitated employers' access to migrant workers across industries and regions while also broadening the international labor pool to reach new, more vulnerable reservoirs of migrants. Moreover, Canada's neoliberal reforms to shift the responsibility and management of TFWs to the private sector without a robust regulatory environment has created new sources of vulnerability among the workforce, resulting in cases of debt bondage and a growing undocumented population. The incorporation of more vulnerable workers and more sources of vulnerability has infused greater competition into the labor market and, consequently, greater precariousness in the farm-work experience of migrants and Canadian citizens alike.

As this chapter shows, attempts to weaken, cheapen, and exploit farm labor have been challenged by trade unions and social justice organizations seeking greater rights for workers and migrants. The AWA/UFCW Canada has taken a prominent role in the development of the formal labor movement, financing legal challenges, funding support centers to provide outreach and advocacy, undertaking a public awareness campaign, and engaging in political lobbying from the local level to the transnational. Particularly noteworthy is how these struggles have transcended labor rights to focus on issues of human mobility and migrant rights, including a reconceptualizing of some of labor's traditional goals that is more attuned to the concerns of an increasingly globally mobile proletariat—in other words, a flexible workforce. Thus, although much of the changes in labor-capital relations within Canada's agriculture and food system appear to have benefited capital, we are also witnessing important changes within the labor movement that hint at a new politics of production responsive to transnational workers, involving a refashioning of demands that transcends labor rights to address the right to move and the conditions under which that movement takes place.

Such struggles face heavy challenges, owing to the structural vulnerability of TFWs and the growing support for anti-immigrant policies within many high-income countries. In Canada, the ongoing challenge of organizing managed migrants, along with events such as the stunning defeat of the UFCW's legal challenge regarding collective bargaining and trade union rights, may also refocus the efforts of the social movement for migrant farmworkers' rights in order to engage more strategically with the politics of global food production and consumption as it impacts food and agriculture workers the world over, an approach that recognizes their increasingly mobile, often transnational lives.

Notes

1. Politics also plays a role in selection, particularly in Jamaica, where SAWP participants are recruited based on their work for governing members of Parliament.

2. Under the SAWP, a worker must be paid a wage rate equal to or greater than (1) the legal wage for agricultural workers in the province of employment; (2) the rate determined by the Canadian government through the SAWP negotiations to be the prevailing wage rate for the type of agricultural work performed in the province of employment; and (3) the rate being paid by the employer to his/her regular seasonal workforce performing the same type of agricultural work.

3. The name of this TMP reflects Canada's National Occupations classification (NOC), which identifies four skill levels that correspond to the type and/or amount of training or education typically required to work in an occupation. Codes C and D categorize those occupations that usually require, at most, a high school diploma or a maximum of two years of job-specific training.

4. Some nationalities may be denied visas. When issuing visas, immigration officers assess the health status of migrant workers and their potential to respect the terms and conditions of the work permit, taking into account the applicants' intentions to become permanent residents, their personal circumstances, and the context of their home countries (Fudge and MacPhail 2009). Employers claim that their requests for workers from some countries have been denied.

5. Field notes, March 2009.

6. The federal government has implemented some measures, but development of these has been slow and led by the provinces, with Manitoba enacting legislation in 2009 to enhance the regulation of employment placement agencies and to create new protections for migrants, particularly regarding recruitment (Sharma 2010). Other provinces have since amended or introduced legislation regarding the right of recruiters to charge fees to workers (Citizenship and Immigration Canada 2010b). Federally, the Canadian government tightened advertising requirements in 2009 and instituted a voluntary scheme in 2010 for employers to demonstrate compliance with the terms of their offers of employment to migrants, a two-year prohibition from hiring migrant workers for noncompliant employers, and an online blacklist of offenders (Citizenship and Immigration Canada 2010a; Fudge and MacPhail 2009; Standing Committee on Citizenship and Immigration 2009).

7. My research found Thai farmworkers paying CAN$11,000 in recruitment fees, an amount corroborated in the press (Carter 2007). The calculation of expected earnings is based on fifty-two weeks of forty hours at the 2007 minimum wage in Ontario, $8 an hour.

8. Groups in this social movement include KAIROS: Canadian Ecumenical Justice Initiatives; Migrante International; the Workers Action Centre; Justicia for Migrant Workers; Canadian Association of Labour Lawyers; Students Against Migrant Exploitation; World Council of Churches; El Sembrador; ENLACE Community Link; and the Canadian Labor Congress.

9. Ontario (Attorney General) v. Fraser. 2011 SCC 20. Ottawa, ON: Judgements of the Supreme Court of Canada.

10. The locations of the centers are British Columbia (Abbotsford, Kelowna, Surrey), Manitoba (Portage la Prairie), Ontario (Leamington, Bradford, Virgil, Simcoe), and Quebec (Saint-Rémi, Saint-Eustache). See http://awa-ata.ca/en/get-in-touch-join-awa/wp-contentuploadsmapsmap_insert1html.

11. Field notes, September 2007.

12. PTNPs, introduced in 1996, are agreements between the government of Canada and provincial or territorial governments and allow them to nominate, usually on the basis of economic or labor needs, immigrants who wish to settle within their boundaries. Provincial nominees are not assessed on the selection factors of the federal government's point system for determining eligibility for Canadian immigration but are assessed on eligibility criteria unique to each PTNP.

13. The CNC is a partisan organization of the Partido Revolucionario Institucional, which is the current ruling party in Mexico.

14. The demonstration in Guatemala City was organized by the Asociación de Guatemaltecos Unidos por Nuestros Derechos (Association of Guatemalans United for Our Rights), a group of former Pilot participants who lost their jobs in Canada.

15. These are Convention no. 87, Freedom of Association and Protection of the Right to Organise, and Convention no. 98, Right to Organise and Collective Bargaining.

5

Guestworkers in the Fabrication and Shipbuilding Industry along the Gulf of Mexico

An Anomaly or a New Source of Labor?

Diane Austin

Historically a strategic industry for commerce and the military, ship-building has benefited from centuries of US federal aid.[1] Unlike industries that have streamlined and automated production, reorganized work, and significantly reduced workforces, however, shipbuilding has remained remarkably static. In 1968, more than two-thirds of all employees were craft workers or operatives (apprentices, helpers, and machine operators), and almost three-fourths were in "blue-collar" jobs (Rubin 1970:20). At the end of the twentieth century, two-thirds of the workforce worked primarily as fitters and welders (Bureau of Export Administration 2001). Fitters put together the pipes and steel plates that make up the vessel structure, and welders secure these plates together; the need to minimize the amount of material applied with each weld, to control both weight and cost, demands highly skilled welders.

Industry officials have considered labor shortages in both skilled and unskilled positions to be a significant problem for at least a century. In the 1970s and continuing to the twenty-first century, analysts have identified high turnover and overspecialization as key workforce problems, especially among production workers. In 1970, for example, turnover rates reached as high as 75 percent annually, and employees with more than five years of seniority were rarely found working more than 1,600 hours per year for the same employer (Rubin 1970:21). High turnover has been attributed to uneven workloads, harsh work environments, the perception of the work as low skilled, and a competitive labor market; overspecialization has been blamed on government contracts (particularly military procurement), union activity, and certification requirements (Bureau of Export Administration 2001; Rubin 1970; Whitehurst 1986). Responses to labor problems have focused on technology transfer in production and management, training, and outsourcing redundant labor (e.g., Office of Technology Assessment 1983).[2] Still, despite innovation in specific companies, such as the introduction of the lean production business model (Bureau of Export Administration 2001) and modular manufacturing (Austal 2009), lack of volume remains a problem, and labor shortages continue to plague the industry; even when offering relatively high wages, companies struggle to attract workers (Austin and Crosthwait 2013).

Recognition of the industry's problems is not new. For more than a century, shipbuilding has been debated, studied, and manipulated. Concerns for maintaining naval capacity and merchant fleets are reflected in federal policy, including responses to increasing competition from foreign shipyards. The Merchant Marine Act of 1920 (commonly called the Jones Act, after Senator Wesley Jones, R-WA) remains the center of US policy in this regard, requiring that all goods transported by water between US ports be carried in US-flag ships constructed in the United States, owned by US citizens, and crewed by US citizens and US permanent residents. The 1936 revision to the act aimed at making domestic yards more competitive with foreign yards by enhancing the market for the construction and maintenance of domestically flagged vessels. The act also encouraged this market by attempting to offset the higher US shipbuilding costs, much of which are attributed to higher labor costs. More recently, pursuant to the Maritime Security Act of 1996, the US government has acquired and maintained a fleet of merchant ships, the "ready reserve fleet," to support military operations worldwide.

The effort to maintain a *productive* workforce for US shipyards has included training as a key component, and both government and industry programs have been developed (Dooley 2001). The federal government has subsidized union apprenticeship programs as well, although these have remained unfunded since 1982 (Maritime Administration 2008) when they came under fire during the Reagan administration (interview, November 2007). Still, US shipbuilding is declining, and worries about capacity and competitiveness persist. Many analysts conclude that the federal policies have undermined innovation, widening the gap between

US and international shipyards (Bureau of Export Administration 2001; Vambery 1968a, 1968b; Whitehurst 1986). Now, many companies move any work not subject to the Jones Act overseas, restructure US jobs in order to hire and fire workers quickly and, in the process, create a large pool of contingent workers without explicit or implicit contracts for long-term employment. There has also been an increased reliance on labor contracts and subcontracted labor (Barker and Christensen 1998; Kalleberg, Reskin, and Hudson 2000; Polivka 1996). Such features often pave the way for guestworkers (Griffith, chapter 10, this volume).

In contrast to US shipbuilding, the offshore petroleum industry spurred expansion in the Gulf of Mexico during the latter half of the twentieth century. In the 1930s and '40s, when the petroleum industry moved into the wetlands and inland lakes and then onto the outer continental shelf, war surplus and fishing vessels delivered people and supplies to the rigs and platforms (Austin et al. 2002). As the offshore petroleum industry grew and moved farther offshore, demand for a range of service vessels (e.g., for seismic exploration and for transport of people, supplies, large equipment, and drilling muds) encouraged the expansion of existing yards and the creation of new ones. Many vessel companies remained small, and these continue to dot the Gulf Coast bayous, but others, such as North American Shipbuilding of Lafourche Parish, grew to become industry leaders (McGuire 2008). In addition to service vessels, finding and producing oil and gas requires large metal structures. Since the 1950s, along with thousands of Gulf drilling rigs, more than 5,500 platforms have been installed, many fabricated in yards located along the coast.

Added to the outsourcing and restructuring of jobs, labor relations in the Gulf Coast shipyards have been affected by corporate enforcement of federal drug-testing requirements and, since September 11, 2001, the requirement that all workers who require access to secure areas of ports carry special biometric documents. Each of these developments has further constricted labor supplies, creating a context for the use of guestworkers.

THE H-2B VISA AND THE US GULF COAST

Outside of shipbuilding, several industries in the US South have relied on guestworkers and the H-2B program since its inception. Using data from the Department of Labor (DOL), McDaniels and Casanova (2005) found that between 1996 and 2001, nationwide, forest management contractors in the southeastern United States were the largest single category of employers in the H-2B program, employing 21 percent of the program participants; nearly the same proportion was hired in housekeeping, maintenance,

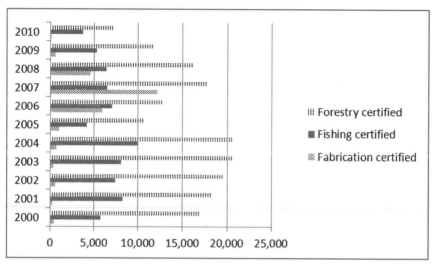

FIGURE 5.1

Certifications for H-2B visas in the timber, fishing, and fabrication and shipbuilding industries.
Forestry *includes forest workers and tree planters;* Fishing *includes fishers, shuckers, cannery workers, processors, fish cleaners, and fishing vessel deckhands;* Fabrication *includes fitters, welders, metal fabricators, pipefitters, riggers, and structural steel workers. Source: Foreign Labor Certification Data Center Online Wage Library (maintained for the US Department of Labor), http://www.flcdatacenter.com. Note that certifications do not substitute for actual entry; they provide a measure of demand.*

and other occupations. These were followed by landscaping/gardening; structural work; processing occupations; plant and animal farming/horticulture; and professional, technical, and managerial jobs. In line with other research on guestworkers (Griffith 2006; Hahamovitch, chapter 1, this volume), McDaniels and Casanova (2005) described contractors who inflated H-2B wages to satisfy the Department of Labor and then recouped those costs by charging exorbitant rates for tools, transportation, and international money transfers. Such wage recovery practices have been reported elsewhere in relation to the offshore petroleum industry (Donato 2004) and agriculture (Hahamovitch, chapter 1, this volume; Martin, chapter 2, this volume).

The first use of H-2B workers in Gulf Coast shipyards occurred in 1996–1997, when Louisiana shipbuilders hired approximately 3,000 foreign workers, primarily from India and Mexico, to fill welder, shipfitter, and electrician positions. One employer, Avondale Shipyards, in a dispute with union leaders, was accused of helping manufacture the shortage by refusing

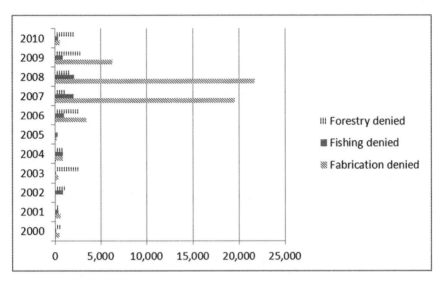

FIGURE 5.2

Denials of H-2B visas in the timber, fishing, and fabrication and shipbuilding industries. Forestry *includes forest workers and tree planters;* Fishing *includes fishers, shuckers, cannery workers, processors, fish cleaners, and fishing vessel deckhands;* Fabrication *includes fitters, welders, metal fabricators, pipefitters, riggers, and structural steel workers. Source: Foreign Labor Certification Data Center Online Wage Library (maintained for the US Department of Labor), http://www.flcdatacenter.com.*

to hire union workers (Priest 2013). In mid-1997, the US Department of Labor determined that the jobs for which the workers were hired did not qualify for the H-2B program because they lasted for the duration of ship-building contracts, which could be three years or more. Yet, in 1998, under pressure from Louisiana politicians, the DOL approved 715 new one-year H-2B visas for welding trainers (Times-Picayune 1997, 1998). No further use of H-2B visas was recorded in the Gulf shipbuilding industry for the next several years.

In general, nationwide, the distribution of H-2B workers among the various industries was relatively stable during the first decade of the twenty-first century, but quite suddenly between 2006 and 2008, the numbers of H-2B workers in the fabrication and shipbuilding industry crept up toward those in the timber industry (figure 5.1). Although the number of certifications in fabrication and shipbuilding remained lower than those in timber, a large number of requests from companies in fabrication and shipbuilding were denied (figure 5.2). Hurricanes Katrina and Rita drove this process.

DIANE AUSTIN

Just months before the storms, in May 2005, the Emergency Supplemental Appropriations Act for Defense, the Global War on Terror, and Tsunami Relief was signed into law, exempting returning workers from the H-2B cap and allowing the program to expand into new areas without siphoning off H-2B workers from other industries. Fabrication and shipbuilding were major beneficiaries.

SHIPBUILDING IN THE GULF OF MEXICO

Given that labor shortages in this industry are not new, the circumstances that led to the rapid increase and precipitous decline in the use of guestworkers require attention. The data used here were gathered during a study of the fabrication and shipbuilding industry in the US Gulf of Mexico conducted by researchers from the Bureau of Applied Research in Anthropology at the University of Arizona for the US Bureau of Ocean Energy Management. Ethnographic fieldwork was carried out by a team of eight researchers between January 2007 and January 2009 in seven Gulf Coast communities from Brownsville, Texas, to Mobile, Alabama (figure 5.3). Researchers lived in each community, or group of nearby communities, for at least four months, taking tours of worksites, attending training classes, and conducting informal and semi-formal interviews and focus groups with employers, workers, community leaders, and other residents. The researchers also returned to each community to present their initial findings and get feedback and additional information in focus groups and individual interviews. Secondary data were drawn from databases from the US Department of Labor, labor recruiter and company websites, local and national media stories, and government documents.

Humans living along the Gulf of Mexico have constructed watercraft since they began to occupy the region tens of thousands of years ago. The modern shipbuilding industry developed with commercial fishing and the military in mind. Even in communities where no military installations remain, ties to war era shipyards are remembered; many sites developed as military facilities were converted to service the offshore petroleum industry. With petroleum's rise after World War II, some shipyards began to fabricate vessels, rigs, and platforms. Some workers who learned to weld during World War II applied their skills in the postwar petroleum industry (Penney 2008).

The growth of wartime shipyards was part of the area's industrial development, with companies lauded for providing large numbers of well-paying local jobs where few were found before. By the end of the 1990s, the Gulf Coast employed 35 percent of the nation's shipyard workers, more than

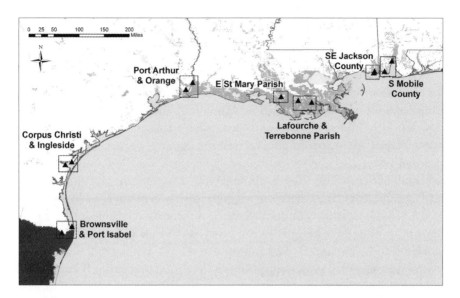

FIGURE 5.3

Map of Gulf Coast study communities. Created by Ben McMahan in 2012 using data packages included with the ArcGIS software suite. Sources used to create these data layers: ArcWorld/ESRI, National Atlas of the United States, Tele Atlas, US Bureau of Transportation Statistics, US Census, and US Geological Survey.

any other region, the work evenly split between the military and commerce (Bureau of Export Administration 2001). Within a decade, though most yards would gladly have done new construction, much of the work was in repair, especially following the 2005 hurricanes in the Gulf. Many companies and workers specialized in either constructing vessels or fabricating rigs or platforms, and some moved back and forth between the two (Austin and Woodson 2012). In addition, several yards operating out of Brownsville dismantled vessels and sold what could be recovered as scrap.[3]

The fishing industry also created demand for vessels. Historically, fishermen built, operated, and repaired their own vessels, and many small-scale fishers continue to do so. However, after World War II, as the industry expanded and moved farther offshore, the need for larger vessels and the availability of steel for construction supported the shift away from wooden vessels. Some locals began to specialize in construction for this industry.

As in other regions of the country, the processes, equipment, and technologies used in shipbuilding have remained relatively unchanged since shipbuilders switched from wood to metal and welding became a critical skill. Throughout most of the twentieth century, shipbuilding work, though challenging, was a valued occupation—passed from father to son and, in some cases, even to daughters. Workers could—and did—respond to slack labor demand in shipbuilding by finding work in related industries nearby and outside the area. An electrician who had retired from a large shipyard in Mississippi stated, "When we finally ran out [of business] in '48, the last ship we built was headed down to Argentina, and me and the one other guy left were laid off.... I was an electrician's apprentice.... And after we were laid off, we were tramping all over the country working. And after the Korean War, I got called back, and when I came back, the shipyard told me to come back because they would make me a supervisor, and three weeks after I came back, they made me a supervisor" (interview, June 2008).

Throughout the twentieth century, shipyards continued to employ tens of thousands of people; in the twenty-first, they offer what many still consider to be among the best jobs in the region. When work is available, employees can work at least sixty hours a week, making relatively large sums of money from overtime. However, ties to the offshore petroleum industry, whose activity fluctuates, have done little to ameliorate the cyclical nature of shipbuilding. Some companies have taken on both military and petroleum industry clients in the hopes of smoothing out the fluctuations, but the needs and requirements of the two are sufficiently different that many companies serve only one group or the other. Thus, the pattern of hiring and laying off large numbers of workers over short time periods has persisted in companies that construct vessels and platforms for the petroleum industry. A sales manager for a mid-size Mississippi shipyard described operations prior to the 1980s downturn, which left many companies bankrupt and people out of work: "But what made us so flexible was, within one week, we could hire a hundred skilled workers. Then, when the work was done, we laid them off. At the end, we didn't try to keep them on. One to two months later, we could rehire. Maybe not the same people.... Word spreads. We had work, and they wanted that kind of work because they wanted to work lots of hours and then take off when they wanted to go hunting or whatever" (interview, June 2008). Labor unions have struggled in the region; only the largest yards are organized.

The past success of companies involved in the petroleum industry, including shipyards, in finding both skilled and unskilled laborers has been attributed to a number of specific characteristics of the region and its population (Austin 2006; Austin et al. 2002; Austin and McGuire 2002). The US South has generally experienced lower rates of outmigration than other parts of the country. The region has long been marked by pockets of extreme poverty, with Louisiana, Mississippi, and Alabama all exceeding the national average in numbers of people living below the poverty level. Coastal regions have tended to fare better than inland regions, due primarily to petroleum and related industries. In coastal communities, levels of education lag far behind state and national averages.[4] With little formal education and experience in the military, fishing, or agriculture, many residents have perceived work in shipyards and related companies as a good option, and they are able to fill employment gaps by hunting, trapping, and fishing.

Since the 1970s, because of the massive downturn in the 1980s and the subsequent reorganization of the petroleum industry, which led to greater levels of subcontracting than ever before, the loyalties that once existed between workers and their employers, as well as the familial ties across generations, have steadily eroded (Austin 2007; Austin et al. 2002). By the twenty-first century, shipyard managers and personnel directors in the Gulf region faced the same challenges as their counterparts elsewhere in the United States. Work in the yards is hard and dangerous; it is perceived to be less desirable than even other petroleum industry jobs, such as working in refineries or on offshore rigs and platforms; and it pays less (Austin and Crosthwait 2013). A bookkeeper at a small shipyard noted, "The shipyards are a stable force, but not a driving force—they just can't compete with the refineries, [which] have the luxury of a benefits package and pay more than the shipyards" (interview, April 2008).

Following national patterns, workforce screening and surveillance, especially for drugs, have become commonplace across the industry, and the recent rise in security measures has affected employment eligibility. The workforce is also aging, with individuals in their sixties and older holding much of the expertise. As is common immediately prior to requesting guestworkers, managers regularly decry the perceived poor-quality labor, complaining also that potential workers will choose either not to work at all or to take lower-paying jobs in the service industry rather than shipyard jobs, even when the latter offer possibilities for advancement. Union leaders argue that the instability in the labor force has been exacerbated by low wages, a lack of apprenticeships, and other workforce development initiatives.

In August and September 2005, Hurricanes Katrina and Rita struck the Gulf Coast, worsening the problems in the shipbuilding industry. In early October, the US secretary of the interior reported that the hurricanes had destroyed 109 platforms and 5 drilling rigs and damaged another 50 platforms and 19 rigs (CBS Business Network 2005). Pressures to get the oil industry back on its feet were great. One local official in Texas's Golden Triangle region related that the first question President George W. Bush asked on his September 2005 visit to view the damage caused by Hurricane Rita was "When will the refineries be back online?" (interview, June 2007). A public relations officer for a shipyard in the Golden Triangle reported going from a labor force of "practically zero" just after Katrina and Rita struck, to a peak of 1,300–1,400 hourly employees within about nine months. During that period, welders were working seven days a week, twelve hours a day, and some were making close to $100,000 per year (interview, March 2008).

MEETING THE LABOR NEEDS OF GULF COAST SHIPBUILDERS

Labor contractors have supplied workers to the offshore petroleum industry, including shipyards, for decades, their recruitment efforts reaching across the United States and to its territories. Many employers have used these contractors; others have tried to avoid the expense, developing strategies to find and retain workers on their own (Austin and Crosthwait 2013). Over the years, these have included manipulating workers' hours; providing training; establishing programs in local high schools to attract young people; establishing programs with local prisons to train and employ individuals in work release programs; developing national recruitment campaigns; attempting to make the workplace more comfortable, such as enclosing outdoor work areas; adopting measures to increase safety; developing modular systems that enable components to be constructed overseas and then brought to Gulf yards to be assembled; increasing the mechanization of routine tasks; and diversifying to include, specifically, African Americans, women, Asian Americans, and, most recently, Latinos. All of these approaches have been met with some success, yet the problem of fluctuating demand for labor remains.

Although Gulf Coast employers have long used guestworkers in fisheries and forestry, shipbuilders did not apply for H-2B workers until almost the twenty-first century. In 1999, Hatco, Inc., a labor contractor from Garland, Texas, applied for certification for 15 arc welders and 56 shipfitters to work in Louisiana. The request was denied, as was one in 2000 for 100 arc welders and 175 shipfitters. As shown in table 5.1, several other requests from the region were also denied. In 2000, the only shipyard to be certified to receive H-2B workers was Todd Pacific Shipyards Corporation in Seattle, Washington; the company requested and was certified for 50 riggers, 47 shipfitters, and 50 welder fitters. There is no record that Todd Pacific requested employees after that year, and outside the Gulf of Mexico, the use of H-2B workers by shipyards has remained small. Initially, as shown in table 5.1, activity in the Gulf of Mexico was limited as well.

TABLE 5.1

Early Requests for H-2B Workers for Gulf Coast Fabrication and Shipbuilding

Year	Company	City	Workers Requested	Action
1999	Hatco, Inc.	Garland, TX	15 arc welders, 56 shipfitters	Denied
2000	Hatco, Inc.	Garland, TX	100 arc welders, 175 shipfitters	Denied
2000	International Marine and Industrial Services	Gautier, MS	40 arc welders	Denied
2000	Freide Goldman Halter	Gulfport, MS	285 pipefitters	Denied
2000	Overseas Ship Services	Miami, FL	100 workers: pipefitters, welder fitters, machinist apprentices, electricians, joiners, metal fabricators	Denied
2001	Lomco Employment Services	Schriever, LA	125 welder fitters	Denied
2001	Ladnier-Hardy Services	Bayou La Batre, AL	10 metal fabricator assemblers	Certified
2001	Don Rhodes Welding Service	Houma, LA	20 machinists	Certified
2002	International Marine and Industrial Services	Gautier, MS	75 arc welders, 35 shipfitters, 10 pipefitters	Denied
2002	Don Rhodes Welding Service	Houma, LA	6 gas welders	Certified

Source: Foreign Labor Certification Data Center Online Wage Library (maintained for the US Department of Labor), http://www.flcdatacenter.com. Note that certifications do not substitute for actual entry; they provide a measure of demand.

The number of requests and certifications continued to inch up slowly until the hurricanes of 2005. Pressure to get the offshore platforms and rigs back to work was tremendous, and the extensive displacement of workers and their families, along with competition from reconstruction efforts, exacerbated already existing labor shortages. Some perceived the H-2B program as a significant part of the solution, with nearly all company owners and administrators who were contacted naming the 2005 hurricanes as the reason they began using H-2B workers (Austin and Crosthwait 2013).

Despite the uniformity of guidelines surrounding H-2B, with similar labor problems facing all Gulf Coast shipyards, across the seven study communities, prior experience with H-2B workers ranged from very extensive to almost nonexistent. Because locals have lived with and supported the shipbuilding industry for many decades, they are accustomed to the ups and downs of the industry, the large-scale efforts to hire workers and the massive layoffs, and the recruitment of workers from beyond their borders. In some places, the recruitment and arrival of foreign workers drew attention, whereas in others, it was hardly noticed.

In most yards, especially the larger ones that employ more than a dozen or so people, workers of different legal status and classification are commonly grouped together. During the study, these included US citizens living in the local communities, US citizens who commuted and returned home periodically, US citizens living in prison, H-2B workers, permanent residents, and undocumented workers. When the H-2B workers came from countries that already supply large numbers of immigrant workers to the industry, they drew little attention. In the Gulf Coast communities studied, H-2B visa workers were drawn from Mexico, Jamaica, the Philippines, India, Pakistan, Romania, and China. Some companies hired the workers directly, and others worked through contractors. For the latter, each week, the employer would provide a list of workers needed and the contract company would send them. Many companies drew on multiple contractors to fulfill their labor needs. A human resources director at one shipyard noted, "We form relationships with agents in that area. For example, once the Romanian agent developed a pool of applicants, [another HR manager] and I went with four craft superintendents, and we tested 262 people in two days and then made offers for skilled workers. Shipfitters, pipefitters, structural welders, and pipe welders. Same thing will happen in Puerto Rico. You can't just go into a country—you have to have an agency relationship there" (interview, June 2008).

To reduce costs and get around issues with contractors, some employers began hiring H-2B workers directly. A recruiter for a mid-size shipyard with a number of large, permanent "Help Wanted" signs dotting the area highways described the process: "First, you advertise in the city you need the workers…and you wait several days, and the job services hold the phone number to see who calls about the job and who could work. Then you find out how many people call, but few ever do…. Then you refer the information to Baton Rouge [the Louisiana state capital], and then after a day, you can recruit from Mexico" (interview, October 2008).

THE "NEED" TO BE FILLED

Everyone discussed the recruitment and employment of H-2B workers in the context of general labor shortages. Whether in support of or against the use of guestworkers, those who discussed the issue noted that the shipyards had trouble finding workers because of competition from other industries and other parts of the country. Work in refineries and on offshore platforms paid much better; looking at petroleum exploration in other parts of the United States and around the world, skilled workers could make more money elsewhere. Other than workers and labor organizers, only a small minority of respondents cited increased wages as the solution to labor shortages, suggesting that company employment policies contribute to the shortages.

To justify importing workers, employers also mentioned labor quality: local workers, supposedly shunning hard work, opted for lower-paying but easier service jobs, worked only long enough to qualify for unemployment compensation, or signed up as if seeking a job, but only to continue getting unemployment benefits. Employers regularly complained that local workers often failed drug screens or welding skills tests. Echoing this, a pastor and labor advocate in Texas noted, "It's not just the price of oil [contributing to the labor shortages]. It's the cursed drug use" (interview, November 2007). In contrast, the director of human resources for a mid-size shipyard observed, "We did pre-employments on all of the Romanians, and every one of them tested negative. I was talking with one of their interpreters, who's now a foreman here, and he told me he knew it was going to be that way because in Romania, if you're caught with an illegal substance, you're looking at twenty-five years in jail. That's a heck of a deterrent, which young people aren't looking at here in the US" (interview, June 2008).

Not everyone agreed that guestworkers were the answer. A labor recruiter for a contract company that did not use guestworkers reflected on the tensions: "At the old company I worked at, we had 150 guys, and we were making a killing on H-2B work, but a lot of times, you have a trained welder on unemployment and a guy on a visa doing that job—it seems like maybe we should kick the visa guys out" (interview, October 2008).

A principal source of profit from hiring H-2B workers, according to some, was that the workers received low base wages and then the difference between those wages and the going wage was classified as per diem for food and lodging; employers did not pay overtime or workers compensation insurance on the per diem. In contrast to the H-2A program for farmworkers, the H-2B program does not require employers to provide housing. However, especially due to the lack of adequate housing following the 2005 hurricanes, many employers did make arrangements to house their workers. As is common among employers of H-2B workers, companies that provided housing generally charged for it, earning back a good portion of the money they were paying out (Griffith 2006). Although many company officials argued that what they provided and charged was decent and fair, some workers and residents questioned the housing conditions. Concerns about housing reflected larger concerns about the H-2B program and the perception and treatment of workers, as illustrated by the case of Signal International.

SIGNAL INTERNATIONAL AND THE H-2B PROGRAM

Signal International is a marine and fabrication company with four yards, two in Pascagoula, Mississippi, one in Orange, Texas, and a marine repair facility in Mobile, Alabama. The company focuses on "offshore drilling rig overhaul, repair, upgrade and conversion" (Marler n.d.). Early in the study period, on March 9, 2007, East Indian H-2B workers were gathered up and held by Signal officials in a predawn raid of their housing facility in Pascagoula. The workers had begun protesting that they had paid recruiters $12,000 to $15,000 each in exchange for what they were told would be high-paying jobs and permanent resident cards and had received neither. On March 11, the workers, now organized as the Signal H2B Employees Organization, issued a statement describing their treatment and requesting help (Signal H2B Employees Organization 2007). This action, and those of the company and others who intervened in the case, became the basis upon which the H-2B program was understood and discussed by many in the Gulf region.

The story began in 2006 with little fanfare. On June 13, 2006, Signal's application for 180 fitters and 110 gas welders for one of its Pascagoula yards was received by the designated state workforce agency for Mississippi, and approximately two months later, on August 20, the company was certified to receive all 290 workers (Department of Labor 2006). The request for Signal was filed by immigration attorney Malvern Burnett, who also represented North American Shipbuilding, Good Jobs, Inc., and other Gulf Coast fabricators and shipbuilders that year. Working with labor recruiter Global Resources, the company was also seeking to employ 300 workers at its Texas yard.

As part of the Texas request, Signal applied to the city of Orange for permission to provide temporary housing on company property, which was located within an industrial zone. A city ordinance prohibited the location of permanent housing within the industrial zone but was silent on the issue of temporary housing. Representatives from the city's fire department, police department, public works department, and code enforcement reviewed the permit application and toured the proposed site. On September 1, 2006, before any guestworkers arrived, the city manager prepared a memo for the city council. The memo included information about the number of workers to be brought to the Texas facility (300), the number being sought for the Mississippi yard (290), the workers' countries of origin (Indian nationals coming from India and the United Arab Emirates), the H-2B visa program, Signal's application, the types of workers being sought, the wages to be paid, the cost of housing and per diem, medical insurance to be provided to the workers, and the steps Signal had taken to advertise for local workers (communications with Pipefitters Local 195 and ads in three local papers and the *Houston Chronicle*). It also addressed potential concerns about the safety of personnel and emergency workers responding to calls at the site, entertainment, the provision of translators for non-English-speaking workers when they were off the property, and access to the site.

The memo recommended that the city council approve temporary housing for a period of eighteen months, subject to review at that point. The memo requested specifically that "trailers used for housing be fitted with a sprinkler system, meet flood plain requirements and be placed so that the finished floor is eight feet [above] Mean Sea Level, meet the International Building Code, and [be] sized properly for the number of occupants" (Oubre 2006). The city had already at the time approved on-site housing for another shipbuilder, but the memo stated, "[The City] did not suggest these requirements because the City felt that it was an isolated incident due to lack of housing. As the City continues to get these requests, Council may want to use the above requirements as the minimum requirements as staff feels there may be more requests in the future.... The Golden Triangle area is experiencing economic growth that it has not experienced in this area in a long time. In order to address this growth, Council is being asked to approve something it would not consider during normal economic activity" (ibid.). Attention to such details about the workers' housing grew out of close relationships between city personnel and leaders of the Interfaith Worker Justice organization (interviews, June and November 2007). The council approved the request for housing, and the Indian workers began arriving in November 2006. They lived in Texas for less than eighteen months.

In Pascagoula, too, Signal decided to house its workers on the yard.[5] At the time, housing was still in very short supply, and there is no evidence that the decision raised the concerns of any local officials. Attempting to assuage local concerns about bringing in foreign workers, Signal advertised and discussed its use of non-immigrant labor as a last-choice response to labor shortages (see Nelson 2007; Roche 2007). The common refrain throughout the Gulf region at the time was that everyone who wanted a job and could pass the drug test already had one. The owner of a mid-size Alabama shipyard reflected on that period: "They were hiring at higher prices to aid in rebuilding, even people to hold signs. That put an upward pressure on [the] wage system, and a number of workers left to chase debris removal" (interview, May 2008).

The Indian workers in Pascagoula objected to their housing conditions soon after their arrival, but those objections were not immediately made public. Initially, all information about the situation at Signal was provided by the company. A January 2, 2007 article in the *Sun Herald* described the Indian workers who would be housed at Signal "in a facility constructed specifically for them." On January 3, Signal issued a statement describing its use of guestworkers, which included the following:

> In autumn of 2006 Signal International began receiving tempo-
> rary guest workers from India to fill first-class welder and fitter
> positions at the Pascagoula shipyard. Currently there are 300
> guest workers on Signal's payroll as full-time employees. They
> receive the same pay and are taxed the same as all other Signal
> craft personnel. Guest workers also pay for their room and board
> during their stay at the company's on-site housing facility, which
> includes a cafeteria, recreation lounges, laundry facilities, and
> bunk-house sleeping quarters. (Roche 2007)

Again, Signal's primary concern was that the company would be criticized for hiring guestworkers rather than locals.

On March 9, 2007, six Indian workers were terminated and then detained in a TV room at their living quarters.[6] They were surrounded by other workers, who issued a statement on behalf of the Signal H2B Employees Organization, and released two days later. They left Pascagoula and, on March 13, joined other Indian and Mexican workers with the Alliance of Guest Workers for Dignity in a protest outside a US Department of Labor office in New Orleans. Locals seemed indifferent to the protest. That same day, in an interview with the author about critical issues in the fabrication and shipbuilding industry, a Mississippi economic development officer talked about workforce problems and noted that a local company had recently brought in 300 workers from India and constructed barracks for them on the yard. She emphasized the services the company was provid-ing, such as taking the workers to church. She also stated, "[The workers] need little compared with what an American worker would expect and are grateful for what they get" (interview, March 2007). When asked whether there had been any negative reactions from community members regarding the workers or their treatment, she responded that there had not. She noted instead that another local company had already begun the process to bring in foreign workers and that, based on a survey conducted by her organization, many local companies said that they would hire 100 skilled workers on the spot, if they could be found.

On March 14, a story appeared in the *Los Angeles Times* about the workers and the New Orleans protest (Simmons 2007). Local press coverage a day later supported the company and repeated some of the same claims about positive treatment, noting that the workers were provided with a chef who could prepare Indian cuisine (Ward 2007). The situation was quickly characterized in the media and by residents and community leaders in one of two ways: (1) as an example of a company and recruiters mistreating workers, under advice from the US government, or (2) as an example of disgruntled workers who had exaggerated their skill levels, had to be demoted to lesser positions at lower wages, and then complained. The full story was far more complicated. For example, several sources noted that the company said that it was holding the six men on the advice of US immigration officials and was going to load them on vans and forcibly deport them (e.g., Beyerstein and Alexandrovna 2007; Parks 2007). The role of the US government remains under investigation. Whatever eventually unfolds, the case has become yet another symbol of the problems with guestworker programs in the fabrication and shipbuilding industry and elsewhere, stimulating a variety of, at times, contradictory reports (figure 5.4).

In April 2007, Signal stated in a letter to the president of Global Resources, the H-2B recruitment company, that it had been told that the fees charged to the workers were much less, demanding that Global Resources reimburse the workers half that fee, their visa fee, and airfare (Ward 2007). In June, *Forbes* magazine noted that the workers had been fired "after complaining about conditions and stirring up discontent at the camp" (Helman 2007). In August 2007, a request by Malvern Burnett for H-2B visas for 118 metal fabricator apprentices and 252 fitters for Signal was denied (Department of Labor 2007). Later, on March 27, 2008, Signal issued this statement: "[Signal will] no longer hire new temporary workers under the H-2B program until it is reformed to better protect foreign workers and U.S. companies that were misled by recruiters" (Hangartner 2008). By then, Signal had transferred all its H-2B workers to one of the Pascagoula yards, leading a city official in Orange, Texas, to note that the community had "finished with that phase" (interview, March 2008).

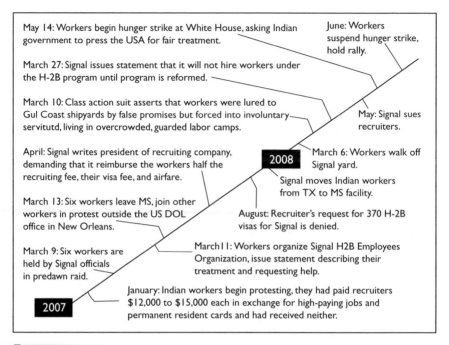

May 14: Workers begin hunger strike at White House, asking Indian government to press the USA for fair treatment.

June: Workers suspend hunger strike, hold rally.

March 27: Signal issues statement that it will not hire workers under the H-2B program until program is reformed.

March 10: Class action suit asserts that workers were lured to Gul Coast shipyards by false promises but forced into involuntary servitutd, living in overcrowded, guarded labor camps.

May: Signal sues recruiters.

April: Signal writes president of recruiting company, demanding that it reimburse the workers half the recruiting fee, their visa fee, and airfare.

2008

March 6: Workers walk off Signal yard.

Signal moves Indian workers from TX to MS facility.

March 13: Six workers leave MS, join other workers in protest outside the US DOL office in New Orleans.

August: Recruiter's request for 370 H-2B visas for Signal is denied.

March 9: Six workers are held by Signal officials in predawn raid.

March 11: Workers organize Signal H2B Employees Organization, issue statement describing their treatment and requesting help.

2007

January: Indian workers begin protesting, they had paid recruiters $12,000 to $15,000 each in exchange for high-paying jobs and permanent resident cards and had received neither.

FIGURE 5.4

Timeline of key events in the Signal case, by Diane Austin.

On March 6, 2008, 89 Signal workers walked off the yard at the company headquarters in Pascagoula (Baker 2008). A group of more than 100 workers then boarded a bus to New Orleans, where, with the help of the New Orleans Workers' Center for Racial Justice, on March 7 they filed a class action complaint (*Kurian et al. v. Signal International, LLC, et al.*) that Signal had defrauded and exploited more than 500 Indian workers in its Pascagoula and Orange yards (Crocker 2008). On March 10, the Southern Poverty Law Center filed a class action suit on behalf of several hundred Indian guestworkers, asserting that the workers were lured by false promises of permanent US residency and had paid tens of thousands of dollars to obtain temporary jobs at Gulf Coast shipyards only to find themselves forced into involuntary servitude and living in overcrowded, guarded labor camps (*David et al. v. Signal International, LLC*). Then, on May 14, 2008, with support from the DC Jobs with Justice, the Southern Poverty Law Center, and the AFL-CIO, 24 of the workers began a hunger strike at the White House, asking the Indian government to press the United States for fair treatment. Signal, in turn, sued both US and Indian recruiters for allegedly misleading the workers (New York Times 2010a).

In June 2010, the US Citizenship and Immigration Services concluded that about 150 of the workers would be granted visas because they had been subject to involuntary servitude and therefore were entitled to visas set aside for victims of human trafficking (New York Times 2010b). Signal responded with a "Recruitment Fraud Alert" posted on its website in 2010. "Signal International, LLC ('Signal') has recently been made aware of fraudulent recruitment activity abroad in Signal's name in the recruitment of foreign nationals," it read. "This fraudulent recruitment activity took place with respect to the recruitment abroad of foreign nationals for H-2B visas." The alert went on to describe how some of the frauds were perpetrated and warned potential workers that the company was no longer in the business of recruiting foreign nationals.

In April 2011, the US Equal Employment Opportunity Commission (EEOC) filed a lawsuit against Signal, charging that the company "violated federal law by subjecting a class of approximately 500 Indian employees to human labor trafficking and a hostile work environment" and that "the living facilities, food and overall living conditions were intolerable, demeaning and unsanitary" (Equal Employment Opportunity Commission 2011:1). The EEOC reported that the Signal case and others were being brought to combat discriminatory practices regarding foreign laborers. Though the EEOC lawsuit was still pending against the company at the time, in January 2012, a US federal judge denied the workers class certification in the *Kurian et al. v. Signal International, LLC, et al.* case, arguing that the workers were free to live off company property and to come and go as they wished and denying that they suffered harm or any threat of harm. With that decision, the only option left to the workers was to sue the company individually, which was deemed by observers to be unlikely (Sohrabji 2012). Nevertheless, on September 5, 2012, the twelve plaintiffs named in *Kurian et al. v. Signal International, LLC, et al.*, filed a motion for leave to file a third amended complaint, seeking to remove the class action allegations and demands for injunctive relief but adding additional allegations and defendants to the case. The plaintiffs' motion was granted on September 21, 2012.

AN ABRUPT HALT

Although Signal's case is unique due to both the activism of the H-2B workers and the public attention it received, the overall story is not. The enthusiastic recruitment of workers, followed by the unmet expectations of workers and often of employers as well, and the withdrawal of employers from the H-2B program are all features common to court cases against employers of guestworkers. As shown in figures 5.1 and 5.2, between 2006 and 2010 after a fairly rapid rise in demand, with much of it met by certifications, the certifications came to an abrupt halt, and the number of requests dropped soon afterward.

What explains the rapid decrease? Despite the general economic downturn in the United States, the construction of rigs and naval vessels continued into 2009, buoying the economies of coastal communities. Amid signs that rig demand would be slowing (Kammerzell 2009), the Gulf Coast employment picture still looked generally good (Judge 2009). Nevertheless, climbing unemployment rates in other regions, along with a return of many area residents to the coast, increased the pool of workers available to employers. By 2010, even before the Deepwater Horizon disaster in the Gulf of Mexico, the economic recession was being felt more broadly, and employers were laying off workers. As noted above, often the H-2B visa workers were the first to go (see Soni and Castellanos 2010). Although this contributed to a reduced demand for H-2B labor (see Legendre 2009), it alone does not explain the rapid drop. Instead, deliberate efforts by workforce development officers at the state workforce agencies led to the sudden halt in certifications for H-2B labor. At the Louisiana Workforce Commission, for example, a veteran staff member was given responsibility for the foreign labor certification program in 2008. She immediately began working with union representatives to monitor job postings for workers in this industry. Together, they would gather the resumes of US citizens qualified for the positions and then forward those to the national processing center with the recommendation that the certification be denied. This process was repeated in all four Gulf states where H-2B workers had been employed in the fabrication and shipbuilding industry. The results were almost immediate. Beginning in 2009, all requests for certification were denied.

DISCUSSION

Workers, employers, and others in the study communities expressed differing perspectives on decisions to employ H-2B workers, not always aligning in predictable ways. Some, for example, made little distinction between the guestworkers and others who had been recruited to their communities, whereas some were quick to point out and address the differences. Generally, employers argued that their negative experiences with the program led them to abandon it as an alternative. Yet, at least one large shipbuilder continued to request H-2B workers into 2010. The incident at Signal had repercussions for other companies and workers. In one case, after a Jamaican worker complained about working conditions, the labor recruiter informed all the Jamaican workers he had recruited and the companies they worked for that they would be sent home. Both employer and employees expressed frustration and anger over that situation.

In general, employers noted that they had been hesitant to become involved in the H-2B program, both because of the monetary costs associated with the process of getting workers, whether by working directly with labor brokers in other countries or with US labor contractors, and because of strong community ties that encourage local hiring (even when the number of locals employed in many of these yards has been low for some time). One labor contractor who was providing labor to companies along the Coastal Bend in Texas explained why his company did not participate in the H-2B program: "There are plenty of residents, citizens, available right now. We haven't tried to go into visas. It's too...I don't know...too complicated. All those procedures and things. We haven't tried. We've been doing good with the guys, the residents, and everything. There's a lot of contractors who go in for visas. They bring Indian guys" (interview, April 2008). Others argued that they had no option: "Hiring is just different now. And it's not just in the craft positions. But in craft, they're just not making them any more. We don't want to bring in H-2B visa Mexicans. We want everyone to be from here. But it's just not possible" (interview, May 2008).

Many of the workers encountered in the Gulf of Mexico had considerable experience working in guestworker programs across the globe, but few organized to protest their circumstances. Chinese workers in southern Alabama, for example, compared their experiences in different countries and noted that though they were treated poorly in the United States in comparison with elsewhere, their wages were better in the United States. One Chinese resident who had befriended some of the workers noted, "Quite a few had been in Japan, Korea. They said in Japan it was so nice. They had their own room, with a fridge. In Korea too. Their living conditions were better in both places. But the pay here was better. They were not complaining.... What they make here in a week is what they make there in a month. That's the real allure for coming here" (interview, October 2008).

Whereas concerns about wages and the fees that workers had to pay were not uniformly expressed, housing was mentioned by almost everyone, employers and workers alike. As when US workers are housed in bunkhouses and labor camps, company housing facilitates connecting workers with jobs and avoids competition with local residents for limited low-cost housing. A representative for a Mississippi shipyard claimed, "We did this [provided worker housing] for two reasons: first, they wouldn't know how to find housing in town and get to work, and, second, it was right after Katrina and the little housing there was needed by local community members. We didn't want to take it up with the workers" (interview, May 2008). Company housing also facilitates shipbuilders' control and oversight of their guestworkers, which, they argue, allows them to ensure that the workers do not jump their visas and to protect the companies' investments of time and money in bringing the workers to the United States and their particular yards.

Both the state and federal governments helped some of the larger companies provide housing. Bollinger Shipyards, which noted that it had to replace 500 workers after the storms and therefore recruited from across the United States and supplemented its usual contract labor workforce with H-2B visa workers, identified "housing and logistics" as the company's biggest problem (Marine Log 2006). The company received assistance from the Louisiana Department of Economic Development and the US Federal Emergency Management Agency in setting up eighty-two trailers and additional bunkhouses in four locations across the Gulf, providing housing for US and H-2B workers. A manager at one yard noted, "I never wanted to get into the business of being a slum landlord, and now I'm dealing with housing stuff, with housing issues" (interview, June 2008).

Not all employers provided housing for workers. In some communities, companies rented out large sections of trailer parks, purchased or rented motels, or left the workers to find their own housing. A southeast Texas yard that hired workers from Mexico contracted sections of a local motel for a limited time until workers developed networks and friendships and found places where they would prefer to live (interview, May 2008). One individual who established a labor-contracting service and recruited workers converted what had been his mother's house into a bunkhouse, putting four workers to a room and charging them each $400 a month rent plus $1 an hour for access to a driver for every hour they worked, whether or not they used the driver. The workers were under contract to be paid $30 an hour, but the labor contractor took $12 an hour, leaving them $18 an hour before housing and transportation costs were taken out. Like most laborers in the region, the workers attempted to earn higher pay by working overtime (interviews, October 2008).

The type of housing that was provided was a visible indicator to the workers and to everyone else in the community of their status. Instead of being treated as the skilled professionals they understood themselves to be, in the Gulf, these workers were treated—by the companies and also by the communities in which they were living—as common laborers. A Filipino worker who had been doing contract welding across the world commented,

"It is like a prison here. We can't go out. Only to Walmart for one hour a week, that is all. We can do no socializing, no drinking. We just sit here—we are like prisoners" (interview, July 2007). Residents, too, commented that the workers were treated like "slaves," "locked up in the compounds," "chained in a room except when they work," and "behind barbed wire" (interviews, March 2007, May and July 2008). One social services provider described yard-owned residential facilities as ranging from "unethically terrible to moderately tolerable" (interview, July 2008).

That US contract workers had become more accustomed to their lower status—and were generally unaccustomed to being provided housing—was reflected in some of their comments. One Mexican American welder from Corpus Christi, who was staying in the same facility as the Filipino workers, noted, "They cook for us, and we can also cook for ourselves. They do our laundry too. It's awesome. You put your clothes out by 6 a.m., [and] they're done by 5 p.m. It's a really good deal. They do all this stuff for you, and then you can work overtime and not worry about having to do your errands" (interview, June 2008). This individual also commented on the pay: "I get $12 an hour now plus overtime, but I can jump up if I become a welder. The Filipinos are getting screwed though! They only make $5 an hour for [a] Class 1 welder!"

CONCLUSION

The use of H-2B workers in the Gulf of Mexico fabrication and ship-building industry during the 2000s followed the general patterns of guest-worker programs described elsewhere in this volume: guestworkers were hired to fill positions perceived as undesirable by US workers. A significant difference, though, is that some of the positions the workers were hired to fill were once highly regarded. Many employers argued that they did not distinguish the H-2B workers from others on their yards and many workers were recruited for skilled labor, but craft workers' experiences in the United States were more like those of the unskilled and low-skilled laborers discussed by others in this volume. Workers and their advocates, even some employers, also noted specific differences in the conditions faced by H-2B workers and other employees, highlighting recruitment practices and the information that workers in the sending countries received, unanticipated costs such as housing charges and other deductions, and the use of deportation and threats of deportation to discipline the workers. The Indian workers at Signal, in collaboration with legal aid and human rights organizations, took action that reached beyond their circumstances in an attempt to address problems they experienced with the H-2B program. Although, as Hahamovitch (chapter 1, this volume) notes, such coordinated resistance to guestworker programs has occurred before, it is rare. Due to the rapid drop in shipbuilders' access to the H-2B program shortly after the legal challenges began, the results of the action by the Signal workers will be hard to measure.

Moreover, the April 2010 explosion of the Deepwater Horizon drilling rig about forty miles off the coast of Louisiana had immediate consequences for the offshore petroleum and fishing industries in the Gulf of Mexico and for the shipbuilders and fabricators that service those industries. A moratorium led to a sudden halt in deepwater drilling. Though activity was beginning to pick up by 2012, the ban on drilling, coming on top of the downturn already being experienced in many coastal communities, led many companies to cut hours and reduce their workforces. The effects of the disaster will be far-reaching, not only on drilling in the Gulf of Mexico but also on workers' perceptions of being part of the offshore petroleum industry, and it is too early to tell whether widespread labor shortages are likely to recur in the near future. Only when they do recur can the surge in requests for guestworkers in the Gulf of Mexico fabrication and shipbuilding industry be fully understood. Was it a one-time response to specific circumstances that created particular needs in a particular industry at a specific place and time, or has the road been paved so that the next increase in demand will be met by mobilization of the networks and contacts established in this phase? And if the industry regains access to the H-2B program, will the experiences of employers, employees, and the communities within which this industry operates play any part in improving the circumstances facing all workers? Given the pressures accompanying demand for rig and vessel repair and construction, it is hard to be optimistic.

Notes

1. The US Office of Management and Budget (OMB) is the federal agency responsible for overseeing the development of industrial classifications. Under the North American Industry Classification System, adopted in 1997, the code for shipbuilding and repair is 33661. The official OMB definition of shipyards is "fixed facilities with drydocks and fabrication equipment capable of building a ship, defined as a watercraft typically suitable or intended for other than personal or recreational use.... Illustrative examples include: barge building; cargo ship building; drilling and production platforms, floating, oil and gas" (US Census 2007).

2. The use of H-2B workers provides an alternative solution: companies effectively insource labor when demand is high without the full obligations to regular employees.

3. Most shipbreaking is done outside the United States, but for security reasons,

the US government stipulates that navy vessels must be dismantled in US yards. The bulk of shipbreaking has shifted to Brownsville.

4. Prior to the 1960s, coastal residents, especially those of Native American and African American descent, had limited educational opportunities. An April 1963 US District Court ruling that the public schools could not discriminate against American Indian students (*Margie Willa Naquin et al. v. Terrebonne Board of Education*, US District Court, Eastern District of Louisiana, Civil Action 13, 291) made it possible for Native American students to attend local public schools in 1964 for the first time (Wallace et al. 2001).

5. The practice of housing fabrication and shipyard workers on the yards increased in frequency throughout 2006 and 2007 as the yards took on more work and brought in more workers (Austin and Crosthwait 2013).

6. According to testimony still being revealed in ongoing lawsuits, ICE officials advised the company's officials how to treat the workers and how to get them out of the country.

PART III

Guest and Host Families and Communities

6

From Perfect to Imperfect Immigrants

*Family Relations and the Managed Migration
of Seafood Workers between Sinaloa, Mexico,
and North Carolina*

David Griffith and Ricardo Contreras

Since the late 1980s, several small communities between the metropolitan centers of Los Mochis and Guasave, Sinaloa—in northwestern Mexico, across the Sea of Cortez from Baja California—have been sending hundreds of workers, primarily women, to seafood-processing plants along the US mid-Atlantic coast. These workers are legally authorized to work in the United States, issued H-2B visas, and contracted for seasonal employment lasting around seven or eight months, from April or May through November or December. Their participation in the mid-Atlantic seafood industry has occurred during a time of generalized crisis in US commercial fisheries, when a combination of political, economic, ecological, and social developments has undermined the abilities of many fishing families and corporate entities to continue to catch, process, and sell the fruits of the sea and near-shore estuaries, sounds, river mouths, and other coastal waters.

During the late 1980s and 1990s, access to legal Mexican labor allowed seafood-processing companies in North Carolina, Virginia, and Maryland to remain in business and even expand, yet several developments combined to cause a decline in seafood-processing plants and employment during the first decade of the twenty-first century. Among these developments was the increasing competition from foreign, including Mexican, imports of lower-cost blue crab meat—some of it from the very region that supplies Mexican workers to mid-Atlantic plants. Imported seafood is high on the list of threats to US commercial fisheries in general, but in this case, the same women who labor in the US crabbing industry have worked and, in some cases, continue to work for its Mexican competitors. At least in part, then, Sinaloa women have contributed to this period of industry contraction, during which many of the US plants that once hired Sinaloa women have closed. This employment has provided the women of this region with a temporary but significant source of income and power in their households, neighborhoods, and communities, but it is unclear whether they will be able to sustain the lifestyles they have grown accustomed to after these opportunities end.

This chapter examines how working-class Mexican women have become available for managed migration that separates, as fully as possible, productive labor from the settings of social reproduction. It considers the individual, local, and regional consequences of that process in Sinaloa, Mexico, and in eastern North Carolina. The construction of this labor force occurred in Sinaloa prior to its transformation into a migrant labor force, yet, ironically, increased participation in the migrant labor force has enabled some women from this region to decrease their participation in the local labor market. For other women, however, migration has not enabled withdrawal from Sinaloa labor markets. This chapter begins with a brief review of work on the construction of rural labor forces and then narrows from a consideration of the uses of slaves, indentured servants, and others to an examination of guestworker programs.

CONSTRUCTING A RURAL LABOR FORCE

Several social scientists and historians have described and analyzed the construction of laboring classes through various political-economic and cultural means (Daniel 1972; Griffith 1993; Griffith and Valdés Pizzini 2002; Hahamovitch 1997; Mintz 1957; Stoler 1985). The analysis of labor force construction in agriculture, fisheries, mining, forestry, food processing, and other rural, seasonal occupations often considers the roles of labor migration and immigrants in such processes. Many native workers will not accept these jobs because of their seasonal character; the current rates of pay and the working conditions; and their being distant from urban centers and thus isolated, which often stimulates the development of labor camps and company towns or the growth of sections of nearby small towns for house workers who come from other regions or other countries. The Otherness of many rural workers and their relative isolation (physically, in labor camps and dormitories, and interpersonally, due to cultural and linguistic differences) may encourage the development of stereotypes—from both workers' and native locals' perspectives. Thus, employers can manipulate images of immigrant workers to locals and images of locals to immigrant workers and influence understandings of work, leisure, and home life, all of which facilitate compliance with workplace regimes and community norms. Using immigrant women further allows employers and others to buttress these images with gendered interpretations, characterizing work and leisure in ways calculated to circumscribe workers' physical movement and social consciousness.

Much of the research on the construction of rural labor markets focuses on the physical and legal mechanics of organizing workers for transport from their homes to worksites and on ensuring compliance with workplace rules and local norms. These studies have examined slavery (Wolf 1982), indentured servitude and debt peonage (Daniel 1972; Stoler 1985), guest-worker programs (Griffith 2006), network recruitment (Massey et al. 1987), and labor contracting (Vandeman 1988), among other methods of securing labor. Smith and Winders (2008) address labor force construction with reference to the growing flexibility of labor; employers conceive of workers' bodies as flexible—bodies that are available to work at a moment's notice, bodies that are reliable, productive, affordable, youthful, disposable, and (usually) male. They argue that such workers cannot simultaneously occupy spaces of social reproduction, since they are living lives that are too dislocated from specific places to participate in family and community formation and maintenance. Cindy Hahamovitch (2003) has described a similar process—"creating perfect immigrants," guestworkers who, historically, were separated from their families; kept largely isolated from the host nation's natives; housed at or near worksites; sent home when injured or noncompliant or after the work ended; and forbidden or discouraged from labor organizing, collective bargaining, or participating in social justice movements of any kind. Under these conditions, guestworkers may be acceptable even to racist, nativist, or anti-immigrant groups because they are legally prohibited from permanent settlement yet can satisfy the needs of employers who desire a captive and malleable labor force.[1]

Guestworker programs were largely restricted to Germany and South Africa prior to the Great Depression, but in the late 1930s and during World War II, interest in and use of guestworker programs rose worldwide. In line with the male bodies that Smith and Winders (2008) view as the most flexible, most guestworker programs were nearly exclusively confined to men. Hahamovitch writes:

> For those governments determined to prevent foreign workers from staying permanently, female migrants represented a serious threat because they could both produce and reproduce. Thus the U.S., South Africa, and Great Britain all took pains to exclude women. U.S. immigration officials learned this lesson the hard way. Bahamian women had been included in the World War II program that brought farmworkers to Florida. When women became pregnant, the managers of federal labor camps had to arrange for their deportation.... Much to the dismay of camp managers, this resulted in "a considerable number of induced abortions," according to the East Coast Field Medical Officer. (Hahamovitch 2003:86)

By the late 1980s, however, some guestworker programs not only included women but also preferred them to men (Hughes, chapter 7, this volume; Preibisch, chapter 4, this volume). The preference for women stemmed from female native workers' holding certain jobs in the economic sectors soliciting guestworkers, such as chambermaids in hotels and crab pickers in seafood-processing plants (Griffith 1993, 2006). In such settings, the jobs guestworkers took had already been gendered; they had already been associated with specific social and cultural expectations and embedded in the unequal power relations between men and women at worksites. Indeed, as Hahamovitch's observations make clear, guestworker programs are heavily gendered, recruiting primarily women *or* primarily men into seasonal occupations, although this may change in occupations like agriculture, with technology that privileges dexterity over strength, such as Canada's greenhouses.

Historically, in the social sciences, the incorporation of foreign workers into US and other developed countries' capitalist labor markets was conceptualized as the articulation of modes of production or, more accurately, the interpenetration of economic formations—Roseberry's (1989) internalization of the external. In this view, foreign workers' economic formations, such as peasant agriculture, subsidized capitalist economic formations by absorbing the bulk of the costs of reproducing the labor force (Griffith 1985). Workers were able to benefit materially from working abroad, usually in the form of building nicer homes, but were not able to accumulate enough productive resources (land, livestock, etc.) to free themselves and their children from the need to work abroad. In this sense, temporary foreign workers reproduced their material conditions of existence rather than altered or improved upon them. In the abstract, their work abroad could be considered reproductive labor, even in cases, such as managed migration, in which the explicit purpose of the migration is to separate productive from reproductive labor. When these migrants are predominantly women, the irony deepens, in that most women make the multiple sacrifices associated with migration specifically to ensure that their children will not have to follow in their footsteps.

This chapter examines the participation of women in a female-dominated guestworker program, considering how it has shaped relationships within households and between the North American mid-Atlantic coast and the northwestern Mexican Sinaloa coast.

METHODOLOGY

This study is based on twenty interviews with women working at Pocosin Crab (a pseudonym), a blue crab processing plant in Herring Creek (a pseudonym), conducted during the summer of 2009; an additional ten interviews were conducted in Virginia in 2011. Fifteen of these workers were interviewed a second time in Sinaloa, Mexico, during December and January 2010, 2011, or 2012, when we also made several observations about their communities and the region as a whole. We have also revisited the seafood plants in North Carolina and Virginia for casual interviews, and we maintain connections with many of these women to this day. In Beaufort County, informants responded to a semi-structured interview guide devoted primarily to questions about experiences working in crab processing and the effects of that work on their family and community relationships. This constituted a complete sample of all the women who worked the entire season at Pocosin Crab. In Sinaloa, we visited women from three different types of communities: coastal fishing communities, inland peasant communities, and large shopping/service center communities along the Pan-American Highway. These same communities were revisited in 2011 and 2012. Table 6.1 presents sociodemographic information about the original twenty participants in our study. All come from Sinaloa—most from one large shopping/service center near the larger metropolis of Guasave—and a large percentage (around 40 percent) are related to one another in some way.

The table shows that the sample includes women with nearly twenty years of experience in the H-2 labor force and some with fewer than three years in the labor force. They have been participating in the temporary work program between one and nineteen years, with 40 percent participating in the program for more than nine seasons. Nine of the twenty are separated, seven are married or living in a common-law arrangement, three are widows,

TABLE 6.1
Guestworkers' Characteristics (N = 20)

Migrant	Age	Years of Schooling	Years as H-2	Marital Status	Number of Children
1	44	3	8	Single	3
2	42	3	2	Widowed	2
3	20	14	2	Separated	0
4	27	2	2	Unión libre	1
5	49	9	14	Separated	3
6	35	6	1	Separated	4
7	58	1	19	Separated	4
8	30	9	11	Widowed	1
9	42	6	13	Separated	4
10	45	6	13	Married	3
11	48	9	1	Separated	5
12	39	4	1	Unión libre	4
13	30	9	1	Married	3
14	53	3	12	Married	5
15	34	9	16	Married	2
16	27	4	6	Married	1
17	29	9	1	Separated	3
18	30	9	7	Separated	2
19	25	6	2	Separated	1
20	66	3	17	Widowed	6

and one is single. Interestingly, the majority are single mothers, separated from spouses, single, or widowed—or what some second-wave feminist scholars would call "emancipated" (Pessar 2003:85)—living with and caring for their children more or less on their own. With the exception of only the youngest woman, all have children, and the one who does not has the most education and is the daughter of one of the elder women at the plant. The sons and daughters of the women vary in age between four years old and forty-seven years old, with a concentration in the zero–six age bracket (nineteen out of fifty-seven).

All of the women work in Guasave in the off-season (December–February), although not regularly. The majority (70 percent) have spent their working lives in a combination of agriculture, crab picking, and shrimp processing. Several have access to minor productive resources in their home communities, such as fishing, small-scale agriculture, or entrepreneurial activities.

THE SENDING SETTING: SINALOA IN
NORTHWESTERN MEXICO

The coastal region between Los Mochis and Guasave is dominated by agribusiness yet also has ties to the sea, and the majority of the region's residents come from the working classes, with jobs in agriculture, fisheries, or related fields. Promotional materials from Sinaloa boast that the state produces 51 percent of Mexico's chickpeas, 43 percent of its cucumbers, 37 percent of its tomatoes, 61 percent of its tuna, 30 percent of its shrimp, and 13 percent of its sardines. Producing these commodities demands farm, packinghouse, and seafood-processing workers; fishers; support personnel ranging from boat builders to truck mechanics to merchants and drivers; and service workers such as domestics, waiters, and cooks in local restaurants. Supporting the agricultural infrastructure of the region are several corporate entities—some local, most foreign—that have converted the majority of the flat land into vast fields of irrigated corn, vegetables, and cotton, along with groves of mangoes and oranges interrupted here and there by greenhouses, experiment stations, livestock confinement operations, and the densely populated *colonias* (nucleated settlements) where the people live. Although some of the communities have retained the title *ejido* and peasant agriculture is still practiced, the region long ago lost its peasant heritage. Nor are there haciendas or *vaqueros* (cowboys), and no quaint, oppressive *latifundia-minifundia* (large or small estate) landscapes of vast ranches or idyllic cane syrup mills (*trapiches*) powered by burros. In addition to working people, smaller classes of merchants, professionals, skilled mechanics, and entrepreneurs inhabit the colonias. Some signs of fabulous wealth are scattered about in the form of expansive homes and luxury automobiles, but most people earn between 70 and 250 pesos per day—the equivalent of around US$7 as a day laborer or US$25 working on a contract to pick a given amount of fruit for the agricultural firms.

Along with being low paying, the work is seasonal and often irregular, interrupted by weather and other ecological and economic factors influencing when crops are cared for and harvested or when fisheries products are available to catch and process, with many tasks mechanized and the coordination between skilled and lesser-skilled labor similar to what Mintz (1985) described on seventeenth-century Caribbean sugar plantations. Under these conditions, workers must be available "just in time" (Smith and Winders 2008:63), as a kind of emergency or rapid response workforce (Fussell 2009). Women we interviewed in Ciudad de Trabajo, a community that has supplied hundreds of women to North Carolina's blue crab processing plants since the late 1980s, reported that prior to migrating to the

United States, they worked approximately half the year in agriculture and half in fisheries. From January to around May or June, they would pick or pack one of a number of crops—usually, tomatoes, peppers, or squash—but around May or June, they would work in a crab processing plant two kilometers north of town. Others worked in plants farther north, between the large city of Los Mochis and the industrialized oil refining and fishing port of Topolobampo, or in smaller plants in fishing communities dotting the coast.

Such work schedules reflect a continuum of work modes in the region, ranging from independent producers (peasant farmers, fishers, artisans)[2] to people who earn most of their income in local food production, to the women and men who work, without their families, as legal managed migrants in the United States and Canada.[3] This continuum follows a rough geography, with the peasant fishers clustered along the coast, the peasant farmers farthest inland, and most of the full-time working-class workers hugging the major north-south thoroughfares connecting Guasave and Los Mochis, overlapping the Pan-American Highway. Three communities that supply workers to North Carolina seafood plants exemplify these distinctions while illustrating that working-class individuals come from all across the region: the coastal town of Puerta la Virgen, Ciudad de Trabajo on the Pan-American Highway, and the inland ejido Rosa Blanca.[4]

* * *

Puerta la Virgen is a long, thin community nestled in a dry mountainous region along the Sea of Cortez. A few kilometers inland, the industrial agricultural fields begin, but just outside the town, the landscape is barren, sandy, and desolate, as though it had been inundated by the sea and rendered infertile. The land is hot, dry, scrubby, parched, and bleached. Around 3,000 households of primarily fishing families populate this community. Its fishing infrastructure is well developed, with a long, sloping concrete shorefront and piers to which lines and lines of fishing vessels are moored up and down the waterfront.

The vessels are small—most are around twenty-three feet in length—and rigged with long nets that are used for shrimp, deepwater stocks (snapper, grouper, grunts), and other species, including blue crabs and white sharks. Vessels crowd the waterfront. People working on fishing nets, applying fiberglass to boats, and manufacturing or maintaining other fishing gear are common sights in the community. Fish landing and marketing infrastructure interrupts the landscape here and there, including a blue crab processing plant where some of the women trained in order to work in

North Carolina crab plants. Everyone knows about the women who work in North Carolina, and some of the men process crayfish in Louisiana.

* * *

Adjacent to the Pan-American Highway, Ciudad de Trabajo is a predominantly working-class community with around 7,000–8,000 households. Most residents work in the processing plants lining the highway or in the fields stretching for miles in all directions. Agribusiness dominates this segment of the Pan-American Highway; in addition to the crops, there are experiment stations, irrigation networks, corporate offices, and processing plants. Along with housing working families, Ciudad serves as a marketing and service center for many of the nearby communities, agribusiness, and the food-processing sector. Its services include restaurants, a supermarket, electronics and furniture stores, bakeries, *tortillerias*, tire shops and auto mechanics, medical services, and schools. Historically, Ciudad and a similar community around fifteen kilometers north, La Sierra, have sent the most women to mid-Atlantic seafood plants, and local informants reported that the majority of women who work in the mid-Atlantic states first received training at a blue crab plant outside Ciudad.

Most also have worked in Sinaloa agriculture. Ciudad does not have a conspicuous peasant base—neither peasant farmers nor fishers—although small gardens and fruit trees are present here and there and people refer to part of the community as an ejido. Migrating to the United States and Canada, both as temporary legal workers and as undocumented, is common here, and informants report that nearly all of the nicest houses in town were built with migrant earnings and remittances.

* * *

A small peasant community around fifteen kilometers east of Guasave, Rosa Blanca is one of three contiguous communities that together house around 2,500–3,500 people. The communities provide opportunities for small-scale peasant agriculture, some cottage industrial brickmaking, and work in a variety of services in nearby Guasave—one of the larger regional marketing and service centers in Sinaloa.

Only between six and eight women from two or three related families in Rosa Blanca work annually in mid-Atlantic seafood processing; the numbers change slightly from one year to the next. Most people in Rosa Blanca engage in multiple livelihoods, unable to support themselves solely from peasant agriculture or brickmaking. They combine these pursuits with work in the fields, the processing sector (including crab), and the service sector in Guasave.

FROM LOCAL TO TRANSNATIONAL WORKING CLASS

Puerta la Virgen, Ciudad de Trabajo, and Rosa Blanca represent some-what distinct communities in terms of livelihood opportunities, yet their women who work in North Carolina crab plants share many of the same experiences. Their participation in the migrant labor force suppresses distinctive dimensions of their social and economic backgrounds that may derive from coming from different home communities. In other words, joining the mid-Atlantic seafood-processing labor force involves a collectivization or homogenization of experiences for these women: they share one technical and one social experience in particular, becoming, in many workers' minds, fictive kin with the others working and living with them in North Carolina.

The technical experience they share is their work in blue crab processing in Sinaloa, either in the plant outside Ciudad de Trabajo or in one of the smaller community plants in Los Mochis or elsewhere. Most recruiters insist that women receive training in these plants prior to migrating, drawing them squarely into the global economy. This occurs because seafood processed in Mexican crab plants is produced for export; the plants must meet international food handling and hygiene standards. As such, these plants train workers in the discipline that is required in order to work in a globalized food industry. Indeed, women interviewed in Sinaloa reported that, in terms of hygiene, Mexican plants are far stricter (*mas estricto*) than US plants, resulting in training superior to what they would receive in the mid-Atlantic region. Interestingly, too, a principal cause of the decline in US seafood production has been competition from imported seafood and farm-raised fish and shellfish from Mexico and elsewhere. Mid-Atlantic blue crab processing plants have not been immune to this; in this sense, Mexican women working in the crab plants in Sinaloa are contributing to the shrinking of their own employment opportunities in the United States—one particularly insidious dimension of globalization and neoliberal trade.

The social experience these women share is related to labor recruitment. In all cases, women entering managed migration streams must go through an intermediary in Mexico, who acts as a labor contractor for the mid-Atlantic seafood plant. Generally, labor contractors are local: Sinaloa women and men who have worked in the US crab plants, can speak some English, have developed a relationship of trust with the plant owner or supervisor, and can recruit workers through network and community ties in Sinaloa—an ability that also requires earning the trust of both potential workers and seafood plant owners. The experience of working with a labor contractor is increasingly relevant to labor forces constructed partially or wholly with migrants, as more and more migrant and ethnically distinct workers are sifted into production regimes via subcontracts (Zlolniski 2006), mimicking the fragmented global production of *maquilas* (factories), free trade zones, and the neoliberal economic policies of globalization (Gunewardena and Kingsolver 2007; Nash and Fernández-Kelly 1983). Simultaneously, subcontracts allow major companies to avoid directly hiring workers, reducing or eliminating the need for employers to comply with labor laws, regulations that prohibit hiring undocumented migrants, and other government oversight that might interfere with a highly flexible labor force.

In the seafood plants, the use of bilingual intermediaries absolves US employers from learning Spanish and even interacting with rank-and-file workers and also inhibits workers from learning English and developing cultural brokerage skills that might eventually become marketable as social or human capital. The distance between employers and workers that this creates is similar to the blindfold of accounting methods between merchants who organized and financed slave trading during the eighteenth century and the structural violence of the trade itself (Siskind 2001), allowing employers to overlook sexual harassment, intimidation, and other workplace violations of human rights. At the same time, labor contractors provide a minimum of protective paternalism to workers as part of the service workers pay for with whatever kickbacks the contractor demands.[5]

Not all labor recruiters involved in H-2B visa occupations are the same, however, and they differ considerably from the more formalized, association-dominated recruitment of the H-2A program and, increasingly, the Canadian SAWP and Pilot programs. In general, seafood workers are recruited very informally, through kinship and network connections, allowing the negotiations between labor recruiter/contractors and workers to become highly personalized and subject to idiosyncratic beliefs and practices. They are not, that is, standardized. Both in this and in previous research, we found that the amounts workers paid to contractors varied from nothing to a flat rate of US$100 to a nickel per pound of picked crab meat. Amounts paid to recruiter/contractors to acquire access to H-2A programs, by contrast, were far more uniform (Griffith 2006).

A third shared experience—one particularly heartrending for most women we interviewed, often stimulating tears while we talked—involves the difficulties associated with separating from one's family, especially one's children, to enter this labor force. In addition to the common human problem of missing loved ones, separation can involve holding family meetings to discuss the separation, causing anxiety and sadness among family members; disputes with spouses or others (often elder male kin) over the prospect of the woman leaving; and, often most difficult for single mothers, arranging for surrogate parents. Penelope,[6] speaking of her relationship with her young son, said, "He's no longer my son, because he calls my mother-in-law Mommy." Others spoke of the estrangement from their children as undermining the children's health, insisting that only mothers could adequately care for their own children. In response to a question about how Naida's absence affected her children, Naida said, "It affects them in every way because they feel sad...and I worry. Are they eating well? Are they eating at all?" In the most extreme case, the couple in charge of the mother's children spent her remittances on themselves, depriving the children of food and causing one to be hospitalized for malnutrition.

The women we interviewed reported several additional problems associated with surrogate parenting. Initially, they suffer over whom to designate as a suitable parent, usually selecting a mother, a sister, a mother-in-law, or another female relative. After that decision has been made, however, they still experience ambivalence, often disagreeing with the surrogate parent over discipline yet feeling that they have to surrender authority while they are away. Other issues include whether they can trust surrogate parents; the misuse of remittances by surrogate parents; the mistreatment of children by surrogate parents; and the general loss of control over children due to the women's long absences.

Workers' willingness to endure separation from their families and from the places of social reproduction is usually due to the structural conditions and sporadic violence they face in Sinaloa. Nearly everyone interviewed in Sinaloa and North Carolina agreed that jobs in Mexico paid just enough to survive, that raising a family in any condition beyond the bare minimum, which does not include educating children beyond the ninth grade, was impossible with local field and factory work. From local perspectives, in other words, the regional political economy is sufficient only to reproduce the labor force. Some women had migrated to other locations in Mexico to improve their earning capability, but these situations, for the most part, proved disappointing. Several were in abusive relationships, living in extreme conditions of despair, or had experienced a crisis such as the death or incarceration of a spouse or other family member, a divorce, or an illness (including substance abuse) in their family.

Maria Elena, for example, started migrating to the United States shortly after her father died, when she and her siblings began fighting over their father's inheritance. Coinciding with these difficulties, her husband sold their house, pocketed the money, and ran off to Tijuana with her sister. Maria Elena had worked in crab picking in Mexico in the past, but her husband had made her quit, insisting on being the family's breadwinner. This worked out fine until her husband's infidelity. Speaking of her migration, she said, "What happened was that my husband began sleeping with my sister. I was still in shock [over the death of my father]. Right now, I'm a little fat, but at the time, I was traumatized and got thin, thin, thin. It coincided with the problems over the inheritance, the fighting with my brothers. I decided to work as a diversion."

Along with her personal problems and their expression in body imagery, Maria Elena reported that after her father's death and her husband's departure, she returned to work in the Mexican crab plant, leaving her children in the care of her other sisters and her mother-in-law. However, with the local earnings, she was not able to support her children, and with childcare already arranged, she decided to migrate to the United States. When her husband learned that she had migrated, he returned to care for the children while she was away and began hoping for reconciliation—something Maria Elena was firmly against. His primary motivation for reconciliation, Maria Elena believed, was to gain access to her US earnings.

At times, several tragic circumstances converged with one another and with local economic conditions, pushing Sinaloa women toward emigration. In some cases, entering the migrant labor force allowed women to leave tragedy behind and experience migration as liberating; this has been true even when guestworkers experienced excessive employer and labor contractor control abroad. Anaceli, for example, suffered the deaths of both her husband and her father in the year before entering the mid-Atlantic seafood-processing workforce. Her two sons were married and caring for families of their own, and she found herself increasingly unable to pay bills with her work in the local crab plant and in the surrounding fields. Depression set in, and a friend encouraged her to work in North Carolina. "I made my decision [to migrate] because of the depression," she said. "My husband had just died and my father had just died and it left me feeling very depressed. A friend wanted me to come with her [to North Carolina], hoping to distract me and leave my depression behind. My children supported the decision, and that's why I came."

In Anaceli's case, working in a North Carolina crab plant did not meet her economic expectations, yet she was able to secure other work in North Carolina, so her emotional condition improved significantly. Less depressed after her emigration, she also experienced more freedom away from her adult sons. Of this she said, "Here, I have more possibilities to get out of debt.... How do you say? I am, like, freer. The decisions I make here are mine. There [in Mexico], I have to confide in my children, asking their opinions about whatever I want to do, and many times, they disagree with me...many times, I feel more pressured."

Both Maria Elena and Anaceli have found some refuge in North Carolina from troubles at home, although they still suffer from ongoing difficulties with their children. Maria Elena's and Anaceli's experiences differ, but both illustrate the overall ambivalence of women in the migrant stream, finding participation in managed migration at once liberating and confining, invigorating and tiring, exciting and boring. Attempts to resolve their ambivalence most often involve establishing relationships of support among those in more or less the same situations: other Sinaloa women working in crab processing in North Carolina.

Women we interviewed routinely spoke of others in the plant as fictive kin, and nearly half have family members working beside them; many who first met in North Carolina continue visiting one another during the winters in Sinaloa. Others from Sinaloa now live in North Carolina: former crab pickers who have dropped out of crab picking and become year-round residents or those who have remained in crab picking but have married local men and still work at the plant during the season. Relations with past crab pickers and those who have settled in the region are enhanced by an increasingly complex, settled Latino population in eastern North Carolina—a population that has founded a range of Spanish-speaking businesses and grassroots organizations, formed elaborate extended families with both legal and undocumented members, and participates in local schools, churches, health care systems, and other institutions. Earlier H-2B workers, after breaking their contracts, have been active participants in the growth and elaboration of this community, as illustrated in more detail in this and other chapters (Peralta, Griffith, and Contreras, chapter 9, this volume). By contrast, Bump, Goździak, and Lowell (chapter 8, this volume) report that similar resident populations of Jamaicans have not developed in Virginia, although Jamaican guestworkers have been migrating to the region to pick apples since the 1940s. Settled communities of Latinos working in the same region, however, have developed.

In one sense, then, after leaving family in Mexico, Sinaloa women reconstitute family in North Carolina, drawing on shared experiences, sentiments, and sympathies, as well as finding material and social support from others in the crab plant's dormitory and, often, in the community. The varied textures of the relations between crab pickers and others in the community emerge from the behaviors of the women during periods when there is little to no work in the plants or during their free time on Sundays. During one prolonged period of little to no work at the crab plant, Anaceli, for example, visited a friend in a nearby community for an extended stay. While she was there, a labor contractor came by to recruit the friend for a crew heading for Myrtle Beach, South Carolina, to paint condominium units. The friend asked Anaceli to join the crew with her, Anaceli called her supervisor at the crab plant and said that she planned to stay with the friend until work in the crab plant picked up, and the women spent the next two weeks painting condominiums in Myrtle Beach. Later that season, Anaceli stayed to work in North Carolina long after the crab-picking work had ended; a year later, she was staying nearly year-round, returning to Sinaloa only briefly to renew her visa.

These behaviors violated Anaceli's contract, which stipulates that she is to work only for the crab plant while in the United States and to return home at the end of the crab-picking season. Yet, guestworkers have, historically, violated their contracts by doing other work in their host countries or dropping out of guestworker labor forces altogether. Dropping out involves becoming an unauthorized migrant in eastern North Carolina, which may encourage increased independence or may encourage a reinsertion of women into traditional gender roles as they establish relationships, some with men, that assist them in avoiding deportation. Women with H-2 visas do have the advantage of securing drivers' licenses and other documents, however, enabling them to open bank accounts, acquire credit cards, satisfy I-9 reporting requirements, secure employment, and remain employed as long as they have valid licenses or continue to work for an employer who filed their I-9 while their licenses were valid. Because their Social Security numbers are valid, additional checks like E-Verify usually will not reveal that they are working illegally. We have learned of several cases of former crab pickers opening their own businesses, usually to cater to the growing Latino population of North Carolina and across the South. By contrast, we have also learned of former crab workers entering into relationships with local Anglo and Latino men and becoming dependent on them in fairly traditional, domestic ways.

The general growth of North Carolina's Latino population—one of the fastest growing in the United States (Massey and Capoferro 2008)—has made dropping out of the labor force and accessing other work, as well as establishing social relations outside the plant, much easier today than it was when women first began coming from Guasave. This changing social context has facilitated greater physical, economic, and social mobility within the state and opened new alternatives for women from Sinaloa. We discuss three alternatives available to them: (1) returning home at the end of the season, as stipulated in their contract; (2) remaining in North Carolina or elsewhere in the United States beyond the contract period but returning to Mexico prior to the beginning of the next year's contract; or (3) remaining in the United States more permanently, eventually joining the ranks of the undocumented. Each alternative involves a different set of social relations among participants in the seafood labor force; members of their households, families, and communities; and other people living in eastern North Carolina.

RETURNING TO MEXICO AT THE END OF THE CONTRACT PERIOD

A worker with nineteen years of experience told us, "Nunca se ha quedado aquí de ilegal. Todo el tiempo se regresa uno y al siguiente año vuelve otra vez" (Never does anyone stay here illegally. Always, one returns and the following year comes back another time). Although this woman was in denial in terms of her fellow crab pickers leaving their contracts, she was not far off. Most women choose the option of returning to Mexico at the end of their contract period, complying with the terms of the contract and the spirit of guestworker programs.

As with participation in general, returning has its challenges and rewards. Most obvious, of course, the women return to their children, partners (if married or living with someone), and other family members, renewing social relations within the family in part by adding to its store of material possessions, improving family housing, and usually carrying gifts for often large numbers of family members and friends. Returning confirms one's place in one's personal social network, enhanced now with gift giving, while reaffirming the state's goals of moving a constructed labor force, en masse, back to its reproductive sphere when its productive labor is no longer needed.

Yet, returning is rarely as smooth as temporary worker program advocates, praising the programs' efficiency, would have us believe. Returning often involves renewed struggles with partners or brings home the consequences of absence in other ways. For example, Lourdes Herrera returned one year to learn that her seventeen-year-old daughter had become pregnant. The father had abandoned her, leaving her alone with her pregnancy and her sadness. "I told her that it would have been better if I had always been with her," Lourdes said, "better if she hadn't done what she did, getting pregnant." Others have returned to find their children less affectionate toward them, seeming to resent them, or less willing to submit to their authority. In some cases, the women do not attempt to exercise any authority over their children, unwilling to taint with discipline the short four months per year they share with them. Instead, they often shower them with gifts, resigned to their children being raised and disciplined by someone else as long as they are working in North Carolina.

In a few cases, the women return to work in the crab plant while in Mexico, but in most cases, they rest, spending their days repairing their relationships with children and other family members and, if earnings allow, overseeing improvements to the house. One woman we visited in Rosa Blanca, for example, was adding a large room onto the back of her house with the help of day laborers and her sons, who had returned from California (where they were undocumented) while she was home for the off-season. Of all those we visited in Mexico while they were home, only one was working in a Mexican crab plant; all others were staying at home with spouses, children, parents, and other relatives, as well as visiting friends throughout the community.

The lack of need or desire to work is understandable when we place home activities within the set of contradictions between the economic benefits of migration and the social costs of distance from one's family. One woman said of her time working in North Carolina, "Well, for us it has been good, economically, because you go, you work, and you are going to arrange your house, your car, and have more comforts. In this way, I'm telling you, it has been good. But one suffers when you're here [in North Carolina], far from your own." Repairing the damage of that suffering often precludes working while at home.

STAYING IN THE UNITED STATES TEMPORARILY

Although the crab plant in Herring Creek closes in late November or early December, the visas issued to the women in the labor force do not expire until the last day of December, offering them a window of time to remain, legally, in the United States. Further, workers can, if they so desire, remain in the United States beyond the end of the year even if they hope to return as an H-2B worker the following season. They need only return to Mexico prior to the beginning of the next year's contract, which in crab usually is not until March or April.

Workers who choose to stay for a time beyond their contracts must have network ties to help them secure housing because most of the workers' dormitories close when the crab plants close; many use these same network ties to secure work. Although this is illegal, it has become an increasingly accessible option with the growth of the Latino community in North Carolina;

similar opportunities are available to any guestworkers who have sizable groups of co-ethnics already living in the United States and who have the means to interact with them. The example of Anaceli above can be seen as an illustration of how this can be accomplished: she acquired work outside her contract during a time in the crab-picking season when the workers were earning only between $30 and $50 per week. Anaceli had been staying on the weekends with one of two friends, former crab workers who had married local men and settled in eastern North Carolina, and during one of her stays, she was able to secure work. She described this as follows: "In the first weeks [in Herring Creek] that we weren't working, I went to work in South Carolina with the friend I was telling you about, because she came from Virginia also because they had no work. We went with a labor contractor who contracted people for painting. We went to paint with him. I worked two weeks and earned $500 and sent them [her children] $400."

Although this occurred during the season, Anaceli remained in the United States beyond December 31 that season, very likely living with one or both of her married friends and able to find additional work through them, and she stayed year-round the following season. Again, this is illegal, but, as noted earlier, the H-2B visa gives one access to identification such as a driver's license, which can be used to access employment at least until the license expires or until one's employer asks for the license after it has expired. Rebecca Crosthwait (2009), studying H-2B workers on oil rigs along the Gulf of Mexico coast, found that workers called their visas *visas libres* (free visas), referring to the fact that they could use them for free access to the US labor market. Conceivably, H-2B workers who work multiple seasons could renew drivers' licenses as often as they expire and, at the end of their careers as H-2B workers, could access other US employment until their licenses expire.

Remaining in the United States temporarily is an option primarily for women who have no children or whose children are grown; this option represents a joint process of altering one's social ties in Mexico while developing and strengthening one's personal social network in the United States. It represents, too, an intermediate form of resistance to state policy, between fully complying with the terms of one's contract and completely breaking with the contract, dropping out of managed migration and settling permanently. At the same time, it is a withdrawal from the responsibilities of the reproductive and nurturing roles of many female guestworkers. By staying in the United States, most who choose this option neglect the later life phases of childcare and domestic activities, which fall to grandmothers and older mothers. Inasmuch as these individuals are critical to traditional reproductive processes, their exercising this option disrupts the expectations of the state, the community, and the family. Women who choose this option also question, with their actions, the social legitimacy of these reproductive roles and their relevance to the lives of working women.

REMAINING IN THE UNITED STATES PERMANENTLY

Besides Anaceli, only one other woman we interviewed during this study remained in the United States following her contract, marrying a man in Herring Creek and possibly staying there permanently. We say "possibly" for two reasons: first, she has been married and divorced once already and has had terrible experiences with men, including male relatives who sexually abused her; second, she has a son still in Mexico, to whom she is extremely dedicated, is currently attempting to bring him to the United States, and seems perfectly willing to take care of him by herself: "This was my dream, to come, to build my house and dedicate myself to my son. Not to dedicate myself to men, looking for a husband.... I always told him [her son], 'I'm your father and your mother.'"

Although only these two women remained more or less permanently after the work ended, we know from previous research that these were not isolated cases (Griffith 2006). One of the oldest Latino business establishments in the eastern North Carolina town of Greenville, a Mexican *tienda* (store), was, prior to the 2008 economic crisis, owned by two sisters who first came to the United States to work in the blue crab industry, carrying H-2B visas. They were in business well over fifteen years, even serving as informal advisors to other Latino entrepreneurs in the city.

A woman we interviewed for a related study (Contreras and Griffith 2012), Vera Gutierrez, related how she began working in crab picking in 1995 as an H-2B worker for an exemplary employer who always made certain that the housing provided was clean, the bedding new, and the refrigerator stocked prior to their arrival. While working for this employer, she began learning English and was eventually placed in charge of arranging visa applications and doing other paperwork, including the other workers' taxes. When this plant closed, she was placed in a plant operated by an employer whom she disliked and who treated the women terribly. A few weeks into the season, she left the plant with the help of women she had met in a neighboring community, then found a job at a textile plant, and later went into business with another Latina, opening an income tax service that is still in operation and successful today, attracting a Latino clientele from across the South.

Griffith (2006) relates similar stories in his research on guestworkers, arguing that this constitutes a form of worker resistance to the restrictive conditions of H-2 contracts. Clearly, remaining in the United States may have become an option for a minority of Sinaloa women, but working off the contract is much more common. Nearly all the women at Pocosin Crab reported working off their contracts during slow times in the crab season, most of them in a nearby blueberry harvest, even saying that their recruiter and supervisor, a man also from Sinaloa, took them to the blueberry groves in the company bus.

Remaining in the United States permanently constitutes the most extreme form of resistance to the terms of temporary foreign workers' contracts and involves at least a partial withdrawal from one's personal social network at home, turning one's back on state, community, family, and reproductive responsibilities. Again, with the growth of a Latino community that maintains transnational ties through money transfers, continued migration and return migration, and modern communication and transportation technologies, how complete or how partial this withdrawal becomes depends on how extensively those leaving their contracts utilize those transnational services. Yet, remaining in the United States, particularly in a new destination like North Carolina, contributes to the region's growing Latino presence, increasing the community's ability to stay in one location rather than submit to the requirements of flexible production. Based on our knowledge of guestworkers who have stayed in the region, it is clear that some rural North Carolina communities owe the origins of their Latino families to former H-2B seafood-processing workers. These workers—by marrying locals, learning about permanent job opportunities, or taking the risk of establishing businesses—have been responsible for a new era of ethnic diversity in a handful of fishing communities along the mid-Atlantic coast.

Just as guestworkers make up a small proportion of the overall low-wage, seasonal labor force yet have a significant impact on that labor force's overall complexion, the above observations also suggest that Mexican women in seafood processing, although only a fraction of a rural community's population—and a temporary one at that—may have a disproportionate impact on that community's demographic profile. In a few cases, at least, they have been founding members of current settled Latino communities and, in some cases, original members of the local Latino business community as well. Further, among anti-immigrant forces, these observations could lead to the conclusion that employers and labor contractors should become more global in their reach, constantly replenishing their work forces with people from different countries as a way of preventing the potential growth of new ethnic communities and increased opportunities for guestworkers to break their contracts. In North Carolina, throughout the South, and in other new migrant destinations (Ansley and Shefner 2009; Massey 2008; Zuñiga and Hernández-León 2005), however, the growth of the Latino community occurred simultaneously with the increasing use of temporary foreign workers in seafood processing and agriculture, fueled by several developments rather than just the use of guestworkers. These community-building processes, in other words, took place in locations without legal temporary foreign workers as vibrantly as they took place in regions that used temporary foreign workers. It is true that, in some small communities, women with H-2B visas from Sinaloa were among the first Mexicans to remain in the United States permanently following the end of their contracts—and thus may have been founding members of a later, larger Latino community—but it is far less clear that these communities would not have emerged eventually anyway, given the growing Latino presence across the United States.

CONCLUSION: FROM PERFECT TO IMPERFECT IMMIGRANTS

Managed migration programs are designed to separate productive from reproductive labor, thereby creating immigrants deemed nearly "perfect" by pro-immigrant groups who advocate for employers seeking a reliable labor force and by anti-immigrant groups who do not wish to see more permanent immigration, immigrant settlement, or the displacement of natives by immigrants in the economy. Yet, managed migration programs often construct labor forces with people who come from communities within the same country and the same region, creating and reinforcing ties between sending and receiving communities and, at times, facilitating settlement. In Sinaloa, the women who work in the mid-Atlantic seafood-processing industry come from at least three kinds of communities with differing opportunities for mixing domestic production (either peasant agriculture or artisanal fisheries) with local jobs in industrial agriculture, seafood processing, or waged employment in service and other economic sectors. Combining international labor migration with small-scale, home-based, or petty capitalist production systems is becoming increasingly common worldwide as small-scale producers are being displaced by free trade, privatization, and other neoliberal economic developments yet are being offered only occasional opportunities through fair trade, microfinancing, innovative marketing, and other economic initiatives spearheaded by organizations interested in human rights and more equitable distributions of wealth.

Few of the women in Ciudad de Trabajo, the most working-class of the three communities, were involved in domestic production activities, but women from the other two communities were—one had her own small store attached to her house, others raised small quantities of fruit and live-stock, and still others were members of fishing families. These few cases are insufficient to draw any general conclusions, of course, but the differences between the three communities described above suggest that some workers in managed migration programs do have access to domestic production. This has important implications for social reproduction, as overseas earnings may also allow some families to maintain domestic production of important commodities—seafood, tomatoes, corn—even after the state has withdrawn its support for such activities. By maintaining a foundation of domestic production, these households embody the integrity of peasant agriculture and artisanal fishing—if at a bare minimum level—which continue to help with the costs of labor's reproduction. In this sense, these households conform to earlier conceptions of the interpenetration of modes of production that means higher tax revenues and greater capital accumulation among states and corporate entities that no longer have to pay all reproductive expenses. Yet, this occurs, as we have seen, unevenly, varying across time, place, and the life cycle.

After guest workers initially become perfect immigrants from a hodge-podge of backgrounds, their personal and community differences succumb to the structural, social, and technical requirements of work in the mid-Atlantic. Yet, the responses of women to these requirements, initially shared, diverge over time based at least on the three alternatives described above. When we combine these observations with those regarding uneven access to domestic production, we can see that the implications for changing or maintaining relations with social reproduction may be quite complex, with some women conforming to contractual obligations, others being less compliant, and still others challenging guestworker models by breaking their contracts and establishing families and businesses in receiving regions. Sinaloa women have become active agents in the growing settlement of Latinos in North Carolina and in the elaboration of this community's ability to remain anchored to the region and to create new places of social reproduction, bound ever more firmly to area churches, schools, and other institutions. By the same token, Sinaloa women have actively transformed the places of social reproduction in their home communities, altering the physical settings of reproduction by constructing and furnishing houses and altering the gender relations by which community members relate to social reproduction. Sinaloa women have subsidized the domestic production operations of peasant farmers and fishers, elaborating the ways that those enterprises participate in social reproduction.

These varied accomplishments of Sinaloa women have not been without costs. It is not entirely clear that, ultimately, their migration will result in anything more than the reproduction of a permanent working class or, worse, a permanent class that can work only under the condition that it submit to being separated, for long periods of time, from the spaces of social reproduction. As noted earlier, scholarly work in the 1970s and 1980s argued that peasant agriculture, artisanal fisheries, and similar enterprises subsidize the economic sectors in which migrants work by allowing migrants to accept wages lower than they need in order to survive and reproduce themselves (Collins 1988; Griffith 2006; Griffith and Valdés Pizzini 2002). Labor migration was but one avenue by which this took place, yet, in some cases, that migration was clearly related to the viability of capitalist enterprises. It is unlikely that North Carolina seafood processors could have remained in business without the H-2B labor force. Similar to the situation of Gulf Coast shipbuilders (Austin, chapter 5, this volume), local labor supplies had begun constricting prior to the use of H-2B workers; following their arrival, rising productivity standards weeded out most of the domestic workers who remained (Griffith 2006). Even with access to H-2B labor, the entire seafood industry has contracted significantly since the 1990s, paralleling the general contraction of US fisheries due to imported and farm-raised fish and seafood, coastal gentrification, habitat destruction, declining fish and shellfish stocks, conservation initiatives, and government restrictions on fishing. Are these the characteristics of an industry thriving from a subsidy?

Whether the work of Sinaloa women subsidizes domestic production activities at home or domestic production activities contribute to the maintenance and reproduction of Sinaloa women and thereby subsidize North Carolina fisheries is less important to our current discussion than the fact that domestic production is a component of their social reproduction. Historically, the formation of working classes was based in part on the restriction of alternative economic opportunities among the people who, over time, became available to work in fields and factories. This is the structural side of the story of Sinaloa women's agency—the location, within community, where structure and agency meet. As long as Sinaloa communities remain involved in domestic production, the women profiled here may have opportunities to enhance the places of social reproduction in ways that could help their children transition out of the working class, providing capital to small-scale producers in their families and communities that may dovetail with microfinancing, technical assistance, fair trade initiatives, and other forms of support for domestic producers. Further, as long as women continue developing, with and without the aid of co-ethnics, alternatives to the narrow terms of temporary work contracts—working off their contracts, remaining in the United States temporarily or permanently after their contracts have ended, forming relations with settled Latinos or US citizens—they complicate the extent to which the 1970s and 1980s models of subsidy and interpenetration of modes of production apply. These women challenge, too, contemporary conceptions of flexible production, asserting their basic human right to have a place where they can stay, a community, a family, and a home. In the eyes of capital and the state, they become imperfect.

Elsewhere, we argue that many Sinaloa women place great emphasis on the education of their children (Contreras and Griffith 2012). This is a testament to their desire that their children not merely reproduce but also improve their social and economic conditions. Although their investment in their children's education may not have the same payoffs, we know from detailed peasant studies and from profiles of fishing communities around the world (Chayanov 1966; Griffith and Valdés Pizzini 2002; Sahlins 1972; Sider 1976) that children constitute critical assets in domestic production operations, providing some of the labor to these operations and the basis for their reproduction and potential growth. In light of the emphasis that Sinaloa women place on motherhood, becoming perfect immigrants may in fact undermine the reproduction of more perfect immigrants by pushing children toward either education or other pursuits in which they are neither disposable nor, for eight months a year, away from home.

Notes

1. Officially, in policy writings, guestworkers are considered to be "non-immigrants," making their presence more palatable to those opposed to immigration in general.

2. Sinaloa has gained a reputation as one of the northern Mexican states that is home to active drug cartels. Those involved in the trade can be considered to be independent producers in the region's informal economy.

3. In addition to working in mid-Atlantic seafood plants, people in Sinaloa work in managed migration programs in crayfish plants in Louisiana, as forestry workers across the southeastern United States, in US agriculture, and in Canada's Seasonal Agricultural Worker Program.

4. The names of the study communities are pseudonyms.

5. In other studies (e.g., Griffith 2006), we learned of contractors who collected

$100 per worker to participate in the program and others who took five cents per pound for each pound of crab meat the worker picked. But in this study, the women said that the contractor, a man from a neighboring community, did not take money from them for his service.

    6. All informants' names are pseudonyms.

7

The Potential and Pitfalls of Social Remittances

Guatemalan Women and Labor
Migration to Canada

Christine Hughes

In a context of growing economic precariousness, increasing numbers of Guatemalans now include international labor migration in their livelihood strategies.Under Canada's Pilot Project for Occupations Requiring Lower Levels of Formal Training (NOC C&D),[1] Guatemala now sends more migrants to Canada than any other country (Citizenship and Immigration Canada 2011). Scholars and activists have paid increasing attention to the experiences of employers and workers participating in this program (Brem 2006; Fudge and MacPhail 2009; Preibisch, chapter 4, this volume; Smart, chapter 3, this volume; Vargas-Foronda 2010a, 2010b). To add to this body of work but also counter its tendencies to adopt an economic focus or to critique working conditions (e.g., Nakache and Kinoshita 2010), this chapter examines the prospects for social, gendered impacts of women labor migrants on their sending communities in Guatemala. Specifically, drawing on fieldwork in Guatemala and Canada, I explore the potential for gender-related social remittances to impact household gender relations in Guatemala. After Levitt (1996), "social remittances" are defined here as ideas, beliefs, values, and practices that flow from receiving-country to sending-country communities in the context of migration.

I first situate the analysis in literature on transnationalism and the gendered impacts of migration, outlining the labor migration schemes in which Guatemalan women participate and sketching the process and site of my fieldwork in Guatemala. I then move to the main analytical components, dividing the process of social remittances into three steps—awareness, adoption, and transmission—and identifying the salient factors at each stage that condition whether Guatemalan women might draw on social remittances to alter household gender relations. With one exception, I found little indication of change in household gender relations linked with women's migration, a finding that conflicts somewhat with Griffith and Contreras's work (chapter 6, this volume) among Mexican women. I argue that key aspects of the women's experiences in Canada and the sociocultural contexts in Guatemala collude to limit how much women can acquire gender-related knowledge in Canada, aspire to apply it to their lives, and can transmit this knowledge to home communities. In exploring these dynamics, this chapter draws attention to the particularities, in highly structured, managed migration schemes, that encourage social continuity more than change.

TRANSNATIONALISM, GENDER, AND MIGRATION

In global migration today, social networks, practices, organizations, and communities span national territories (Goldring and Krishnamurti 2007), encouraging individuals' simultaneous connection to more than one society (Glick Schiller, Basch, and Blanc 1995). Integral to transnationalism, indeed constituting the cross-border ties that render it an undeniable feature of globalization today, are flows not only of money but also of ideas, values, beliefs, and practices (Ramírez, García Domínguez, and Míguez Morais 2005). Such flows have increased in extent and intensity with advances in communication and transportation technologies (Levitt 1998), as well as with increases in temporary or circular migration. In recognition of these developments in migration, some scholars have focused on the implications of these flows, including those related to gender (Kunz 2008; Levitt 1998; Vullnetari and King 2011).

Since the 1970s, migration scholarship has increasingly acknowledged and examined women's experiences (Pessar and Mahler 2003), reflecting the increasing feminization of international migration, which has both quantitative and qualitative aspects (Ramírez, García Domínguez, and Míguez Morais 2005). International migrants worldwide number approximately 210 million, and women account for half of these (Franck and Spehar 2010). More women are moving independently and for economic reasons, in search of income-earning opportunities to improve their lives and those of their families (José Alcalá 2006).[2] Thus, international migration is not a domain dominated by men, and migrant women are no longer primarily followers of male family members. Migration scholarship acknowledges this by treating female migrants as privileged subjects in their own right (Monzón 2009).[3]

Both informing and emerging from these examinations of women's international migration is an understanding of the importance of gender to migration (Lutz 2010 ; Piper 2005). "Gender" is understood here as an ideological, social construct that encompasses the culturally ascribed characteristics of and differences between females and males (Lindsey 1994; Luxton 2006; Pessar and Mahler 2003; Siltanen and Doucet 2008). Gender is key to organizing all spheres of personal and social life (Hurtig, Montoya, and Frazier 2002), including identities, practices, interactions, and institutions (Wharton 2005). The reasons for, experiences in, and outcomes of migration are always gendered; gender identities, roles, and relations both impact and are potentially impacted by migration (Boehm 2008; Pessar and Mahler 2003; Ramírez, García Domínguez, and Míguez Morais 2005).[4]

This chapter addresses how migration may contribute to changing gender relations (Asis 2005 ; Piper 2005). Specifically, I draw on the growing body of research concerned with how migration may impact patriarchal household gender roles and relations, especially when one partner migrates and the other does not (see, for instance, Boehm 2008; Menjívar and Agadjanian 2007; Resurreccion and Van Khanh 2007; Weinstein Bever 2002). Studies have demonstrated that when women migrate and men remain behind, certain key interrelated processes can, under certain circumstances, contribute to a weakening of men's power in patriarchal households. These processes include an increased sense of personal independence and empowerment among women (Hugo 2000), a break with the idea that women's place is in the home and men are the proper breadwinners (Asis 2005), increases in women's contributions to the household economy (Chant and Craske 2003; Kunz 2008; Menjívar 2006), and the transfer of gender-related ideas and practices (José Alcalá 2006; Levitt 1998; Ramírez, García Domínguez, and Míguez Morais 2005). Although these processes and their impacts are, admittedly, interrelated, here I focus on the last process, that is, social remittances. Social remittances— nontangible transmissions of ideas, behaviors, values, and identities— have the potential for sociocultural transformation: "The flow of ideas can have far-reaching effects on social norms" (United Nations Development Programme 2009:71).

Examining social remittances from a gender perspective focuses attention on the potential for migrant women to learn about new gendered ideologies and practices and to transmit them to home communities, potentially contributing to changes in gender relations in both migrant and nonmigrant households (Levitt 1996, 1998; United Nations Development Programme 2009). Specifically, this process starts with personal change when migrants, through gradual acculturation to "dissimilar worlds" (Menjívar 1999:602), learn about gender-related ideas and practices and selectively incorporate them into their lives (Lindstrom and Muñoz-Franco 2005). Through communication, visits, and return migration, migrants share these ideas and practices with their home communities (José Alcalá 2006; Levitt 1998; Ramírez, García Domínguez, and Míguez Morais 2005).

A few authors examining Guatemalan women's migration have explored social remittances, focusing on the "transformative" potential found in significant changes in the social, political, economic, and cultural environments that migrants experience (Lindstrom and Muñoz-Franco 2005:278; Menjívar 1999). Through migration to the United States, Guatemalan women may learn about contraceptive use (Lindstrom and Muñoz-Franco 2005), how domestic violence is addressed (Taylor, Moran-Taylor, and Rodman Ruiz 2006), and that US men participate more in housework than Guatemalan men (Menjívar 1999). In the case of contraceptive use, Lindstrom and Muñoz-Franco (2005) found that migrants' contraceptive knowledge spreads to nonmigrant kin and friends.

Although the possibility of these effects exists, this chapter problematizes the potential of migration to weaken the patriarchal nature of household gender relations, in line with other research (e.g., Resurreccion and Van Khanh 2007; Taylor, Moran-Taylor, and Rodman Ruiz 2006). Just as the impacts of economic remittances depend on a number of factors (Ramírez, García Domínguez, and Míguez Morais 2005; Vullnetari and King 2011), so, too, do the outcomes of social remittances and the possibility of gathering and transmitting the contents of social remittances in the first place.[5] A number of mediating factors complicate the gendered impacts of women's migration. Levitt (1998) helpfully delineates several such factors specific to the creation, transmission, and impact stages of the social remittances process, including patterns of interaction with the host society, the ways in which ideas or practices are transmitted, the fit between social remittances and other sociocultural messages, and the balance of power between those who stand to gain and those who stand to lose from social change. This chapter draws on a qualitative case study to illuminate the aspects of the experiences of female migrants and their family members that seem most responsible for limiting the likelihood and impact of social remittances.

CANADA'S LOW-SKILL PILOT PROJECT

Whereas international labor migration is not a new phenomenon for Guatemalans (Little 2005; Montes 2009), the labor migration examined here dates only to 2003, in large part facilitated by the shifts in Canada's immigration policies outlined by Smart (chapter 3) and Preibisch in this volume. Specifically, this chapter focuses on Guatemalan farmworkers brought into Canada under the Pilot program (Preibisch, chapter 4, this volume), often dubbed the Low-Skill Pilot Project.

Although Guatemalans arrive and work under the regulatory framework of the Pilot, their migration has been facilitated in large part by the International Organization for Migration (IOM), an intergovernmental body that signed memorandums of understanding with three agricultural producer organizations in Canada that manage foreign agricultural labor (Vargas-Foronda 2010b).[6] Unlike the SAWP, these are not bilateral agreements between Canada and Guatemala (International Organization for Migration 2008b; Reed 2008). The IOM manages the recruitment and preparation of workers in Guatemala, responding to requests from the agricultural producer organizations with which memorandums have been signed and that, in turn, act on behalf of employers who have received approval from the Canadian government to contract for migrant workers. The government of Guatemala plays a "support role" (Field 2010), with the Ministry of Labor assisting in recruiting workers and evaluating contracts and the Ministry of Foreign Relations assisting workers in Canada through consular services (Mantsch 2010).

Guatemalans' migration under the Pilot has grown significantly since a small group of 215 migrants (180 men and 35 women) went to Canada in 2003 (Vargas-Foronda 2010b). In 2009, 3,800 Guatemalans arrived to labor in Canadian fields and greenhouses, followed by almost 4,300 in 2010 (Citizenship and Immigration Canada 2011). Guatemalan women have accounted for 3–5 percent of total workers, depending on the year in question. In 2010, women made up 170 of the 4,280 Guatemalan workers who arrived in Canada to work in agricultural occupations (Citizenship and Immigration Canada 2011).

CASE STUDY AND FIELDWORK

The migrants' perspectives informing this analysis were garnered through interview-based fieldwork undertaken primarily from February to May 2010 in Guatemala and some follow-up contact with a few of the same migrant women in Canada when they returned to work there in the following months. While in Guatemala, I lived in an indigenous farming village,

CHRISTINE HUGHES

Vista Hermosa,[7] in the Central Highlands area of Tecpán, and carried out semi-structured interviews of one to two hours in length with forty-five individuals, including twenty-nine migrants (fourteen men and fifteen women) and sixteen partners of migrants (fifteen women and one man).[8]

The female migrants who constitute the focus of this chapter were Kaqchikel Maya, and their marital status at the time of migration was equally divided among single, married and common-law equivalent (*unión libre*), and separated. All the married or separated women had one or more children, and the single women, living at home with their parents, were childless. The women ranged in age from early twenties to mid-forties, and their educational attainment in all but two cases was limited to sixth grade or less, resulting in a few of them being functionally illiterate. The number of times they had been to Canada as temporary workers varied from one to three. They worked in three Canadian provinces—Alberta, Ontario, and Quebec—primarily in field crops but also in greenhouses, on contracts ranging from four to seven months.

How social remittances affect household gender relations in this community depends in large part on the arrangement of gender relations in general. Similar to other indigenous communities in Guatemala (Bachrach Ehlers 1991; Carter 2004; Taylor, Moran-Taylor, and Rodman Ruiz 2006), relations in Vista Hermosa are patriarchal, exhibiting a fairly rigid, gendered division of labor and overall male authority in the household.[9] Women generally devote themselves to reproductive labor (care of the household and associated tasks), and men spend most days outside the home, earning the bulk of the family's income, usually through agriculture. If women engage in income-earning activities or other pursuits that require them to leave the house, they must not neglect their primary area of responsibility, which is the daily maintenance of the household. With respect to household-level authority over decision making and financial management, like Carter (2004), I found that male control is not absolute. Asked who is in charge overall in her household, one woman said, "The one who's in charge is the man. It's them that have the say," but how much say women versus men have depends on the matter in question and how it aligns with gendered areas of responsibility.

Single, childless women in Vista Hermosa live with their parents until marriage (which tends to occur in women's late teens or early twenties), and their actions and choices are largely subject to the authority of their fathers and older male siblings. They fall in line with their mothers and sisters in the gendered division of labor. Some earn an income and, depending on the family's economic needs, can put a part of those earnings toward their own present or future expenses. In the study reported here, women who have separated from partners generally have paid employment to provide for their children, but if they return to their parents' home, they continue to feel subject to their father's authority. Overall, male authority characterizes households in Vista Hermosa; men tend to be the public face of households and restrict women's freedom with respect to mobility, reproduction, and use of labor power.

In examining how women's migration might contribute to changing household gender dynamics, I investigated two of the three types of social remittances that Levitt (1998:934) delineates: normative structures (ideas, values, and beliefs) and "systems of practice," the actions that normative structures shape.[10] Initially, I asked women about the configuration of household gender dynamics—namely, men's and women's practices, or the division of labor, and authority over decisions and budgetary matters—and subsequently examined how social remittances have been contributing to those dynamics, noting any changes resulting from them.[11] To explore social remittances, I inquired into the differences that women noticed between Canada and Guatemala, considering what these may have to do with gender, and asked women about personal changes that may have resulted from their experiences in Canada: whether they felt any differently about themselves, had noted any changes in their behavior, or had had such changes noted by friends or family. I then inquired into what information about their experiences in Canada the women would transmit to family and friends at home, particularly through telephone communication while in Canada and in person upon their return, and whether there had been any changes to elements of household gender relations compared with before their migration to Canada.

THE STAGES OF SOCIAL REMITTANCES

I argue that three key requirements must be met for women to transfer social remittances and for those to have gendered impacts in their home communities. I draw on Levitt's three-stage model of social remittances—creation, transmission, and impact—but I examine the creation stage more closely than Levitt does, focusing on both exposure to and take-up of gender-related ideas and practices as the first two requirements, followed by transmission and impact. The first requirement is that women be aware of or learn about the social differences between places of origin and destination. Second, they need to aspire after or adopt the social "stuff" they are exposed to or at least assign to the differences they observe some importance or relevance to their lives. And, third, women must remit that social knowledge, through communication channels or return migration, in ways that influence gender relations. I summarize the outcomes I discovered at each stage, illuminating certain aspects of women's experiences in both Canada and Guatemala that frustrated the realization of gender-related social remittances.

Awareness and Learning

For women to remit social knowledge about gender, they first have to acquire it. This requires that their personal and social circumstances permit them to learn about gender-related differences between origin and destination society contexts. The degree to which they will do so depends much on the extent and nature of their contact with the host society (Levitt 1998), as well as, I argue, the reasons for their migration.

I investigated this stage of the potential social remittances process by asking the women what differences they had noticed between Canada and Guatemala and, if necessary, asking directly about gender-related differences. Some women had indeed made observations about women or gender relations in Canada. For instance, they noted that some supervisors or farm owners are female, which would generally not be the case at an agricultural workplace in Guatemala. During trips to nearby towns to shop and bank, some women observed that Canadian women dress differently than women in Guatemala and seem friendlier and more sociable to strangers. Remarks about gender relations particular to the household were rare. One woman noticed that couples in Canada have fewer children than in Guatemala, and a couple of women commented that many Canadian women hold paid employment outside the home or have their own businesses.

I found that I had to ask directly about these gender-related observations, however, and much more frequent or emphasized than observations about gender were remarks about other differences they noted between their home and Canadian society.[12] Overall, the women did not or were not able to comment on gender-related differences between Canada and Guatemala to a significant extent. The reasons for this, I argue, have to do with factors that influence what they saw and what they noticed in Canada, including their limited contact with Canadian society, a common circumstance among guestworkers, and the reasons for their migration. Levitt maintains that "more contact with the host society means greater exposure to its different features, more reflection on existing practices, and a greater potential for incorporating new routines" (1998:930–931). Migrants' contact with host societies depends on the social organization of their working and living conditions in the countries of destination (Menjívar 1999). With whom do they work and live? To whom do they talk? What "structures of opportunity" (ibid.:602) do their daily social interactions provide for learning about sociocultural differences between home and host societies?

Pointing to the potential for gender-related social remittances under certain conditions, Menjívar (1999) cites the example of a Guatemalan woman in domestic employment in the urban United States who, by working and living in the home of an American family, comes to realize that the man of the house contributes more to the housework than men in Guatemala do. Such a realization would generally not occur to the migrant women discussed here, whose working and private lives provide relatively little contact with their Canadian host society in general, let alone with a Canadian household.

A few circumstances produce this reality. First, the majority of employers hiring Guatemalan migrants provide accommodations for employees on the workplace premises. Second, by and large, these women work alongside other Guatemalans and often Mexicans; rarely do they labor alongside Canadian workers, and when they do, their limited command of English or French makes conversation virtually impossible. Third, because of restrictions on their mobility and freedom of association, migrant women have little contact with Canadians outside working hours. Many women said that they were not allowed to receive visitors at the farm and, because of work schedules, the distance to the nearest town with amenities, the cost of transportation in rural areas, and protectionism on the part of employers, they would leave the farm relatively rarely. Once every one or two weeks, they would be transported to a nearby town and spend a few hours tending to their shopping and banking errands. Contact with Canadians during this time would be limited to smiles and simple greetings, and contact was sometimes actively discouraged by farm staff.[13]

In Levitt's typology of patterns of interaction with the host society, such circumstances place these Guatemalan women in the category of "recipient observers," who cannot "actively explore their world because the structure of their lives [does] not bring them close enough to it" (1998:931). A comparative look at Levitt's research and mine demonstrates the importance of the conditions of migrants' lives and work in countries of destination when considering the potential for social remittances. Levitt (1996) documented changes in gender identity among some female emigrants from the Dominican Republic to the United States, but those migrants lived fuller, less isolated lives and enjoyed more social citizenship opportunities than the women in my study, for whom certain linguistic, geographic, and restrictive circumstances largely precluded any substantial or formal opportunities to learn about different ways of "doing gender" (West and Zimmerman 2007) in Canada.

Although the isolated nature of their existence in Canada is likely the dominant factor in their limited gender-related observations, that the women noted relatively little in the way of gender-related differences also stems from the reasons for their migration. Monzón (2009) maintains that the gender-related impacts of migration will depend in part on why people migrate. Whereas migrants' circumstances in destination societies may limit what they are *able* to observe, the reasons for migration influence what migrants *notice* or concentrate on in countries of destination. It is important to consider not only exposure to gender-related differences and learning opportunities but also migrants' propensity to be aware of or take note of those aspects of their experiences.

The motivations driving Guatemalan women's migration have become more diverse, including the effects of armed conflict, poverty and lack of work, family difficulties, and domestic violence (Monzón 2009), but the primary factor tends to be economic necessity. Women's migration for work "reflects the difficult economic situation that they confront, which obligates them to search for sources of work" (MENAMIG 2006:29). In all but one case, the women interviewed cited economic necessity as the main and usually only reason for wanting to migrate to Canada. Reflecting on their reasons for migrating, women said that they pay most attention to the dynamics of their work and emphasized the money-earning aspects of their experiences. Aside from the reproductive work required to sustain themselves and to keep in regular contact with family at home, most concerns while in Canada are secondary, if not distant or nonexistent. One of the more highly educated women said that she would be interested to know more about Canadian politics and society but felt that she had to maintain her focus on her work in Canada: "What interests us is the work and what they pay us." The economic reasons for migrating and the concomitant focus on earning money influence their goals as migrants and what they get out of migration.

It may not be possible to separate the women's reasons for migration from their social isolation in Canada in terms of their mutual influence on women's observations and perceptions, yet the economic reasons for their migration and the resulting monetary concerns largely preclude consideration of the nonmonetary ways their experiences in Canada influence them. The focus on work is made even more acute by certain aspects of their employment relations and the precariousness of their work in Canada (Hughes 2012).

The first requirement for realizing social remittances—that women learn about or take note of gender-related differences—was met only to a limited degree among these Guatemalan women. Restrictions on their contact with Canadian society, coupled with the economic reasons for their migration, limit these women's learning about gender in Canada and therefore acquiring the substance of potential gender-related social remittances.

Aspirations and Adoption

Despite limited opportunities and the demands on their attention, it is certainly not the case that the women had noticed nothing about women and gender in Canada. Drawing on some of the gendered differences they did take note of, this section explores a second requirement in the process of social remittances: that women take up or aspire to the gender-related differences they notice or at least consider them important or relevant to their lives.

Taylor and colleagues argue that through Guatemalan women's employment in the United States and exposure to American culture, "their views about traditional gender roles, relations, and ideologies at home inevitably change" (2006:55). I question this inevitability. Compared with women in my study, those in Taylor, Moran-Taylor, and Rodman Ruiz's research had more exposure to the host country's culture, but I argue that more than a lack of exposure conditions the potential for such gender-related personal change. Countering assertions about inevitable change and highlighting issues of reflexivity and desire, other research suggests that Guatemalan women do not necessarily aspire to or wish to emulate what they see or learn. Menjívar (1999) suggests that indigenous domestic workers did not want to incorporate into their lives the gendered behaviors they saw among men in their US employers' homes.

Similarly, women in my study did not identify with or wish to emulate the behaviors of Canadian women. When I asked which aspects of life in Canada they wished could be replicated in Guatemala, no issues related to gender or women arose. I asked one of the women what she thought of one of the differences she noted, that young Canadian women seemed more *libres* (free) than she felt as a Guatemalan woman. She commented that it was just different and she respected those women but did not necessarily want things to be different for her in Guatemala: she had "*ningún pensamiento así*" (no thoughts like that). To the extent possible, the women also continued to wear indigenous Guatemalan clothing in Canada. They, by and large, detested wearing the pants required for their work uniforms and returned to their *traje* (woven or embroidered skirt, blouse, and belt) after work and during outings to town, with hardly any adjustments for cold Canadian winters. Furthermore, few of the women thought that they had changed as a person, in thought or behavior, because of their migration to Canada. One single woman said that she returned feeling more independent from her mother's guidance, but this was an exception to the responses overall, which focused on physical changes, like returning paler or having lost or gained weight. Quite telling, one woman said, "What can I change?"

Responses such as these limit the potential for gender-related social remittances, because realizing such remittances relies on personal changes involving shifts in one's aspirations or the incorporation of new elements into one's thinking and practices. It is important, therefore, to explore the factors influencing migrants' acceptance of new ideas and practices. Migrants are not mere sponges whose subjectivities change through simple exposure to social influences in their surroundings. Levitt similarly points out that "migrants do not absorb all aspects of their new lives unselectively" (1998:943). Social actors engage in reflexivity, in thinking about and strategizing in their lives, in response to changing experiences. Based on this reflexivity, they may or may not develop concerns or aspirations about certain aspects of their lives (Archer 2007). Quite possibly, migrants actively enact or resist changes to their gendered selves and practices, depending on how those potential changes align with what they consider important. How social actors engage in reflexivity and react to experiences or influence, however, is conditioned in part by aspects of their subjectivities (Adams 2006) or their "interpretive frames" (Levitt 1998). In scholarship on subjectivities, Bourdieu calls this conditioning force "habitus," one's set of dispositions that provide a sense of what is possible. Habitus disposes us to "shape [our] aspirations according to concrete indices of the accessible and inaccessible, of what is and is not 'for us'" (Bourdieu 1990:64).

Aspects of social actors' subjectivity that influence their perceptions and interpretations derive in large part from the sociocultural milieu, and their social location within that milieu, in their countries of origin. Menjívar suggests that we look to migrant women's home cultures and social locations to explain why women may not aspire to gender-related examples in destination societies. For instance, Guatemalan domestic workers in the United States "may perceive their social worlds as too distant from those of their employers" (Menjívar 1999:620) and therefore not aspire to arrange their own household's gendered division of labor like that of their US employers. She argues that their ideologies related to gender (as well as ethnicity and other axes of differentiation) highly influence their perceptions. In a similar vein, Verena Stolcke contends that cultural values informing gender hierarchies affect "subjective responses" to other options of how to live (qtd. in Carey 2006:63). Bourdieu is again insightful here for showing the conditioning links between "outside" and "inside," how aspects of an actor's milieu come to shape her subjectivities. He argues that structural aspects of "fields"—sets of social relations—highly condition the habitus, often in ways that actors are not conscious of (Bourdieu and Wacquant 1992).

What aspects of Guatemalan indigenous women's social location influence their perceptions? In the example of the domestic worker, Menjívar points to the "local expression" of patriarchal ideologies in the migrant's community of origin, which in Guatemala involves real and perceived differences between indigenous and Ladina women (Menjívar 1999:603).[14] Ideologies related to both gender and ethnicity emerged as influential in my study. With respect to ethnicity, a degree of "us versus them," or insider-outsider discourse, emerged in the women's remarks about Canada and their experiences. When asked what differences she had noted between Canada and Guatemala, one woman remarked, "It's different because here we're indigenous and there it's mostly Ladinas. That's the difference." This suggests that she maps onto Canadian society ethnocultural relations pertinent in Guatemala. It also suggests her lack of identification with Canadian women, being an indigenous woman familiar with Guatemala's history of conflict between indigenous and non-indigenous groups. The comments of this woman and others revealed their rootedness and pride in being indigenous, which likely contributed to their active resistance to adopting Canadian women's styles of dress and other markers of Canadian gender. Two women explicitly indicated to me that their *trajes* represent and embody their culture and they believe that it is very important to conserve this cultural identity in Canada and to feel as much like themselves as they can while away from Guatemala.

Certain aspects of local gender ideologies also influence the perceptions and interpretive frames of women from Vista Hermosa. Key among these are that married women should devote themselves primarily to being caretakers of their children and partners, and I perceived a sense of pride and competence among women in such roles. Many women acknowledged the difficulties and long days that being primary caretakers entailed and that certain conveniences could ease their hardships, but I sensed little desire for substantial changes to the gendered routine of their daily lives. Guatemalan women may understand how they are oppressed by patriarchy among other axes of oppression (Martinez-Salazar 2005) yet still understand their work as complementary to that of men, both being "vital to the functioning of the community" (Carey 2006:14). In line with what I perceived among women in my study, other literature suggests that Kaqchikel women also derive esteem from their work, partly due to the adverse conditions under which they carry out their responsibilities (Fischer and Hendrickson 2003). Fischer and Hendrickson claim that a "dignified stoicism" (ibid.:11) characterizes the performance of household work by Kaqchikel women, a quality that most men, if only implicitly, acknowledge.[15] The social rules to which women have become accustomed in Guatemala and which encourage the gender roles from which women derive competence and pride likely color their perceptions of Canadian women's gender practices.

As for young single women in Vista Hermosa, it is expected that they will be under greater influence of their parents until an older age than might be the case in Canada and that they will refrain from sexual relations before marriage. Young women leaving the direct control of their parents for Canada—having more independence, when looked at objectively—do not necessarily identify with their Canadian counterparts. One of the young single women in the study said that she does not feel freer in Canada than in Guatemala because she feels the continued involvement in her life of her parents and their influence over her actions and choices. This should not be interpreted as an unwelcome aspect of this young migrant woman's life, but as a transnational form of care, support, and connection to her family, as well as reflective of her obligations to them. This particular woman goes to Canada in part to help her parents meet the family's needs, and if she were not to behave in keeping with their expectations, she would be breaking the trust that they (reluctantly) put in her to go to Canada.

Gender-related aspects of women's environments in Guatemala, operational over a lifetime, exercise a strong influence over their subjectivities and resist being dislodged, despite exposure to possibly contradictory influences. With reference to habitus, Bourdieu claims that it becomes "not something that one has...but something that one is" (1990:7) and, barring a substantial disruption, exhibits considerable staying power through time and as individuals pass through new spaces. There is the potential for migration to contribute to a shift in migrants' interpretive frames (Levitt 1998) or habitus (Kelly and Lusis 2006; McKay 2001) because of new experiences, but the disproportionate weight of early experiences can make aspects of migrants' preexisting subjectivities "as difficult to shift as any natural attribute" (Lovell 2000:31).

The cross-border continuity of premigration dispositions and identities as Guatemalan women was fostered by the temporary nature of their migration and by frequent telephone communication. They emphasized that they were in Canada only a short time, always with an eye to going home, and they talked by phone with family members as often as daily. It remains to be seen whether spending more time in Canada will have a greater effect on female migrants' gendered selves.

In short, simply being in Canada, where people are different and behave in some unfamiliar ways, did not tend to lead these Guatemalan migrant women to aspire to or emulate what they saw or learned about. Clearly, these women are capable of reflecting on social differences and of imagining how their lives could be different with respect to gender, yet the weight of sociocultural influences conditions such reflection and imagining, very likely precluding their assigning importance to Canadian ideas of gender or changing their own gendered subjectivities. Thus, this study problematizes the ethnocentric Western notion that women participating in migration to more "developed" countries will or should see the gender practices and roles in destination societies as more desirable than those in their communities of origin. Both because of reasons explicitly articulated—such as wanting to preserve their sense of cultural identity—and less-than-conscious influences on their perceptions, these women may resist the adoption of gendered cultural resources available in countries such as Canada.

Possibilities for Transmission

The third requirement in gender-related social remittance processes is women's ability and desire to transmit new ideas and practices to their home communities. Because the interviews revealed relatively little in the way of gender-related knowledge or resulting personal change, we should perhaps expect little in the way of gender-related social remittances actually occurring. Indeed, my research indicated that household gender practices or relations changed very little, if at all, after the women rejoined their families in Guatemala. The women said that their household division of labor and authority "returned to normal" or were the same as premigration arrangements. No change can be as analytically interesting and insightful as change, however, and the study revealed challenges that the women might face if they wanted to transmit gender-related knowledge or to effect gender-related change in their households.

Levitt (1998) explains that migrants transmit social remittances through two main avenues: telephone communication and in person when migrants visit or return home. I examine accounts of phone conversations and return migration here in terms of the prospects of remitting gender-related ideas and practices. The women certainly talked frequently by phone with their family members in Guatemala but generally were not remitting gender-related knowledge. Instead, their conversations, as recounted to me, ranged over topics of personal well-being and family or household affairs, with mothers devoting a considerable portion of their time talking to children or to partners about parenting issues. Among topics related to Canada, women would talk about their work and, less frequently, their outings. When asked about differences between Canada and Guatemala, they focused on the weather, land, and sunset times. The topics and trajectories of the conversations—specifically, the absence of gender-related issues— certainly in part reflect the findings discussed in the previous two sections about awareness and the take-up of gender-related differences. However, the nature of their conversations also reflects other factors. First, they had limited time to talk—often a maximum of fifteen minutes—to multiple family members. Second, important aspects of transnationalism and their continued attachment to family and home emerged. Their conversations focused on the topics that were easiest to relate to the person called or that provided connection across distance.

The second avenue of remittance—return migration—may permit women to remit new gender-related knowledge and practices through talking with people or acting differently upon their return. When women arm themselves with new ideas and aspire to put them into practice in their households or communities, they can often drive processes of social change (Monzón 2009). However, in research on Guatemalan migrants, Taylor and colleagues found that "it is a rare case where women translate their personal transformations into new relationships with men" (2006:58). My interviews revealed little in the way of cultural diffusion through in-person communication or personal behavior. As noted above, the women generally did not think that they behaved differently upon their return, and conversations with friends and family upon return—as recounted in interviews—tended to focus on "what it was like there" and "how things went."

Although most of the women had little to share in terms of gender-related remittances, one needs to also consider the structural conditions in which such remittances and potential gender-related social change could occur. Monzón argues, "The effects of migration are linked closely with the gendered condition" (2009:226); in other words, the local context is a key factor in shaping social remittance processes (Menjívar 1999). In their research, Taylor and colleagues (2006:58) found influential the "rigid structure and social norms" regarding gender in Guatemala, which continue to tip the balance of household and relationship power decidedly toward men. In Vista Hermosa, similarly, certain aspects of the gendered condition make it difficult for women to communicate, much less act out, new gender-related ideas and practices.[16]

If women did want to communicate or enact new gender-related knowledge or practices, men would likely resist changes to the gendered division of household labor, and the conditioning effects of gossip would hinder transmission. In the first instance, let us consider a social remittance related to the gendered division of housework: one migrant woman noted that men do more cooking for the family in Canada than men do in Guatemala. Suppose that she wanted her husband to adopt more responsibility for food preparation after she returned home. It is important to consider what he did while she was in Canada. Normally the domains of women, childcare, cleaning, and cooking still need to be done in women's absence, and perhaps if men took on these chores while their wives were away, learning the value of this work to the household's functioning and family well-being (Resurreccion and Van Khanh 2007), men might be more open to women's injection of new ideas or gender practices. Research suggests, however, that few men take up traditionally women's tasks. Whereas women often expand their roles in the course of migration, the men left behind "cling to their old roles" (Asis 2005:119), leaving reproductive labor to be done by other female relatives. Migration studies involving Guatemala have found this to be the case (Bernhard, Landolt, and Goldring 2005; Carey 2006; Taylor, Moran-Taylor, and Rodman Ruiz 2006), with Carey arguing that men assuming women's responsibilities would be "considered irrational" and would mean that men "were choosing subordination" (2006:17, 115).

In Vista Hermosa, indeed, few men assumed responsibility for "women's work" in migrant women's absence. Childrearing and household chores were generally assumed by grandmothers or sisters and, less often, by paid, non-kin domestic help. Although some men assumed more responsibility for parenting, they particularly avoided domestic tasks such as cooking and cleaning. So resistant were men to doing such housework that the same woman cited above, who had noted men's involvement in food preparation in Canada, said that she would not have been able to migrate if it were not for her sisters-in-law, who saw that her husband had his food prepared and his clothes washed: "If maybe we were in a house apart [from the family], I wouldn't have gone, because he's a man and the men here [in Guatemala] work less in the kitchen than there [in Canada]."

Although my study suggested that one could reasonably question the extent to which men would have the time, given their day-long agricultural work and the learned abilities necessary to perform these household tasks, community gossip also arose as a conditioning influence on gender-related behaviors. The community seemed to represent a "shame culture," "in which people—for better or for worse—mind each other's business" (Adler Hellman 2008:199). It became discernible to me over the course of my fieldwork while living in Vista Hermosa that gossip was rampant and sometimes hurtful. People sometimes found fodder for gossip in hearsay that women or men were acting outside their expected household roles. "People talk badly about that sort of thing," one village woman related to me. She explained that there was social pressure and that there would be "talk" if people behaved in ways out of the customary.

In addition to or aside from men's resistance to changing the gendered division of labor and the conditioning effects of gossip, women may not desire such change (Vullnetari and King 2011). Women's competence in and attachment to their gender roles and practices, as discussed above, should not be forgotten. The "return to normal" seemed to be, overall, acceptable and desirable to returning Guatemalan women. One newlywed said, in reference to her return and taking up her wifely roles again, "I feel fine because I know it's my husband, and I feel fine having to attend to him again." This reflects Resurreccion and Van Khanh's contention that it is problematic for women to let go of roles that they understand to be "an intrinsic part of their obligation as women" (2007:219). Just as men may feel "unnatural" or emasculated by performing women's work, women may take exception to men performing tasks in the sphere of activity from which women derive esteem and pride.

To conclude, then, in my study, the third requirement for the realization of social remittances—that migrant women successfully enact or transmit gender-related ideas—was largely precluded. Of particular importance were women's attachment to their roles and the gendered conditions of their home communities, which, like Vista Hermosa, encourage a "return to normal" and would likely stymie those women who might aspire to effect gender-related social change in their households and communities.

AN EXCEPTIONAL CASE AND FUTURE RESEARCH

Among the migrant women interviewed in Vista Hermosa, one stands out as representing the possibilities that migration to Canada and social remittances hold for loosening patriarchal gender relations. Brenda (a pseudonym) cited having noticed or learned in Canada that Canadian families are generally much smaller than Guatemalan ones, that women have fewer children: "There, sometimes they have only one child. Here, no, the majority of the families are big." She realized that this was important for a family's standard of living and for being able to provide for children's basic needs and post-primary education. She said, "[It would be better] to have only one or two children so that they have better opportunities... different from us." She had shared these observations and thoughts with her husband—who had also worked in Canada: "We had thought about two, but better just one." She also thought that although she does not consider herself the right person to do it, there should be increased efforts in Guatemala to educate women about the benefits of and tools available for family planning. Thus, Brenda seems to have met all three conditions discussed in the preceding sections: she took note of a key gender-related difference, thought it important to incorporate into her life, and transmitted this new idea or value to her husband—if not (yet) to her wider community—on whom it seems to have had an impact.

It should be noted that other factors may be at play in this case that suggest the need for further research. Brenda had higher educational attainment than any other woman interviewed, through which she may have acquired knowledge about lower birthrates in more developed countries and the benefits of family planning, and her husband had also migrated and made observations about family size in Canada, which likely influenced his receptiveness to the idea of having a smaller family.[17] Future research might do well to account for these types of factors in order to identify with more precision the circumstances that foster or discourage the likelihood and influence of gendered social remittances.

Further research could also examine gender-related social remittances by male migrants from villages such as Vista Hermosa. Many of the same inhibiting factors discussed here would likely apply to male remitters, with potentially important exceptions. First, while living in Canada, they perform household work that they normally would not do in Guatemala. There is limited evidence among Vista Hermosa households to suggest that this may contribute to men coming to better understand and value this type of work or to help their female partners more with it. Such possibilities are important to consider, given that Levitt (1998) suggests that if gender-related social remittance patterns are more intense or thick—that is, if more people are conveying similar practices or ideas more frequently—those social remittances are more likely to have an impact on both migrant and nonmigrant households. The second difference for men is that they are, arguably, in a position of more power than women to effect changes in household labor and authority arrangements, so shifts in men's ways of thinking and acting possibly have greater impact potential.

A longitudinal, comparative study in a village like Vista Hermosa would also prove valuable. There is no end in sight for Guatemalan migration to

Canada, nor is there a shortage of Canadian employers willing to contract foreign labor. This study, conducted seven years into Vista Hermosa's participation in the Pilot, revealed little in the way of gender-related social remittances, but as more of the village's residents migrate to Canada or as many of them do so repeatedly, we could see more discernible—although, no doubt, incremental—shifts in patriarchal gender relations stemming from social remittances.

CONCLUSION

This chapter examines the potential for women's labor migration to Canada to contribute to changes in household-level patriarchal gender arrangements in Guatemala through social remittances. Three conditions need to be met for gendered social remittances to be realized and have an impact, and in this case, these requirements have largely not been fulfilled. First, with limited contact with Canadians and the desire to work as much as possible, migrant women in Canada did not have the opportunity or inclination to notice or learn about many gender-related differences between Canada and Guatemala. Second, any gender-related differences they may have noticed did not seem relevant to their lives: the migrant women's enculturated and transnationalized social location, related to gender and ethnicity, contributed to this lack of take-up through both less-than-conscious conditioning and active resistance. Third, the women may have held tightly to the gender roles to which they were accustomed, but should women wish to remit gender-related ideas or practices upon their return, they would likely face men's resistance and the weight of community discourses.

Overall, this study contributes to bodies of work examining the dynamics and social impacts of Canada's low-skill labor migration program, adding to the gender and migration scholarship the experiences of women participating in managed migration. Focusing on conditions in Canada and Guatemala and transnationalized elements of gender, it problematizes the notion of migration being a "gender transformative odyssey" (Preibisch 2005:91), at least through the means of social remittances. For studies on the social impacts of migration, it perhaps most poignantly draws attention to the importance of differences among types of migration in terms of their conditioning effects on gender-related social change. It calls for other studies that have documented the realization and impact of gendered social remittances (e.g., José Alcalá 2006; Levitt 1996; Ramírez, García Domínguez, and Míguez Morais 2005) to perhaps moderate their claims in consideration of the particularities of managed migration. This highly structured instance of labor migration from Guatemala to Canada, in which migrant women's experiences are highly controlled, their exposure to Canadian society minimized, and their attachments to home maintained, has contributed thus far to minimal social disruption with regard to gender.

Acknowledgments

This research was supported by the Social Sciences and Humanities Research Council of Canada (SSHRC). Many thanks to Laura Macdonald and Christina Gabriel for their feedback on early versions of this chapter.

Notes

1. *NOC* refers to the National Occupations Code, used by Canada's federal government to categorize and stratify different types of employment.

2. In addition to or instead of economic reasons, women may seek "safer, more enabling environments" abroad in order to escape gendered forms of oppression, such as domestic violence (Asis 2005:115).

3. This is not to deny in the least that many women find themselves in forced international migration flows as refugees or as victims of trafficking, but to draw attention to women's status as independent labor migrants.

4. For instance, the relatively small number of women among Guatemalan agricultural migrants to Canada reflects gender-based assumptions among Canadian farmers about which workers are appropriate for which types of work (Preibisch and Encalada Grez 2010), as well as the importance assigned in Guatemala to women's roles as mothers and housewives, which results in their having less freedom than men to leave home. Pratt discusses this hindrance of women's international movement in terms of "spatial stickiness," which is influenced by the division of labor and power in households (Pratt and Yeoh 2003:161).

5. Admitting of some exactitude, I reserve the term "remittances"—based in the word "remit" (to send)—for ideas, practices, and the like, that actually get sent or transferred or that flow from one place to another, or the process of such sending. I differentiate content—ideas, practices, and the like—from social remittances in order to acknowledge the possibility that migrants may learn about, gather, or acquire this content but not remit it. Put differently, social remittances have a spatiotemporal aspect that differentiates them from their substance, which, until such time as it actually flows, remains the stuff of a would-be or potential remittance only.

6. These producer organizations and their respective provinces are FERME in Quebec, FARMS in Ontario, and WALI in Alberta and British Columbia. FERME is the Fondation des Entreprises en Recrutement de la Main-D'œuvre Agricole Étrangère,

FARMS is Foreign Agricultural Resource Management Services, and WALI is the Western Agricultural Labour Initiative. The IOM's role has changed with respect to migrant labor in Quebec. FERME opened an office in Guatemala City to facilitate the migration of Guatemalans to Quebec and to another farm in western Canada, without the assistance of the IOM. Also, WALI no longer processes foreign worker applications; employers in western Canada now deal with the IOM directly.

7. I use a pseudonym for the village name in order to protect the identities of study participants.

8. That there was only one man among the partners interviewed is explained by the facts that only five of the female migrants were married (whereas all the male migrants represented were married) and it was difficult to interview the men because they were often out of the house during the daytime hours, when interviews could be conducted.

9. Some research has suggested that gender relations in indigenous households tend to be less patriarchal than in non-indigenous households in Guatemala, exhibiting more egalitarianism with respect to the division of labor and authority (Carey 2006; Chant and Craske 2003; Menjívar 2006).

10. Levitt's third type of social remittance is social capital. I did not find that key aspects of social capital—such as social networks and the use of status and prestige for one's advantage—were relevant to the experiences of migrant women in my study.

11. It is not possible in a qualitative study to attribute cause and effect with respect to gender-related social change, given that a host of other factors and influences may come into play. If respondents cited changes in their household gender relations, I privileged their perspectives on whether and how migration may be contributing to those shifts.

12. Among these were that vehicles respect pedestrians, people can walk in the streets without fearing for their safety, places and infrastructure look different, people are wealthy, and housework or farmwork is performed differently or with different implements.

13. I address issues of employers' direct restrictions on women's freedom of mobility and association in Canada in Hughes 2012.

14. Ladinos are the non-indigenous population in Guatemala, descendants of the mixing in colonial times of Spanish and Mayan populations.

15. This is not to ignore the ways in which patriarchal systems and ideologies circumscribe the agency of Kaqchikel women (Carey 2006), but to adjust the view of them as miserable or fully subjugated at home (Martinez-Salazar 2005).

16. Levitt (1996, 1998) draws our attention to several factors that condition the transmission and impact of social remittances. Although not directly investigated in

this study, the following factors in particular may be influential in the case of Vista Hermosa: the gendered division of household and community power between the senders and receivers of social remittances (in the case of women's migration); and other types of messages, discourses, or practices related to gender that are circulating or being enacted in the community—for instance, in the churches or in women's groups—and would support or contradict the substance of potential social remittances.

17. Other material conditions also may come into play in decisions regarding family planning, such as the family's anticipated livelihood; relatedly, the need for family labor power in the case of peasant agriculture; and the household income level expected.

8

Global Trends, Local Outcomes

Globalization and the Foreign-Born Temporary Labor Force in the Shenandoah Valley Apple Industry

Micah N. Bump, Elżbieta M. Goździak, and B. Lindsay Lowell

In this chapter, we present the Shenandoah Valley, Virginia, apple industry as a case study of dependence on temporary worker programs, contributing a local perspective to the national policy debate on temporary worker programs while enhancing the understanding of the dynamics of temporary worker programs, global market forces, and changing settlement patterns and their impact on different US locations. Our detailed focus on a single commodity illustrates how the fate of temporary foreign workers in local areas is intimately tied to global and national trends beyond the control of apple growers or apple workers, subject to international trade and increased competition among different sectors of the food industry. At the same time, the chapter shows how local responses to global forces influence the demand for foreign labor and the ability of a local growers association to keep meeting workers' housing needs and the demands of government paperwork, drawing on a history of exemplary enlightened management.

Since the late 1940s, apple growers in the Shenandoah Valley have relied on government-authorized temporary worker programs to access foreign-born labor from the Caribbean to pick fruit during the annual apple harvest. Although temporary worker programs have been criticized for causing illegal migration and poor working conditions (Martin 2001; Meissner 2004), the decades-long reliance on Caribbean labor in the

Shenandoah Valley industry has neither spurred increased numbers of unauthorized workers nor led to a permanent illegal resident population. And though not trouble free, the camp and the grower association we study provide adequate if somewhat basic working and living conditions for the temporary workforce.

The ability of the Shenandoah Valley apple growers to avoid an illegalization of their workforce while meeting basic working and housing standards can be attributed to several factors. First, Shenandoah Valley growers shifted relatively smoothly from the British West Indies Labor Program (BWILP) in the 1940s to what eventually became the current H-2A program and were able to maintain continual access to seasonal Caribbean workers. Second, the Frederick County (Virginia) Fruit Growers Association has owned, managed, and operated a migrant workers camp since the 1940s. The early institutionalization of the growers association and its operation of the camp have permitted area growers to pool resources for decades to meet the housing and paperwork requirements of the temporary worker programs. Third, the principal sending country of the temporary workers is Jamaica. Jamaicans, unlike Latino migrants who have settled permanently in the Shenandoah since the 1990s (Bump 2005), have limited support networks as there is no Jamaican immigrant community in the immediate vicinity. Moreover, Jamaican-born migrants as a whole are an insignificant portion of the undocumented population (Hoefer, Rytina, and Baker 2008). Fourth and last, a single apple grower in the Shenandoah Valley with a large operation has consistently sponsored more than 200 workers per year during the twenty-first century. This has provided stability to the operation of the migrant worker camp during an increasingly difficult period for the apple industry. From US policy makers' and growers' perspectives, all of these factors reinforce the successful temporary worker program in the Shenandoah Valley because the workers are managed well within the framework of the program and they return to their home countries. As for the workers, we argue that they return to the camp year after year because the working conditions are tolerable and their earnings are superior to what they might earn at home.

Despite the long-term success of the temporary worker program in the Shenandoah Valley, its future is uncertain. The national economic boom of the 1990s and early 2000s—with its very low unemployment rates, increased industrialization, and increased development pressures on farmland—affected the US apple industry. At the same time, China rapidly emerged as a major exporter of apples and apple juice, directly affecting US apple growers and workers. The confluence of these factors forced many apple growers, nationwide and in the Shenandoah Valley, to shut down operations, alter production and marketing strategies, or hold down wages and other costs to survive.

The competition from China and increased development pressures on farmland mean that production costs must decrease in order for US growers to remain competitive. In some instances, US apple growers have attempted to decrease costs by shifting to a predominantly Mexican-born, mostly undocumented workforce. For example, in the eastern panhandle of West Virginia, close to the Shenandoah Valley, what had been H-2A camps became "Mexicanized" as mostly undocumented Mexican workers "crowded out" Jamaican temporary workers (Schrecongost 1999).[1] Although growers in the Shenandoah Valley also employ Mexican-born workers, through both the H-2A program and the domestic migrant and seasonal worker streams,[2] Jamaican H-2A workers continue to constitute the majority. Instead of decreasing reliance on Jamaican H-2A workers, as in West Virginia, the increased competition and pressure to improve productivity intensified the long-standing reliance of Shenandoah apple growers on foreign-born H-2A guestworkers. The dependence on H-2As has remained despite a new permanent settlement pattern that emerged during the economic boom of the 1990s, when many former seasonal and migrant farmworkers found year-round employment opportunities in nearby poultry-processing plants, as well as in construction, landscaping, plastics manufacturing, and non-poultry food processing (Bump 2005). The Jamaican H-2A workers have neither migrated into these jobs nor settled permanently in the Shenandoah Valley. Rather, the new source of labor primarily is unauthorized Mexicans who are drawn to the poultry plants, but they have not supplanted the Jamaican apple workers even though they cost less, offer greater flexibility, and report that they prefer apple to poultry jobs.

Even with access to H-2A workers, several large apple producers in the Shenandoah Valley have abandoned their operations since the 1990s, resulting in reduced demand for all types of temporary apple pickers. Growers who continue to maintain orchards have increased productivity to the extent possible under the current system by planting higher-yield trees. Access to workers appears not to be a major problem because of the institutionalization of the H-2A program, although growers are unanimous in their frustration with the time-consuming bureaucracy of the program. And although other fruit industries have increased productivity and competitiveness through technological advances, as the apple industry has seen improvement in tree varieties, the mechanical picking and sorting technology

FIGURE 8.1

"Apple Capital of the World." Photo by Micah N. Bump.

for apples has enjoyed limited success. Given the expense of technological solutions, apple growers have sought alternatives such as producing for niche local markets, opening farm stands, switching to "pick-your-own" operations, and seeking new export partners. What consequences these approaches will have on the use of temporary workers and whether they will be successful remain to be seen.

DECADES OF DEPENDENCE ON FOREIGN APPLE PICKERS

A sign—"Virginia Apples from the Apple Capital of the World"—posted at the city limits, greets visitors coming to Winchester, Virginia (figure 8.1). Although the dwindling number of apple growers and decreased apple production in Winchester and the surrounding Frederick County cast doubt on the modern-day accuracy of this title, the apple industry remains an important part of the local economy and a source of local civic pride. Labor

Day continues to usher in the start of apple-picking season, as it has for the past 150 years. And each time this perennial cycle repeats, local apple growers look beyond the valley for workers to handpick their crops.

Finding the seasonal labor to carry out the intense apple harvest work has challenged apple growers in the Shenandoah Valley for more than a century. By the early 1900s, the apple industry was the main employer in the Shenandoah Valley, and people were employed in processing, packing, and apple picking during the harvest. Farmers with smaller operations would help large orchard owners with the harvest to earn extra money. However, as a result of labor shortages during and after World War I, growers were forced to look farther for workers and turned to local and out-of-state women, who "saved the apple crop" (Eddy 2005). The economic crises and resulting labor surpluses of the 1930s provided a brief respite, but the employment of migrant workers can be dated to this decade (Eddy 2005; Heppel, Spano, and Torres 1997). The availability of a suitable workforce to pick apples became a major concern during World War II, when growers used a variety of workers, including soldiers home on leave, local boy scouts and housewives, and German prisoners of war imprisoned in what is today Frederick County's largest H-2A labor camp (Griffith 1986; Heppel, Spano, and Torres 1997).

In 1943, a local apple grower remarked, "Our labor troubles, in my judgment, have been 'on the make' for many years. Certainly in Piedmont Virginia an ample supply of good labor has been hard to get for a long time.... That gaunt figure with the tobacco-stained jaw and battered hat, asking for a job at the back door, is gone forever" (Heppel, Spano, and Torres 1997). This shortage was confirmed by Tupper Dorsey, a local grower whose family has been in the apple business since the 1920s: "World War II put a demand on the men. So they had to find other labor, and they used German POWs for harvest work" (interview, 2004).[3] The use of POWs lasted only a short time, but in the 1940s, a prison was constructed in Winchester, Virginia, to house them. Altered and enlarged, this site is still used today as the migrant worker camp for the Frederick County Fruit Growers Association. The camp is built on a hill, is surrounded by a high chain-link fence, and can accommodate up to 1,000 workers. There are several buildings on the camp grounds, which resemble old military barracks. The accommodations are simple, with concrete block walls, concrete floors, metal bed frames, and communal eating and washing facilities (figure 8.2).

The history of the Frederick County Fruit Growers Association's migrant worker camp highlights the dependence of local growers on foreign-born temporary workers and provides a good illustration of the

FIGURE 8.2

The Frederick County Fruit Growers Association's migrant labor camp. Photo by Micah N. Bump.

evolution of the temporary workforce used to pick apples in the northern Shenandoah Valley. Virginia was not immune to the difficulty in accessing farm labor up and down the East Coast during World War II, with growers claiming labor shortages as young workers left for war or to join the war effort. Whereas some argue that labor was in short supply only because growers refused to raise wages or improve working conditions in response to a tightening labor market, growers claimed that fruit would rot in the orchards if new supplies of farm labor were not developed (Griffith 1987; Hahamovitch 2011).

In response, the US government established the British West Indies Temporary Alien Labor Program (BWITALP). This was a temporary agricultural worker program, similar in design to the larger bracero program, which drew on Mexican workers, and it established the practice of contracting for temporary labor from the Caribbean. Under the BWITALP, which officially operated from 1943 through 1947, workers from Jamaica, the Bahamas, St. Lucia, St. Vincent, Dominica, and Barbados were brought to the United States for temporary work in agriculture. Although the program was developed primarily for southern Florida's sugar producers, apple growers also benefited. The fact that these workers spoke English was seen as an advantage over the Mexican workers in the bracero program. When the BWILP ended in 1947, Congress converted it "into a temporary-worker program, as allowed under the provisions of the Immigration Act of 1917"; this became the precursor to the H-2 and eventually the H-2A program (Briggs 2004).

The data presented in figure 8.3, which show the Frederick County Fruit

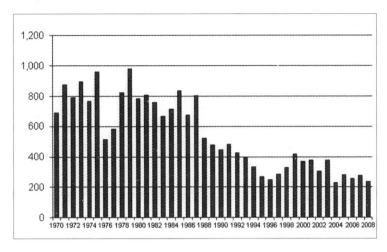

FIGURE 8.3

Jamaican H-2A workers employed at the Frederick County Fruit Growers Association's Winchester labor camp, 1970–2008. Source: data provided to authors by Carol Burke, executive secretary of the Frederick County Fruit Growers Association, 2009.

Growers Association's heavy reliance on Jamaican H-2A workers since the 1970s,[4] reflects the legacy of the BWITALP. According to Percy Williams, an eighty-seven-year-old African American man who worked as a camp supervisor for more than fifty years, from 1955 to 2006, there were always Jamaicans and other Caribbean people in the camp (interview, 2004). He estimated that half the workforce was from the Caribbean. One of his first tasks in 1955 was "to build a fence to separate domestic workers from the Caribbean workers" (ibid.). In the 1950s and 1960s, he said, there would be approximately 300 Jamaicans on one side of the camp and a mixture of African Americans, whites, and sometimes Puerto Ricans, about 300 in total, on the other side of the camp. He said that the fence was necessary because "people didn't get along good...they liked to fight a lot" (ibid.).

The growers association has tried to recruit domestic workers repeatedly over the years, supposedly with little success. However, there were times when Puerto Ricans were brought in to replace Jamaican pickers but were rejected by local growers (Griffith 1986). Carol Burke, the executive secretary of the association, started her job in the 1960s and said that at that time, the association "sent buses all over the South to pick up workers" (interview, 2004). Williams confirmed this observation, stating that "in 1965, they [the growers] went everywhere [to recruit workers]—Mississippi, North Carolina, and South Carolina." The US policy toward Haitians and

Puerto Ricans has periodically resulted in these populations appearing among the harvest workers. Burke remarked that "bunches of Haitian boat people came [to the camp] in the early 1980s. They were granted parole into the country, and they were eligible right away for employment. Even if they had high-paid jobs or were lawyers in Haiti, when they came, they were picking apples somewhere" (interview, 2004). There are few Haitians and no Puerto Ricans now. Williams stated, "Now [in the fall of 2006] it's mostly Mexicans and Jamaicans. Not as many Haitians any more. They [Haitians] have jobs in hospitals and nursing homes" (interview, 2006).

INCREASED DEPENDENCE ON FOREIGN TEMPORARY LABOR, BUT FEWER WORKERS

Modern growers in the Shenandoah Valley still complain of a shortage of domestically available workers and use the government-endorsed temporary H-2A agricultural program to fill their harvest workforce every fall. Dorsey commented, "[I can't] think of the last time someone came to [my] office looking for work.... It is difficult to find a person who can do the work who is willing to do the work" (interview, 2004). Of course, this may imply that there is a high productivity standard that effectively screens out otherwise willing local workers (see Martin, chapter 2, this volume). In addition to the largely Jamaican workforce, the growers association has employed a small number of H-2A Mexicans in recent years. Burke noted that the rest of the workforce is "domestics," whom she described as US-domiciled Haitians and Mexicans, who come to Virginia from Florida on private contracts (interview, 2004).

Although H-2A temporary workers from Jamaica and Mexico do not account for the entire harvest workforce at the Frederick County Fruit Growers Association camp, the data presented in figure 8.4 show that the dependence of the local growers on H-2As has intensified in the twenty-first century. Between 1988 and 1997, H-2As accounted for an average of 51.8 percent of the total harvest workforce. From 1998 to 2008, however, the average share of H-2A workers increased to 65.1 percent of the entire workforce. Extrapolating from earlier research, we find that the increased reliance on H-2A workers can be explained, in part, by trends in new immigrant settlement in the Shenandoah Valley, with many former seasonal and migrant farmworkers—but not Jamaican H-2As—finding year-round employment in local food-processing plants, construction, landscaping, plastics manufacturing, and service industries (Bump 2005). Ironically, unauthorized Mexican workers drawn to local food processing have not moved to supplant the Jamaicans, even though they express a preference

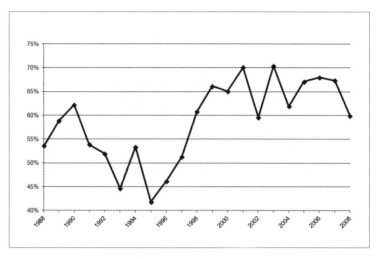

FIGURE 8.4

H-2A workers' share of the total Frederick County Fruit Growers Association apple harvest workforce, 1988–2008. Source: data provided to authors by Carol Burke, executive secretary of the Frederick County Fruit Growers Association, 2009.

for apple over processing jobs (interview, 2004). At the same time, prior to 2007, rock-bottom unemployment rates at less than 3 percent created significant competition for labor among all of these sectors, making it yet more difficult to find local or "domestic" workers among the growing, low-skilled labor pool who would pick apples (Bump 2005).

In contrast to the rapid growth of Latinos in the Shenandoah Valley since the 1990s, Jamaicans have not settled permanently in the area (Goździak and Bump 2008). In 2000, the US Census counted fewer than 100 Jamaicans in Winchester and Frederick County, and more recent government surveys do not contain a sample large enough for an accurate estimate. It is plausible that Jamaican H-2A apple pickers working in the Shenandoah Valley since the 1990s settled in other areas of the United States with larger Jamaican communities,[5] but our qualitative research indicates that most prefer to return to Jamaica after the picking season. Carol Burke, who fills out the H-2A petitions for many workers, stated that although the association has no way to be certain that all the H-2As return home, the fact that so many of the same people come back each year leads her to believe that this is the case for the majority (interview, 2004).

For instance, Anthony Smith, a forty-year-old man from Jamaica, has been coming to Winchester to pick apples for several years. He flies from

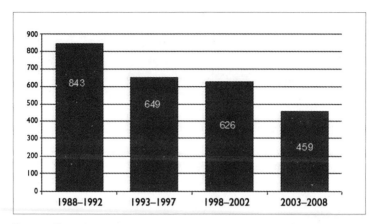

FIGURE 8.5

Average number of harvest workers at the Frederick County Fruit Growers
Association's labor camp, 1988–2008. Source: data provided to authors by
Carol Burke, executive secretary of the Frederick County Fruit Growers
Association, 2009.

Jamaica to Miami and then takes a bus up the coast. He complains about
the work and the living accommodations, saying, "The food's bad. Living
conditions are bad. You have to come out of your house to go to the bath-
room." Yet, Smith also said that necessity keeps him coming back. "Carrying
loads [of apples] is hard work, but I need the money, so I keep coming
back" (qtd. in Kane 2008). The money that Smith and his colleagues make,
$9.70 per hour, according to the 2012 wage fixed by the US Department of
Labor, does not all return home in monetary form. Every year, at the end
of the picking season, the Jamaican H-2A workers fill the trailers of several
large trucks with appliances, televisions, stereos, and other goods to bring
back to the island (Griffith 1983).

LOWER NUMBERS OF WORKERS AT THE CAMP

Although the Frederick County Fruit Growers Association's temporary
worker data indicate an increased dependence on H-2A workers, the data
presented in figure 8.5 show that the overall number of workers employed
at the camp has fallen in recent years. From 1988 to 1992, an average of 843
workers were housed at the migrant camp each fall for the picking season.
Over the next fifteen years, however, this number fell by 46 percent, or
almost half of the average workforce from the late 1980s and early 1990s.

As demonstrated in figure 8.6, all three types of workers housed at
the association's migrant camp have experienced this decline. The starkest

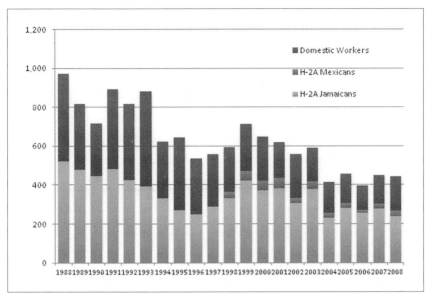

FIGURE 8.6

The total Frederick County Fruit Growers Association apple harvest workforce by worker type, 1988–2008. Source: data provided to authors by Carol Burke, executive secretary of the Frederick County Fruit Growers Association, 2009.

decline occurred among the domestic workers; between 1988 and 1992, an average of 372 domestic workers were employed at the camp, but between 2003 and 2008, this number dipped to 156. Jamaican H-2A workers also declined, but not as steeply or steadily. Between 1988 and 1992, an average of 470 Jamaican H-2As were housed at the camp, but between 2003 and 2008, this number fell to 276. Mexican H-2As, much smaller in number and with less history at the labor camp, ranged between 13 and 52 between 1998 and 2008, tending to be fewer in more recent years. As shown elsewhere in this volume and in previous research, the difference between Mexicans and Jamaicans may be due to the growth of co-ethnic populations in the region (Bump 2005; Griffith and Contreras, chapter 6, this volume).

LOWER PRODUCTION DECREASES DEMAND FOR FOREIGN LABOR

That fewer workers show up in the Frederick County Fruit Growers Association's migrant camp each fall indicates that the local apple industry is struggling. Dorsey traces the changes in the apple industry back to the 1980s (interview, 2004): "[With few exceptions,] the apple business hasn't

195

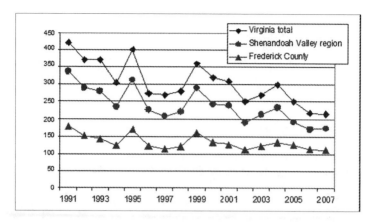

FIGURE 8.7

Virginia apple production, 1991–2007 (in millions of pounds). Source: US Department of Agriculture 2005.

been good since 1985. Although 1996 was a good year.... Things got bad due to overproduction and the price structure. In 1990, China didn't grow what the US does, but now they do. We don't import the [Chinese] fruit to the US, but they export to the same countries we sold to. It's a world system" (ibid.). In his view, both domestic overproduction of apples and increased globalization of the apple market changed things.

Indeed, a look at the numbers shows that the heyday of apple growing in the Shenandoah Valley is a thing of the past. The data presented in figure 8.7 show that production of apples in Virginia has declined since the early 1990s, with the total pounds of commercial apples produced falling by 49 percent between 1991 and 2007. Virginia's apple industry is driven by production in the Shenandoah Valley, which accounts for 75–80 percent of the annual Virginia crop, and the valley's production drop has propelled the statewide downward trend. Reduced production has been paralleled by decreases in the number of Virginia apple growers and in the total acreage dedicated to apples. The data presented in table 8.1 show that the number of Virginia apple growers fell by 40 percent between 1987 and 2005 and the total number of acres for apple growing dropped by 51 percent over the same period.

Locally, in the Shenandoah Valley, the number of growers has also declined. Burke indicated that in the late 1980s, twenty to thirty growers would house workers at the camp, but in the past few years, this number has dropped to nine. In an action that is perhaps most symbolic of the state of the apple industry in the Shenandoah Valley, Harry F. Byrd III, grandson

TABLE 8.1

Number of Apple Growers and Acres Dedicated to Apples in Virginia

Year	Growers	Total Acres
1987	343	23,352
1992	315	21,517
1997	264	18,589
2001	233	16,438
2005	206	11,403

Source: US Department of Agriculture 2005

of the "Apple King of America," Harry F. Byrd Sr., decided that apples had no future. He uprooted the apple trees in the orchard that his grandfather planted more than 100 years ago, and he leased another 900-acre orchard in Clarke County to a farmer. Diane Kearns, a local grower, commented on this situation: "[He] threw his hands up this year and tore out his trees. The whole industry is suffering, and I want to be upbeat, but it's going down the tubes." She added that her family's company, Fruit Hill Orchards, which she operates with her father, Robert Solenberger, was not in it for "economic returns" these days, but because they "like it." Some of the smaller growers are "being backed into a corner and have only their land left" (interview, 2004; Griffith 2009a). Other examples of long-time producers leaving the business are not uncommon. At one time, Joe Robinson's family grew apples on as many as 1,500 acres, but they quit in 2000 after a century in the business (Edwards 2001).

Apple growing, just like any other agricultural venture, has always been affected by numerous factors, including the high cost of pesticides, cicada invasions, natural disasters, the availability of bees for pollination, and local and global market forces. Locally, increased development pressure during the housing boom of the late 1990s and 2000s, resulting in residential sprawl into apple-growing country, and increased global competition from China both have greatly influenced the apple-growing industry in the Shenandoah Valley.

INCREASED LOCAL DEVELOPMENT PRESSURES ON FARMLAND

The Shenandoah Valley, with its idyllic rural landscapes, rich history, and strong economy, has seen slow, steady population growth since the

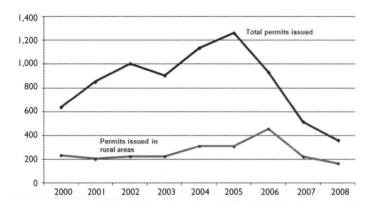

FIGURE 8.8

New residential building permits issued in Frederick County, Virginia, 2000–2008.
Source: authors' tabulations based on data presented in the Frederick County,
Virginia, Land Use Planning and Development Annual Reports, 2005, 2008,
http://www.co.frederick.va.us/planning.

mid-twentieth century. The abundance of open land and the proximity of
the valley to major urban centers, especially Washington, DC, made the
area particularly susceptible to development pressures during the housing
boom of the late 1990s and 2000s. Development pressures were very intense
in the northern region of the valley, which is strategically located around
the intersection of I-81 and I-66 in northern Virginia, the latter connecting
directly to the DC metropolitan area.

The intensification of development pressures is reflected not only in
the population growth but also in new residential construction in Frederick
County since the late 1990s. Between 1970 and 2000, the county experienced
an average annual population growth of 2.9 percent (Frederick County,
Virginia 2008). From 2000 to 2006, this rate was 3.17 percent. Figure 8.8
shows the rapid upward trend in new residential housing permits that were
issued in Frederick County between 2000 and 2005 and the decline when
the housing market began to contract. Between 2000 and 2008, the county
issued an average of 845 new residential permits per year, with close to 40
percent of them in rural areas. Many of these "rural areas" were former
farms sold to developers. Along with new housing developments taking
land out of agricultural production, their proximity to farmland presents a
challenge to growers who use pesticides. Kearns stated, "You don't want to
spray the people next door [with pesticides]."

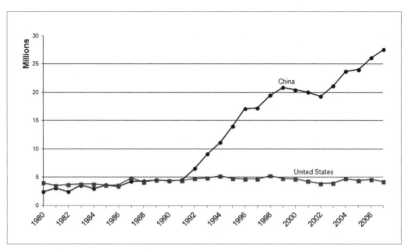

FIGURE 8.9

Chinese and US apple production, 1980–2007 (in millions of tons). Source: authors'
tabulations based on data from the Food and Agriculture Organization of the United
Nations' FAOSTAT–ProdSTAT module. The FAOSTAT–ProdSTAT module contains
detailed agricultural production, area/stock, and yield data from 1961,
http://faostat3.fao.org/home/index.html.

GLOBAL COMPETITION: CHINA ENTERS AND QUICKLY DOMINATES THE WORLD APPLE MARKET

Global commodity markets have also greatly affected apple production
in the Shenandoah Valley. Kearns confirmed that global competition, particularly with China, has played a major role in the local apple industry's
decline. In 2004, Kearns, Solenberger, and executives of the Winchester-
based National Fruit Product Company traveled to China to have a first-
hand look at what growers in the Shenandoah Valley, and elsewhere, were
up against.

The data presented in figure 8.9 show that between 1991 and 2007,
China went from almost no production to approximately 30 million tons of
apples a year. In 2007, China produced 27.5 million metric tons of apples,
about 60 percent of the world's supply and approximately seven times the
US production of about 4.2 metric tons that year. Although apple production in China is burgeoning, Kearns said, the rapid growth has not affected
the US fresh apple market. Markets in the United States are closed to
Chinese fresh apples due to the USDA's Animal and Plant Health Inspection
Service, which has generated a list of pathogens found in Chinese apples
but not present in US orchards.

China has, however, been exporting apple juice concentrate, which has affected many apple growers in the Winchester–Frederick County area who produce apples for processing. In May 2003, Phil Glaize, owner of Glaize Orchards, testified before Congress on this issue: "A flood of cheap apple juice concentrate imports driven by...China is significantly reducing prices that U.S. growers receive for their processing apples.... This has significantly harmed apple growers in Virginia" (Glaize 2003). Another business affected by this development is the National Fruit Product Company, an apple-processing plant located in Winchester across the street from the migrant worker camp. National Fruit primarily produces freshly pressed juice, which requires fresh apples, but it now also buys Chinese concentrate for blending purposes, which may, unfortunately, be undermining local producers. Until recently, the company had processing plants in Colorado, Michigan, and North Carolina, but it has downsized, including eliminating its growing operations. Kearns stressed the importance of the relationship that local growers have with National Fruit: "We need National Fruit, we can't survive without them" (Edwards 2001).

Jim Cranney, vice president of the U.S. Apple Association, indicated that the industry can do little about structural changes in the world economy, reinforcing the fact that labor demand in agriculture, including the demand for temporary foreign workers, is vulnerable to several forces that have little to do with whether workers are from Jamaica, Mexico, or Virginia. Cranney traced a number of developments since the late 1980s that have strained the industry. The expansion of the US apple supply in the late 1980s and early 1990s, when a thriving apple market and high prices induced growers to plant more trees, placed considerable stress on the US apple market. So, too, has the importation of Chinese apple juice concentrate (Edwards 2001).

Not everyone agrees that China is to blame for low US apple juice prices. Agricultural economist Des O'Rourke, the publisher of the *World Apple Report*, thinks that China gets too much blame, arguing, "Countries such as Chile, Argentina, and Poland can match the Chinese price most of the time" (Eddy 2008). Increased fuel costs have also impacted the price of apple juice concentrate. In 2007, the price of Chinese apple juice concentrate reached an all-time high of $2,000 per ton. Just a few years earlier, the price had hovered around $500 per ton (ibid.). Nevertheless, Chinese apple juice exports are displacing shipments from traditional global suppliers.

GLOBAL COMPETITION AND TEMPORARY WORKERS IN SHENANDOAH APPLES

The introduction of Chinese and other foreign apple juice concentrate to the world market has significantly altered apple production and processing practices in the United States, mostly to the detriment of US producers and processors. Understanding the consequences of Chinese apples for the US market, the U.S. Apple Association, based in Washington, DC, has lobbied to keep the United States' doors closed to Chinese fresh apples. However, the agricultural economist O'Rourke does not believe that such a trade barrier will last forever: "It's just a matter of time, there's no question. After all, they've been selling them in Canada for five or six years with no problems" (Eddy 2008). Glaize, who is a board member of the U.S. Apple Association, said, "We understand that we can't export our apples to China and then tell them they can't export their apples here" (Tompkins 2007). The different paths taken by local growers to adapt to increased competition from China will dictate the nature of the demand for foreign temporary workers in the apple industry. Many growers have already responded with marketing and technological solutions; as long as they remain in business, demand for foreign-born apple workers will continue.

Although many growers are abandoning apple production altogether and others are diversifying into other crops, there are a couple of orchardists who are still holding on, but they are changing the target markets for their apples by focusing less on processing apples. For instance, John Marker and his wife, Carolyn Marker, remarked that "their swath of trees, grass, and dirt—about 1,000 acres—represents more than just a livelihood" and they were "not about to let this birthright disappear before the sixth and recently born seventh generation can take over" (Martel 2004:5). However, they knew that they needed another source of income to survive the sagging apple market. Thus, in 2000, the couple started a farm market on their property to sell fruits, vegetables, jams, and baked goods. This market has enabled them to survive. Marker said, "We made the decision that we want to stay here on the farm, and that was one of the decisions that led to us building this Farm Market seven years ago" (Tompkins 2007).

Glaize has taken a different approach. He focuses on exploiting the competitive advantages of Shenandoah Valley apples—the area's high-quality soil yields a superior product (Tompkins 2007). His high-quality apples sell to Virginia and Pennsylvania supermarket chains (Tompkins 2007). Today, producing for local consumption is a new market and may underpin continued demand, especially in light of increased consumer interest in eating local foods. He also exports his crop to several countries in Central and South America and to India. Glaize indicated that this has enabled him to stay in business, but this approach is risky because there are so many factors that can affect his crop (Tompkins 2007). Still, like taking advantage of the local foods movement, the focus on quality production is a response to rising consumer interest in high-quality (even if higher-priced) foods (Pollan 2001).

Kearns said that Fruit Hill has not altered its business significantly to meet the competition from China because the sheer size of its orchards has kept the company in business. Fruit Hill Orchards, comprising 2,800 acres in West Virginia's Berkeley and Jefferson Counties and in Virginia's Frederick and Shenandoah Counties, is one of the top ten orchards by acreage nationally. Kearns said that the company is able to stay in business: "[Because] we are large and have a lot of land." Fruit Hill has rental houses on its land, some of which are occupied by employees. It has also invested in a warehouse and has a part interest in "cold storage." She said, "We want to stay in agriculture. We can swap land [if it is land in the path of development] and move farther out." The company has also put in more peaches and no apples for a few years. There is a trend toward "niche agriculture," she said. Kearns mentioned that she would like to partner with someone in some niche market because she does not have the time to do this on her own: "We're maxed out in management. There are only four of us, but we could partner with someone" (interview, 2004).

All of the major growers in the area have taken advantage of the Shenandoah Valley's superb natural growing conditions as a way to stave off the increased competition from China. The conditions have allowed growers to plant higher-density orchards, which have compensated for dwindling acreage (Tompkins 2007). Marker explained that "older orchards put 40 trees to an acre, utilizing larger apple trees that took eight to 10 years to come into bearing and up to 18 to reach full production. Now, orchard owners are planting 300 to 500 dwarf or semi-dwarf trees per acre. These smaller trees bear apples within three years and come into full production in six." Marker said that the payoff is a quicker return on your money and remarked, "[We have] found over the years that there's not near as many acres here in Frederick County now as there was of apples, but our production is still fairly close to the same" (ibid.).

The data from the Frederick County Fruit Growers Association, of which Marker is a member, confirm this observation. Figure 8.10 shows that the association's members had approximately half the number of acres dedicated to apple trees in 2008 than they did in 1988. But despite losing

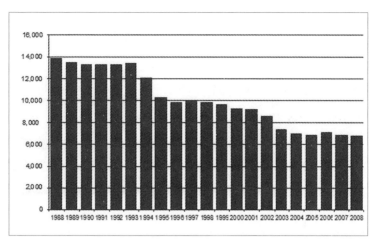

FIGURE 8.10

Acres of apple trees of the Frederick County Fruit Growers Association, 1988–2008.
Source: data provided to authors by Carol Burke, executive secretary of the Frederick
County Fruit Growers Association, 2009.

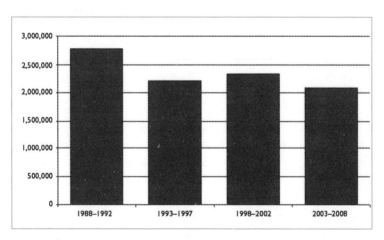

FIGURE 8.11

Average number of bushels of apples harvested by the Frederick County Fruit Growers
Association, 1988–2008. Source: data provided to authors by Carol Burke,
executive secretary of the Frederick County Fruit Growers Association, 2009.

half of the apple tree acreage, as figure 8.11 shows, production fell by only about 25 percent over the same period of time. The higher-density planting of apple trees has allowed fruit growers to get a higher yield of harvested apples per fruit picker. Figure 8.12 shows the increased yield. Between 1988

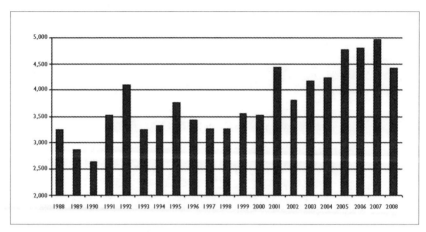

FIGURE 8.12

Bushels of apples per harvest worker: Frederick County Fruit Growers Association, 1988–
2008. Source: data provided to authors by Carol Burke, executive secretary of the Frederick
County Fruit Growers Association, 2009.

and 1992, the average harvest worker picked 3,273 bushels of apples during the picking season. By 2003–2008, this average had jumped to 4,557
bushels. This addition of 1,284 bushels per worker represents a 39 percent
increase over the two-decade span. Clearly, increased productivity has
meant a decline in numbers of apple workers.

But despite the production-per-worker improvements and the quicker
return garnered by planting higher-density orchards, the cost of apple
production in the Shenandoah Valley remains higher than in China.
Glaize said, "It's not really a level playing field" because China has certain
inherent advantages over US growers. As is the case with other industries,
China has access to cheaper labor than is available in the United States,
and Chinese growers do not have to meet the stringent safety standards set
forth in USDA growing regulations (Tompkins 2007). So the Jamaicans in
the Shenandoah apple industry are, to some degree, in competition with
Chinese workers.

Glaize, Marker, and Kearns all stressed the importance of access to
affordable labor as the key to remaining competitive. Glaize, who sits
on the board of the lobbying group the U.S. Apple Association, stated,
"[Immigration reform] is at the forefront of everything we're doing right
now, given the fact that whatever we do to produce our crop, if we can't pick
it, it's all for naught" (Tompkins 2007). He explained that this is why the
U.S. Apple Association's focus is almost entirely on getting the AgJOBS act

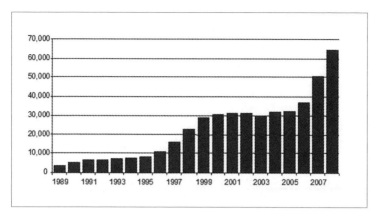

FIGURE 8.13

*H-2A visas issued, fiscal years 1989–2008. Source: Authors' tabulations of data
provided by the US Department of State.*

passed (Martin, chapter 2, this volume), which would streamline the process for approving and hiring foreign temporary labor and allow undocumented agricultural workers currently in the United States to regularize
their status to work in agriculture. Marker and Kearns stressed that reform
is necessary because "it has become more difficult" in the twenty-first century to get people on time to the Shenandoah Valley for the picking season.
Even though the number of H-2A visas issued has increased steadily in the
twenty-first century (figure 8.13), growers in the Shenandoah Valley feel
that they are not able to get the workers they need when they need them.
Glaize observed, "I know that we lost apples to the ground last year because
we were chronically [10 percent short on pickers, and] we weren't the only
grower that experienced that" (Tompkins 2007). Referring to the harvest,
Kearns said, "It's an issue of timeliness."

Worker availability at the needed time is crucial, but according to
Kearns, "the price of labor is the biggest kicker." She said that the prohibitive cost of the H-2A program is what kept some growers from participating in it. She commented that when the National Fruit Company had
its own orchards for processing apples, it "didn't use the H-2A program
because it is too expensive." She was referring to the program's certification process, which involves a US employer convincing the Department of
Labor, on a job-by-job basis, that there are insufficient US workers to fill job
vacancies and that employment of foreign-born workers will not adversely
affect the wages and working conditions of US workers performing similar

Table 8.2

H-2A Average Hourly Rates in Leading Apple States (by Employer Applicant)

	2006	2007	2008
Washington	$9.03	$9.77	$9.94
New York	$9.16	$9.50	$9.50
Michigan	$9.18	$9.65	$9.70
California	$8.93	$9.20	$9.72
Pennsylvania	$8.48	$9.00	$9.34
Virginia	$8.24	$8.51	$9.02

Source: US Department of Labor, Foreign Labor Certification Data Center, http://www.flcdatacenter.com

jobs. Certification keeps the border gate closed to guestworkers until the government certifies that US workers are not and will not be available at a stipulated wage and housing package to fill the vacant jobs. Despite the concerns Virginia growers have about the cost of H-2A labor, table 8.2 shows that Virginia apple growers pay a lower average hourly wage to their H-2A workers than growers in other states.

Once employers pass the certification process, they need to pay the transportation costs to get the workers to the site. According to Burke, "it costs the growers approximately $600 per worker to bring a worker from Jamaica by air and bus. They pay $350 to $400 to bring Mexicans by bus from Monterrey and Laredo." The camp in Winchester is also supported by fees paid by members of the growers association. As the apple industry diminishes and the number of members decreases, the cost per grower of running the labor camp rises. Despite these conditions, the growers association greatly benefits from having an existing housing facility available for the workers each fall, and housing has been a key factor contributing to the decades-long relationship with Caribbean labor.

Providing government-approved housing for seasonal workers is a significant startup cost that precludes taking advantage of the H-2A program for the first time. For instance, as shown in table 8.3, compared with their counterparts in Virginia, Washington apple growers use fewer H-2A worker per bushel, despite their higher apple production. In Washington, the startup costs for using the H-2A program have been prohibitive—especially for smaller growers. Doug Pauly, an operations manager at the Northern Fruit Company in Wenatchee, Washington, said that boosting labor crews by using the federal H-2A program is not a viable solution for a small

TABLE 8.3

H-2A Fruit Workers Certified in Leading Apple States (by Employer Applicant)

Year		Applications (#)	Workers (#)	Applications (%)	Workers (%)
2006	Washington	6	629	1.5	6.2
	New York	120	2,178	29.4	21.6
	Michigan	3	18	0.7	0.2
	California	23	1,154	5.6	11.5
	Pennsylvania	3	19	0.7	0.2
	Virginia	18	607	4.4	6.0
	All other states	236	5,461	57.7	54.3
	Total	409	10,066	100.0	100.0
2007	Washington	22	1,697	4.6	12.3
	New York	128	2,533	26.6	18.3
	Michigan	1	6	0.2	0
	California	13	1,406	2.7	10.2
	Pennsylvania	3	15	0.6	0.1
	Virginia	17	735	3.5	5.3
	All other states	298	7,440	61.8	53.8
	Total	482	13,832	100.0	100.0
2008	Washington	27	2,070	6.8	18.5
	New York	125	2,312	31.5	20.6
	Michigan	2	12	0.5	0.1
	California	18	1,672	4.5	14.9
	Pennsylvania	4	31	1.0	0.3
	Virginia	21	774	5.3	6.9
	All other states	200	4,339	50.4	38.7
	Totals	397	11,210	100.0	100.0

Source: US Department of Labor, Foreign Labor Certification Data Center, http://www
.flcdatacenter.com

company like Northern because "just the idea of putting in new hous-ing, and all the hassle and fine print that comes with that is daunting" (Robinson 2007). Despite these "daunting" hassles, the data on H-2A cer-tifications show that in 2008, Washington and California both began to increase their use of H-2A workers in the fruit industry.

None of the interviewees in the Shenandoah Valley mentioned mecha-nization as a serious alternative to manual labor or as a way to increase productivity by reducing labor costs. However, industry researchers and leaders indicate that the US fruit industry will remain economically viable only if it delivers premium-quality fruit while reducing production and processing costs. The most viable way to achieve lower costs is to use technology to "minimize low-skill tasks, enhance worker productivity and safety, reduce production and handling costs, decrease seasonality of labor, and maximize fruit quality delivered to the consumer" (Washington State University 2009).

Research and development in the apple industry has focused on partially mechanizing pruning, thinning, and picking; experimenting with orchard design; and growing apples on shorter trees to facilitate harvesting speed. Short-term efforts have involved "evaluating mechanized platforms which position workers to improve labor efficiency" (Robinson 2007). However, these have not been successful in harvesting because greater bruising occurs with mechanized bin fillers than with the current bucket-and-ladder system. "Longer term efforts are aimed at developing machine vision and robotic machines to mechanize pruning and harvest" (ibid.). Although advances in computer technology have made this more of a reality, current research suggests that a robotic harvester is still years away from mass production, due to the "complexity of identifying the fruit location, detaching the fruit without bruising, and transporting the fruit to the bin without bruising" (ibid.). Thus, in the near term, it seems certain that the remaining apple growers in the Shenandoah Valley will continue the more than half-century tradition of relying on foreign-born temporary workers to pick their apple crop.

CONCLUSION

This case is well in line with the argument that H-2As provide employers with control over their labor (Hahamovitch, chapter 1, this volume; Martin, chapter 2, this volume). Nevertheless, even if not a workers' paradise, the Shenandoah apple industry appears to be a case of enlightened management. This employer choice, to a large degree, was made possible by the historical institutionalization of the Jamaican H-2As decades ago in the Frederick County Fruit Growers Association's migrant camp. Like the nearby POW camp in Frederick, Maryland, the Shenandoah camp was sold at auction after the end of World War II. Unlike the Frederick camp and others, which were soon dismantled, the Shenandoah camp provided the basis for the ongoing use of temporary Jamaican workers for the apple industry (Cotter 2012).

This preference for H-2As over domestic workers is similar to that found in other settings where they provide greater reliability and predictability. In addition to the H-2A contract, the migrant camp underpins that reliability, through the camp's construction of space, fences, and transportation. This has been institutionalized over time in the historic separation of domestic and foreign workers and the program's reliance on returning, willing Jamaican workers. Our observation that the camp is adequate was echoed in an earlier evaluation of Virginia camps, three-quarters of which had serious violations, but the report found that in "Winchester, migrant housing was not a problem for most growers as a number of them belong to the Frederick County Fruit Growers' Association, which has a cooperative migrant labor camp" (Commonwealth of Virginia 1989).

Our reference to enlightened management refers to the fact that the camp provides an adequate living environment, compared with other camps in the area, and the continuation of the H-2A program at the camp was an express strategy of the leadership of the growers association (interviews, 2004). What is more, the growers saw the program as a means of procuring dependable labor in a manner that is time tested, but they also expressed concern that these workers, from a developing country, be able to continue to rely on these jobs—even though that commitment was driven by their dedication to their inherited apple businesses. This balance of employer dependence without excessive labor control has also been found in a family-controlled apple farm in upstate New York, so perhaps rare, "benevolent" employers are at the core of such practices (Griffith 2006). Recall that H-2A camps with similar histories in the area have been replaced by a migrant and unauthorized workforce for whom working and living conditions are not good (Schrecongost 1999).

Apple growers are pressured to reduce prices by both local and global forces. The impacts of local development, problematic in the Shenandoah Valley, can be seen in other industries, such as seafood (Griffith and Contreras, chapter 6, this volume). As in other industries, many apple growers have turned to lower-cost unauthorized workers. At the same time, there is the globalization of fruit production and lower-cost labor markets abroad. The Chinese have access to cheaper labor, as do the Poles and Chileans, so the Shenandoah Valley's imported Jamaican workforce is in competition with labor around the world. The growers, as we have seen, have pursued alternatives in this competition (see Trupo, Alwang, and Lamie n.d.). They have increased their productivity by planting new groves, they are emphasizing the high quality of their eating apples, and they are taking advantage of the growing demand for local produce and farmers markets. Not only does globalization undermine US employers' competitive position, but it also can lead to creative strategies and technologies. The H-2A workers, on the other hand, have precious few alternatives and therefore remain a "reliable" source of labor. Their future employment and working conditions are intrinsically bound up with how employers deal with the forces of globalization and with US policies. Perhaps the value of the current case study is that it demonstrates some promise for creative employers to optimize their survival through enlightened management.

Notes

1. H-2A workers are not US residents and can be employed only when a shortage of labor exists in a particular region. They are prohibited by law from taking other employment within the United States upon completion of their contracts. Employers must pay for H-2A workers' transportation to and from their countries of origin, must provide them with housing, and must pay them a guaranteed wage.

2. Migrant farmworkers are US residents who travel from their permanent residence to their place of work and are unable to return home the same day. Commonly, migrant farmworkers are residents of Florida or Texas who travel to Virginia for summer employment. Seasonal farmworkers are non-immigrant workers. They return to their permanent place of residence the same day. They earn the majority of their annual income from farmwork, and they work at least twenty-five days per year, but not year-round, for the same employer. Many seasonal farmworkers are former migrant farmworkers who have settled in the community and continue to perform farmwork.

3. Micah Bump interview with Tupper Dorsey, September 13, 2004.

4. Burke noted that in the 1950s and '60s and in part of the '70s, Bahamians also worked at the camp. However, their records referred to them only as from the "West Indies," and since the 1970s, most of the Caribbean H-2 workers have been Jamaican.

5. The overall Jamaican-born population in the United States grew by 9.6 percent, or 58,740 people, between 2000 and 2007. Much of this growth occurred in Florida, where the Jamaican-born population grew by 19.5 percent, or 34,134 people.

9

A History of Activism

The Organizational Work of Juvencio Rocha Peralta

**Juvencio Rocha Peralta, David Griffith,
and Ricardo Contreras**

This account is based on a life history interview with Juvencio Rocha
Peralta, a community activist and founder of the Asociación de Mexicanos
en Carolina del Norte (AMEXCAN), an organization widely known across
North Carolina and in many other parts of the United States, Mexico, and
Central America for its work promoting culture, leadership, and education
on behalf of Mexicans, Central Americans, and other Latino immigrants
in North Carolina and beyond. Although he was never a guestworker,
Juvencio has been an instrumental participant in the settlement of Latinos
in rural North Carolina—a state that has witnessed some of the heaviest
use of guestworkers through the H-2A and H-2B visa programs. Juvencio
has facilitated general Latino access to local institutions that have enabled
guestworkers like Anaceli (Griffith and Contreras, chapter 6, this volume)
to find work outside their guestworker contract and to take steps toward
permanent residence. Juvencio's story is further relevant to the fate of managed migrants in North Carolina in that he has been a tireless advocate for
improved Latino access to health, education, employment, and other services and has done outreach work directed toward migrant laborers in agriculture and fisheries. His work raising North Carolina citizens' awareness
of the contributions that Latinos have made to the state has been essential to the continued use of guestworkers in agriculture, fisheries, forestry,
tourism, and other economic sectors there.

In general, Juvencio's account highlights a critical dimension of the guestworker experience: the work of Latino community formation and advocacy among long-time Latino residents in rural North Carolina. Juvencio's experience as an immigrant and, eventually, as an immigrant advocate in North Carolina began in the tobacco, sweet potato, and cucumber harvests—where he worked alongside guestworkers and other migrant farmworkers. This and his subsequent work in the poultry industry and his experiences as a business student and an outreach worker for a community college were all instrumental in his perceptions of and responses to injustices facing immigrant Latinos, guestworkers, undocumented workers, and settled legal immigrants alike. His understanding of the depths of discrimination and his efforts to promote appreciation for and understanding of Latino culture have built bridges between immigrant and native communities in North Carolina and inspired many young Latinos to leadership and advocacy.

THE GROWTH OF AWARENESS AND AMEXCAN

At the age of sixteen, in 1978, Juvencio Rocha Peralta migrated from Mexico to North Carolina to live with one of his uncles from Veracruz and work in tobacco, sweet potatoes, cucumbers, and other harvests. It was not his first migration. Two years earlier, as the crisis facing Mexican small peasant farmers deepened, displacing many *ejiditarios*, or tillers of community lands, Juvencio was forced from his father's fields into the internal migrant circuit in Mexico, working in agricultural harvests. Although he was only fourteen at the time, he had already been working for eight years. Raised in a poor family in a poor community, of his childhood he said, "I had to work very early, at six years of age.... I grew up very quickly. At fourteen, I left the village to look for work in other places." The village was Agua Dulce, Papantla—a small ejido outside the larger city of Poza Rica in Mexico's oil-rich Veracruz, where Cortés landed and burned his ships in 1501. Juvencio's father, a farmer, worked his own lands but was, like so many others, devastated by the deterioration of the Mexican agricultural economy in the mid-1970s, which forced his children to look for work elsewhere. Juvencio's mother, a powerful influence in his life, kept the family "always united," teaching her children the importance of kindness and awareness of their roots. "She influenced me fundamentally," he said.

Juvencio's arrival in North Carolina in 1978 preceded the vast settlement of Latinos in the state, which began in the mid- to late 1980s. At that time, most of the Mexicans and other Latinos working in North Carolina agriculture migrated through the state. Juvencio was fortunate, he said, finding work on local farms where he could stay through the year. "My father grew tobacco," he said, which made Juvencio particularly well suited to tending a crop that many tobacco farmers claim takes thirteen months a year to grow. He was fortunate, too, that he had a network of uncles who had migrated to North Carolina during the 1970s and who, in the rural county of Duplin in southeastern North Carolina, could find work not only on farms but also in the expansive poultry industry of the region. "At first, it was a little difficult. I remember that I was almost crying all the time for two years—apart from my family, apart from my people. There weren't many Latinos there. It was difficult."

But this difficulty strengthened him. Perhaps because there were not as many Latinos in North Carolina at that time, he had to learn English and was fortunate to meet North Americans who were willing to teach him. He also seized the opportunity to learn more about agriculture in the region, improving his chances of employment without having to migrate from state to state. Still, work in agriculture was limited and seasonal, plagued with periods of idleness between harvests or due to weather—exactly the sorts of problems that lead to high turnover. The occupational alternative open to him was in the construction industry, but this, too, posed a challenge. "To be able to leave agriculture to work in construction was difficult because at that time, we [Latinos] were few in number and, for example in North Carolina, the only opportunities were in agricultural labor, construction, or services." He added, "For me, it was a matter of professional development, to make the transition from working in agriculture to working in construction." In so doing, Juvencio's experience would foreshadow that of many of his fellow Latinos over the coming years, including Latino guest-workers: entering the state's labor market through agriculture but transitioning, in time, to construction. When Juvencio made that transition, however, in the early 1980s, still a teenager, the Latino population in the state and in construction was still thin. Of this experience he says, "For me, to be able to move into construction presented the opportunity to have my own car, my own apartment, and these kinds of things." More important, the move made him more responsible, giving him, in his words, "the power to go to school." Of this fundamental transition, the stepping-stone to school, he says, "For me, what I looked for was what I wanted."

With this transition, he moved again, from Duplin County to the larger metropolitan Pitt County, where he began attending Pitt Community College. This transition, too, foreshadowed the experiences of many Latinos: settling out of agricultural labor, moving from a rural to an urban area. Juvencio's experience reflects that of managed migrants who settle out of seasonal occupations in agriculture and fisheries—occupations based in rural areas with few opportunities, particularly for the undocumented. Most guestworkers we have encountered who have broken with their contracts in North Carolina, have settled in larger metropolitan areas, where opportunities to establish businesses or find work are greater.

Shortly after making the move from the country to the city, Juvencio had an accident on the job and was incapacitated for a year. Although he was undocumented at the time, the company he worked for agreed to compensate him for the injury, providing his salary for a year. During this time, he worked toward legalization, with the company helping him to take advantage of what he called the "Reagan amnesty" to receive temporary work authorization at the age of twenty-one, in 1983. This ended a five-year period in the United States without documents, freeing him to begin working toward an education and laying the organizational groundwork for his future activism. He began studying at Pitt Community College, taking business courses and working toward permanent legal status, familiarizing himself with the local and federal government bureaucracies. It is a testament to Juvencio's developing political skills that just two months after initiating this process, with assistance from a local congressman's office, he secured a green card.[1]

With his documentation, he began working for the Pitt County Department of Transportation four days a week as a driver while still attending Pitt Community College. Over the next two years, he secured his GED and a degree in business; he continued working for the DOT for six years, initially transporting cargo and later establishing weight limits for buses carrying agricultural labor. When he worked in the county through the 1980s, as the transition from African American to Latino labor was taking place in the surrounding fields, what he witnessed prepared him for leadership. "For many years," he said, "I had been experiencing many incidents that, from my point of view, were injustices. For example, when I worked in construction, most of the workers were white North American, a few blacks, so they called me names. They called me 'wetback,' they called me 'nigger,' they called me those types of things. After this, I began investigating the meanings of these terms, asking, why do such injustices exist in this society?"

Already Juvencio had learned that injustices were not confined to the construction industry but permeated even some branches of society that, supposedly, work against prejudice and discrimination. Always having a desire to help children, Juvencio once approached the Greenville Boys and Girls Club. "I went to apply for a volunteer position with them, but they didn't accept me." Although they said that it was because he did not have a Social Security number and did not seem very strong, he believed that the real reason was that he was Latino. Determined to use his free time volunteering, he applied to help out with the Greenville Special Olympics, working with children with special needs, and there he was accepted. While working with the children, he perceived injustices directed toward them too. Ironically, these injustices often came from within their own families. "How could their own parents," he asked, "discriminate against their own children?"

Working against injustice, he dove into the programs designed for them, including football, softball, and other sports. Eventually assigned six children to work with especially, he taught them all they could learn and became an activist for them. Dedicating himself to volunteerism thus prepared him for later social activism, giving him the opportunity to advocate on behalf of the children in the program. As is common among leaders, Juvencio's early community service with the children snowballed into other opportunities, including the Pitt County AIDS Service Organization (PiCASO), whose members invited Juvencio to join them in their fight against sexually transmitted diseases in the county. In his work with PiCASO, he was witness to more discrimination and racism. "Most of the people were African Americans," he said, "or people with few resources— most were also women—and they experienced racism and discrimination. Some couldn't access services, food, housing—all those kinds of things." Hearing about and witnessing this, he became newly inspired to advocate on behalf of the dispossessed, the discriminated against, the downtrodden, asking, "How could this exist in a country that [is] so rich?"

Working primarily in education and health, he began at this time to direct his efforts toward helping the growing Latino population in the state. Two of his first projects were to organize soccer tournaments on weekends and to locate ESL classes for farmworkers. "During this time," he said, "the majority of Latinos in eastern North Carolina were still working in agriculture, so along with the soccer, we organized classes in English and instruction in how to become legal." By this time, in the late 1990s, the principal guestworker programs in the state—in agriculture, fisheries, and forestry—were well established, having grown in concert with the growth and elaboration of the Latino population across rural North Carolina. At this time, too, in response to growing public attention—good and bad— directed toward the Latino population, he began meeting with other Latino leaders and others interested in the welfare of the state's Latinos, traveling to the state capital, Raleigh, three to four times per month. However, this was costly in terms of expenses for gas, meals, and such, and at the same time, he continued to perceive that Latinos in the eastern part of the state had many, many needs. "There arrived a moment at which I had to concentrate my work, my services, in this region [eastern North Carolina]."

"In 1999, we had Hurricane Floyd," he remembered, "one of the largest natural disasters in the history of North Carolina." Following the hurricane was an even more devastating flood. "The county wasn't prepared for its people, and they didn't understand our community. At this moment, we felt as if, with regard to human rights, we were an afterthought, of the second class. The county wanted to provide for North Americans first and only later provide for immigrants. In Pitt County, there was a county commissioner who said, 'Let's give the leftovers to the immigrants, and let's take care of our people first.'" In response to sentiments like this, Juvencio and three others founded the North Carolina Latino Coalition. Out of this effort came several activities—marches, meetings with politicians, discussions—that collectively led the governor's office and the state to consider the needs of this new population, including establishing a Latino advisory group for the governor.

"This was a critical moment for the state of North Carolina," he said, especially with the recognition by the Mexican government of North Carolina as a new destination for its people. There began to spread through the community a general recognition that North Carolina did not have Latino leaders. There was thus a need to develop Latino leadership in the state—leadership capable of responding to the growing Latino population. "At that time, we began to organize as a group of Mexicans," he said, adding that they were bolstered by the 2000 Census figures, which showed that North Carolina was home to one of the fastest-growing Latino populations in the United States. "We called the Mexican government, and, in part because the Census figures had reported a great increase in the Mexican population, the government listened to us and established a consulate here in the state to see to the needs of Mexicans."

"At this time, we began to formalize the organization that today is known as AMEXCAN." This was possible because of the good relations the organizers had with the Mexican consulate, giving them a basis from which they could link Mexicans in North Carolina with the consulate's suite of services. "We began working on more and more of a transnational project," he said, "between the two different governments—Mexico and the United States. This was also a time of a great change in the Mexican government. The ruling party switched from PRI [Institutional Revolutionary Party] to PAN [National Action Party], and the new president, [Vicente] Fox, formed the Institute of Mexicans Abroad." This moved the issue of Mexican-US migration to the forefront of government policy, thus creating an opportunity for Juvencio and leaders like him to represent the Mexicans living in North Carolina. "I was the first Mexican in North Carolina to occupy the position—the *cargo*—of advisor [to the Mexican government]."[2]

Juvencio held this position for three years, considering it a great opportunity to provide valuable services to the local Mexican population while representing the government of Vicente Fox. "It opened up for me a national experience," he said, "but also a transnational experience of seeing the problems of both sides." This was a period (2000–2005) of great expansion of the Mexican population in North Carolina and its diversification into many different economic sectors, with many opportunities. "In this stage [of the development of the Mexican population], several actors came forward with their own ideas about the [Latino] community, some of whom were more for themselves and some of whom were more for the community." Most of the Latino leadership, however, was concentrated in Raleigh, whereas many of the Latino workers and virtually all of the state's guestworkers were distributed over the rural landscape, many in the eastern part of the state (Griffith and Contreras, chapter 6, this volume). "There were only two of us in the east," he said, "me in Pitt County and another in Halifax. The rest were in the Triangle [the central region where Durham, Raleigh, and Chapel Hill are located]. I began working at the grassroots. Several initiatives came from this, for example, courses in leadership in Duplin, in Wilmington, groups that became part of AMEXCAN. Another group was formed in Newton Grove."

This geographical expansion across the eastern part of the state entailed organizational changes as well. Organizers began working particularly hard in Duplin County—one of the largest in terms of proportion of Latinos in the population. "AMEXCAN moved to Duplin and established partnerships with the county, with the college [Mount Olive College], and with the cooperative extension service, and then we began to work. Inside the organization, we began to work concrete projects—for example, in agriculture [for farmworkers], in the Festival de la Raza. We began promoting leadership, education, and other very concrete projects. We worked across this region—in Duplin, Wayne, Sampson." Along with the poultry industry, this region was pickling cucumber country, where H-2A workers harvested much of the cucumber crop and eventually became members of the Farm Labor Organizing Committee (FLOC). As the FLOC organized H-2A workers, Juvencio and other AMEXCAN leaders achieved the momentum that enabled them to make the most of their own personal resources and past experiences, marshaling what social scientists refer to as social capital to work in behalf of the community. At that time, AMEXCAN consisted of nine core individuals, each with experience in a different kind of organization—*el pueblo*, community development centers, nonprofits— and from these experiences, they acquired leadership skills that were valuable at the grassroots level.

Struggling with insufficient resources, they formed partnerships with various entities in the county. "We went to the county commissioners and presented the idea of the organization and appealed for their help." By this time, they had already formed good relations with some county commissioners and had agreements with the county. "The director of county community development invited us to his office, and we told [him] we were working without pay, without anything." They continued working for Latinos in the county even when they received no help, in particular, working to promote Latino culture. There were Latinos from many countries— Salvadorans, Guatemalans, Hondurans—in the county at that time, and Juvencio and the others promoted the idea of "We are equals." They began holding a wide range of cultural events—dances, music, and so forth. "This was a region very rich in Latino culture," he said, "but we were different."

Because Juvencio's activism during this time was entirely voluntary, he had to work full-time to support himself and to pay the expenses associated with AMEXCAN that could not be covered with other resources. He worked for Waccamaw Turkeys (a pseudonym), a turkey-processing factory in the county and, like other poultry-processing plants, a principal employer of Latino immigrants. As part of the company's human resources staff, he worked in its housing program. During this time, like companies hiring guestworkers, Waccamaw Turkeys provided housing, primarily for its Latino immigrant workers, and Juvencio's position involved assigning housing to new recruits, which enabled a close association with workers' daily lives and stimulated him to focus on the needs of Latinos in the plant and elsewhere. "They had 3,000 employees," he said, "and 75 percent of these employees were Latino." The business solicited his ideas about how to initiate projects that would reflect the interests of the Latino community. One day, the president of the company came to him and said that, as the largest company in the county and a main employer of Latinos, they needed a spokesperson for the Latino community. Juvencio became that spokesperson. "They gave me the responsibility and the flexibility to assist the company with the task of developing various activities for the Latino community." This fit into his principal responsibility of assigning housing to workers and enhanced their living situations with different social activities.

Although the company drew heavily on the Latino population, it did not import guestworkers from Mexico. Nevertheless, both providing housing to workers and organizing social activities for them constitute common methods by which companies control labor, replicating managed migration–like conditions, and Juvencio's involvement in this raised his awareness about the efforts of companies to manage the lives of the Latinos they hired. And Waccamaw Turkeys did import workers from afar, bringing in Puerto Ricans (who are US citizens) to work in the plant. Juvencio knew of the H-2 program, but the only labor-importing scheme that he became familiar with was the Puerto Rican program. "But they discontinued this program because it wasn't working. At the same time, there were famous labor contractors who went from state to state recruiting people to work on farms. Waccamaw Turkeys contracted with these labor contractors to recruit seasonal workers to the business during periods of peak labor demand. They would get people from Mexico, from other states, from all over."

Duplin County also had large numbers of H-2A workers who worked on the farms near the turkey plant and who stayed when their contracts ended (see Griffith and Contreras, chapter 6, this volume). "They arrived but didn't return," he said. "They arrived [to work in agriculture] in Greene County. They arrived to work in crab. But many didn't return." Instead, they would come to the turkey-processing plant to work. "They found that they could earn a little more [at the plant] than they could on contract, and during this time, the plant wasn't too restrictive in relation to documentation. Many workers with H-2 visas worked with Social Security numbers and could easily get drivers' licenses. They made the transition to establishing themselves with this status and went to work in these types of businesses, including pickle companies and all the businesses that process turkeys, chickens, hogs."

To Juvencio, those with H-2 visas seemed to have higher levels of education than the rest of the Latino immigrants. They also seemed to come mostly from states in Mexico that had industrial zones—or, at least, neighborhood industrial zones—or they came from the southern or central states.[3] Just like other Latino immigrants in the state, however, the H-2 workers who left their employers, breaking the terms of their contracts, or stayed in the state after their work was finished took advantage of the activities of AMEXCAN. "Some among them integrated themselves into AMEXCAN," he said, "working to promote various activities. They became part of the efforts to develop culture, leadership, and other activities, volunteering [with AMEXCAN]. They were able to be effective on account of their [higher] levels of education."

Juvencio worked for eleven years for Waccamaw Turkeys, from 1995 to 2006, using his position to improve relations between Latino workers and the company and to expand his base of leadership and his knowledge of the Latino population in eastern North Carolina. Duplin was an ideal place to begin his work with the community and to begin AMEXCAN, which he had co-founded in 2000. As noted earlier, Duplin had a higher proportion of Latinos (over 15 percent) than many other counties in North Carolina, due to the number of farms and farm-related processing industries that hired them. It was there that AMEXCAN began establishing partnerships. "We collaborated with community colleges, with Mount Olive College [on the border of Wayne and Duplin Counties], and with many county departments—social services, health, and other departments that provided services to the community. We signed agreements or established collaborations with them. Mount Olive College helped us a great deal, and Mt. Olive Pickle helped also," Juvencio said, indicating that he sought out resources from diverse sources—public, private, business, industry, health care, education—but not all equally. "Our strongest collaborations were with community colleges," he said, "with Lenoir Community College, with Pitt Community College, with Brunswick Community College—most in the field of education. They gave us space for the Latino community."

During this time, he said, the economy of the state was booming—much of the growth due to the labor of Latinos—and the availability of resources was much greater than it would become later, after the economic crisis beginning in 2008. Many resources came from the state and from the private sector, providing opportunities for Latinos, including Juvencio himself. In 2006, he left Waccamaw Turkeys to work with Lenoir Community College specifically to provide outreach to the Latino community across the eastern portion of the state. "My role at Lenoir Community College was to coordinate programs for Latinos, establishing occupational programs, careers, and everything associated with a basic education," he said. "This was a great opportunity for them to develop [better relations with the Latino community], but then the economic crisis hit and they eliminated the programs for Latinos."

Of his time at Lenoir Community College, however, he said that he was able to learn how to negotiate two different agendas, because he was working both for the college and for AMEXCAN—in a paid position for the former and a voluntary position for the latter. He also learned more about the varied needs of the community and the ways in which various agencies addressed those needs. "At times, the agencies had their own agendas and we had our own agendas," he said, "and we were more…more revolutionary and so could run against the interests of the public agencies." He had the sense that he was more outspoken than the college wanted him to be at times, which he felt posed a threat to the administration. With the elimination of the programs for Latinos came the elimination of Juvencio's job. Following his dismissal, he was able, he said, "to view Lenoir County panoramically. Lenoir is a county controlled by the [white] majority, and the minority has no power. It is kept very much in check. They don't want to initiate progress in the areas where the minority lives. They resist change, progress." When he began to be interviewed about immigration, he felt that he encountered a great deal of negative reaction because many in Lenoir County were against immigration. He would say, "We need immigration reform. We need to legalize those without documents.... Many didn't like this." Many in the county were further threatened, he believed, because he was saying these things as part of his work with a community college, exposing many of the county's youth to his ideas. Those in the college administration began saying, "He's not part of our team. He's not part of us." Juvencio explained, "We were progressive leaders, human rights leaders, and they weren't going to tolerate what was going to go against them."

Reflecting on this time, he recalls now that it was very stressful for him, that he was denying himself and his family, his health and his person, in his position working for the county. Yet, as noted earlier, his relations were not restricted to Lenoir Community College. Through his relations with Pitt Community College, he was able to secure space for AMEXCAN's offices and the various training sessions the group would provide over the next few years. These included educating the local Latino population about diabetes and developing local community health workers. It was in the offices at Pitt Community College that Juvencio established himself after leaving Lenoir Community College, and with the transition, he began working at a different level, organizing meetings and working more in the transnational community, most importantly, with NALAC (National Association of Latino Arts and Culture).

Now, looking toward the future, Juvencio envisions securing resources for AMEXCAN that will allow him to work for the organization full-time. Part of his new direction involves increasing his transnational work, traveling to Agua Dulce and other locations in Mexico, as well as continuing his work in eastern North Carolina. "NALAC is an organization with a transnational vision," he said. "It is helping me position myself in both places, both sides of the border, and from this has come the opportunity to participate in meetings and trips. During this time, I also had the opportunity to work with East Carolina University on a transnational project—on something concrete—looking at the total panorama of migration from Mexico. Now, NALAC is looking at remittances from the United States to Mexico and from the United States to El Salvador." This project is part of an attempt to begin changing the government of Mexico. "We have to change the federal government, the state governments, and the local governments," he said. As part of this, he is trying to initiate projects between sending and receiving communities, again emphasizing his growing interest in the transnational community and building on, "models from Michoacán, Zacatecas, and Guanajuato." He wishes to apply some of these models to Veracruz, which does not have a history of transnational projects.

Although there are challenges in terms of working in the local settings of eastern North Carolina and working in transnational settings, Juvencio believes that political changes are possible in both settings. Through transnational connections, local communities can achieve the strength they need to effect political change. Currently, in Juvencio's mind, they have not achieved this. But they will. "I believe that in the next five years," he said, "I'll be working with progressive groups at the state level, at the national level, and also at the transnational level." Through this work, he hopes to open spaces for immigrants to advocate for their own human rights.

* * *

Being neither an H-2 worker himself nor directly involved with managed migration, Juvencio nevertheless has expanded the social environment for Latinos in North Carolina in ways that have benefited the state's H-2 workers. In line with the transnationalism of managed migration, he has also enhanced the region's international and national connections with Latinos living in Mexico, Central America, and other parts of the United States. His activism has been instrumental in facilitating the settlement of the Latino community and its ability to resist methods of keeping Latinos confined to specific occupations and neighborhoods, opening educational opportunities and paving pathways toward improved health, justice, and social legitimacy. The evolution of his activism, from its roots in personal experience to its later manifestations in partnerships with community colleges and county offices, may have been a slow process, but the gradual accumulation of support has certainly served to increase the awareness of average North Carolinians regarding the myriad problems facing the state's Latino community, including those in the state working on temporary contracts. In like fashion, the FLOC in North Carolina and the UFCW and AWA Canada have been able to piece together support for union efforts that have organized guestworkers through a combination of direct advocacy and partnerships, along with more subtle, public support.

Such developments are critical to the health of managed migration programs particularly now, as states withdraw from worker protections and companies attempt ever more comprehensive methods of controlling labor. Advocacy and partnering have not yet come to all managed migration contexts. The isolation of many managed migrants often means that awareness of their presence evolves slowly, coming to the public's attention only after an egregious incident of abuse or other exceptional developments make the headlines (Griffith, chapter 10, this volume). The advocacy of Juvencio Rocha Peralta has been a quiet, effective testament that awareness need not emerge sensationally, through tragic headlines, but can gradually bring ever-denser networks of aware and caring people to the defense of human rights.

Notes

1. This is remarkable, given this particular congressman's record. A Republican, he is known for switching positions based on popular opinion instead of principle and, in the early twenty-first century, would never help an undocumented immigrant acquire a green card, because the North Carolina Republican establishment is generally opposed to immigration.

2. The use of the word "cargo" is significant as a reference to the civil-religious hierarchy known as the "cargo system" in Mexico, in which community members serve their communities for periods of a year or longer, often at great personal expense yet receiving the benefits of recognition and prestige (Cancian 1969).

3. Juvencio's impressions here conform to some observations others have made concerning the sending regions for workers with H-2 visas and those who enter Canada with temporary visas. Women in the crab industry with H-2B visas, for example, come from either Sinaloa—a zone of industry and industrial agriculture—or from the southern state of Tabasco, whereas Oaxaca, Michoacán, and central Mexico are major suppliers of H-2A workers.

10

Conclusion

Promises of Guestworker Programs

David Griffith

As an alternative to human trafficking and undocumented international labor migration, managed migration holds the promise of constructing labor forces to perform needed, designated economic services across North America without the bondage, exploitation, risk, emotional duress, and physical violence that plague the use of migrant labor beyond the reach of the law. Labor rights advocates, government officials, and industry representatives cling to the hope that they will be able to craft legislation (e.g., AgJOBS; see Martin, chapter 2, this volume) that, if passed, would supposedly protect guestworkers' rights and allow a path toward citizenship while ensuring the continued flexibility and reliability that make guestworkers highly desired in the first place. Whether or not such legislation passes, managed migration has risen high enough on the labor relations landscape that labor unions, human rights organizations, grassroots social movements, and local and regional institutions like worker centers and faith-based organizations have taken an interest in the welfare of guestworkers (Griffith 2009b; Preibisch, chapter 4, this volume; Southern Poverty Law Center 2007). The visibility of guestworkers and managed migration programs, in the short term at least, is likely to increase, especially if guestworker abuse, long a sordid by-product of managed migration, continues, is brought to light, and touches the hearts of the public.

It is next to inevitable that the infamous abuses of guestworkers will continue as long as managed migration is structured as it has been in both the United States and Canada, with workers tied to individual employers, extreme economic and power disparities between sending and receiving states and between employers and workers, weak state oversight, and a lack of equivalent employment promises in sending countries. I use the word "promises" because it is often the mere promise of employment and high wages that stimulates guestworkers to enter managed migration streams. Although the majority of employers honor these promises—some more fully and with more respect for workers' rights than others—the way managed migration is structured allows unscrupulous employers and labor contractors to break those promises rather easily, often with severe consequences for guestworkers yet few repercussions for the employers or labor contractors.

Examples of abuses are legion. In 2007, thirty Thai workers recruited to work on North Carolina farms ended up in New Orleans for the Hurricane Katrina cleanup, living in condemned housing and receiving nothing after paying over $10,000 to labor recruiters to acquire H-2 visas (Greenhouse 2007). To come up with this cash, many had taken out usurious loans in their home countries, using their farms as collateral. One of the most egregious cases of abuse involved two workers at the state fair in Syracuse, New York, who had been recruited in Zacatecas, Mexico, with the promise of making more than $10 per hour only to find themselves serving food to fairgoers for sixteen to eighteen hours a day with few breaks for food or water, sleeping in beds infested with bedbugs, and receiving no pay because their employer claimed that they were in training. Only when one of the workers fell sick from the bedbugs did the case come to the public's attention via hospital staff and a local workers center in upstate New York.

I emphasize that these are not rare or isolated cases. Managed migration programs across North America and the world are shot through with various kinds of abuse—most of it tied to wage theft, labor control, or the maintenance of workplace power disparities. The Florida sugar industry, Martin has noted, had a policy of annually firing a handful of workers just to enforce productivity standards. Through such measures, workers come to compete with one another to reach ever-higher productivity levels and ever more compliant postures vis-à-vis wages and working conditions. Paralleling the competition between workers at job sites has been an increasing competition among sending countries for placements in Canada and the United States, between women and men, and between labor recruiters and labor-contracting firms hoping to emerge as the next large supplier of cheap, compliant, global labor. Similar competition between the United States and Canada or between employers for scarce guestworkers—which could result in raising wages or improving working conditions and programs overall—has not occurred. With employers ever more able to access workers from around the world, the supply of compliant guestworkers seems endless. Caps on numbers of guestworkers allowed into North American labor markets limit the supply, of course, but this has not translated into upward pressures on wages, instead, merely limiting employer participation.

Based on the volume contributors' experience with and knowledge of guestworker programs, the temptation to consider designing a humane and equitable guestworker program is great. Yet, the chapters show that the design of guestworker programs rarely dictates how employers utilize them or how workers experience them. Particularly vulnerable to manipulation are the labor-recruiting practices in sending countries, where state oversight is largely nonexistent (especially in the absence of bilateral agreements) and high levels of economic deprivation encourage various insidious methods of accessing highly desirable jobs abroad. Even where state officials have attempted to protect workers, as with Oliver Stanley in Jamaica (Hahamovitch, chapter 1, this volume), the power of states and private interests opposed to specific worker protections has been far too great. With the growing privatization of guestworker programs and practices, we can expect not only more abuse but also more frequent transfer of costs of recruitment, housing, and transportation from employers and recruiters to workers.

Yet, at the core of the problems guestworker programs face is the bald fact that, compared with economic opportunities in most guestworkers' home countries, jobs in the United States and Canada are highly desired, pay well, finance improvements in their quality of life and that of their families, and offer the slender hope that subsequent generations may not have to seek onerous work that separates them from their families. But the potential for income from overseas employment to improve job prospects in sending countries has yet to be realized. On the contrary, most sending countries' economic opportunities have been narrowing rather than widening, with the recent economic crises and longer-term economic adjustments in the form of neoliberal market reforms and the withdrawal of government support from basic commodities like coffee, corn, and beans.

As long as vast disparities between pay in guestworkers' sending and receiving countries exist, communities that currently supply guestworkers probably will continue to serve as reproductive centers and reservoirs for guestworkers in the future, however much the occasional individual family may improve its standard of living, quality of life, and social class position. Since many of the guestworker-supplying regions are centers of peasant agriculture, artisanal fisheries, and services supporting industrial agriculture, tourism, and manufacturing, the possibility of narrowing the wage gap between sending and receiving regions remains slim, dependent on sustained sending-state intervention or nongovernmental organizations' support in the form of fair trade initiatives, microfinancing that has not become usurious, or international assistance in tapping into new markets or sources of income.

The principal players in North American managed migration have been agribusiness and the food industry. This comes as little surprise to those who have studied agriculture, food processing, and other rural industries that have long utilized workers from disadvantaged backgrounds. Along with pioneering managed migration, such employers and their representatives were among the first to develop complex recruiting systems and subcontracting arrangements. These labor market innovations fragmented labor forces while shifting immigrants and other disadvantaged workers into farm and food production tasks in ways that enabled wage theft and transferred the costs of mobilizing and reproducing workers from capital to labor. Instead of being challenged effectively by human rights organizations or the labor union movement and beaten back to the underbelly of the economy, food industry labor practices have moved from the fringes to the center of neoliberal capitalist economies. In this volume, Austin (chapter 5) gives us the most explicit case of this, with the shipbuilding and petroleum industries embracing managed migration with gusto before underwriting their own decertification. Smart's discussion (chapter 3) also indicates the spread of managed migration and similar labor practices out of agriculture and into the general Canadian economy.

With each instance of the expansion of managed migration, the potential exists for increased program visibility, community interest in managed migrants, and activism leading to greater state oversight. Most promising are those efforts that organize workers transnationally (Griffith 2009b; Preibisch, chapter 4, this volume), drawing community members and organizations in sending and receiving regions into the problems facing guestworkers and the challenges of addressing those problems without losing the economic opportunity that managed migration can provide. Employers' access to labor from many parts of the globe is noted in the chapters as one of the key barriers to activism, yet the contributors also show that even where new workers from new sending regions have entered managed migration streams, as in the US Gulf shipbuilding industry, labor activism drawing on the local community has emerged.

Managed migrants' relationships with their receiving communities are neither simple nor linear, in some cases, leading to settled enclaves of former guestworkers and, in others, keeping them confined to specific places and times in a given year. In the Shenandoah Valley, Jamaican guestworkers seem not to have established ethnic enclaves even after migrating to the region for more than half a century, whereas nearby, in North Carolina, the settlement of guestworkers in Latino enclaves has occurred in many places through many social paths. By contrast, Aaraon Díaz Mendiburo (2010) argues, Jamaican guestworkers can take advantage of vibrant Caribbean enclaves in Toronto, yet Latino workers in Canada have no such similar opportunities. Local histories, moreover, influence how guestworkers are received and treated and what changes they experience in their work abroad. Hahamovitch (2011; chapter 1, this volume) quite convincingly describes the differences between the Jim Crow South, Michigan, New Jersey—where, even with a British accent, a black man was still discriminated against—and midwestern locations like Wisconsin, where Jamaicans were treated very nearly as celebrities. Her work demonstrates, too, the importance of political-economic pressures in sending states in sculpting specific dimensions of guestworker programs, as when Jamaican politicians, hungry for patronage, pressured colonial secretary Stanley to lift his ban on sending Jamaican guestworkers to the South. Further, when in the South, workers experienced hardships that influenced the US guestworker program overall, shifting the treatment of workers from the hands of enlightened farmers in the North to "gun-toting labor bosses" in the South (Hahamovitch, chapter 1, this volume).

Both the varied local responses to guestworkers and the guestworkers' interactions with the communities where they work, call into question the racial, ethnic, and gender stereotypes that often develop around managed migrants and that lead employers to develop preferences for one type of worker over another. Preibisch (chapter 4, this volume) describes the growing interest in female Guatemalans among Leamington greenhouse owners, supposedly based on beliefs that women care for the plants more gently, but also because they appear to be highly pliant and compliant. Perhaps in line with these views, Hughes's chapter 7 suggests that, among these same Guatemalan women, their experiences abroad have not, by and large, shaken their conformity to traditional gender roles in their home communities, in part because those roles provide them with a sense of accomplishment and identity within their families. Canadian women's gender roles seem, for the most part, irrelevant to women's lives in Guatemala. Such behaviors are not, however, due entirely to gender. The Mexican crab workers that Griffith and Contreras describe (chapter 6, this volume) have utilized the power of their increased earnings to challenge traditional gender relations in their home communities and families. Indeed, some have taken the opportunity of their work abroad to leave abusive relationships for good or to establish households independent of parents, sons, and other figures in their lives who might attempt to enforce patriarchal authority (Contreras and Griffith 2012). Many of the women from Mexico have had many more years of experience in guestworker programs than have the Guatemalan women Hughes discusses (chapter 7, this volume); it may be that more and more Guatemalan women will challenge traditional gender roles at home as their years abroad stretch from one or two seasons to their entire working lives. In any case, these findings call into question gender and other stereotypes that employers and labor contractors develop to justify the differential hiring and treatment of guestworkers. Yet, it is highly likely that these stereotypes will not only continue but also proliferate as employers access an increasing array of workers from different cultural, national, and gender backgrounds.

Several developments in the North American economy in the twenty-first century predispose US and Canadian employers to pressure for expanded guestworker programs that do not bind them to bilateral agreements, allowing them to shop the world for workers. The fragmentation of commodity production sites, the further processing and value-adding of food and other products, the deskilling of tasks, the erosion of labor union power, the greater frequency of and more lasting devastation from natural disasters, and the increasing use of labor contracting across economic sectors have all precipitated the importing of immigrants, legally and illegally, from an ever-greater number of countries abroad. With growing employer interest in guestworker programs, the challenge facing labor advocates is how to ensure that these neither contribute to the insecurity of domestic workers nor create a permanent underclass of temporary foreign workers isolated from labor advocacy and held captive in dead-end jobs. Encouraging developments in union activity in Canada and the United States—transnational organizing, for example, or the increasing push to raise public awareness of guestworker abuse—and the interests of non-union human rights organizations in the welfare of guestworkers and low-wage workers generally constitute innovative ways of circumventing the power emanating from capital and parts of the state. However, these activities remain scattered geographically and are often no match for the blacklisting, threats, conservative legislative initiatives, Supreme Court rulings, and physical violence that continue to threaten workers' power. Nevertheless, the negative practices that have dogged guestworker programs from the beginning are forcing labor advocates into new social spaces and geographies. Just as employment practices pioneered by guestworker programs have moved from the fringes to the core of neoliberal capitalism, perhaps the strategies that labor unions and advocates are developing to ensure social justice and human rights for guestworkers will move from the margins of our political economies to the center of our humanity.

Two weeks prior to writing this, Ricardo Contreras, Brianna Castro, and I visited a handful of guestworkers in northern Virginia, in a region on the western shores of the Chesapeake Bay known as the Northern Neck. The designation "neck" refers to its geographic location between two rivers —the Potomac and the Rappahannock—which, combined with the sheltered harbors lining the bay, has endowed the region with a surplus of waterfront land and sheltered water access for its fishing and seafood-processing industries and, increasingly, for real estate development. It is rural and sparsely populated, with little economic opportunity and the typical widening gap between rich and poor created by the gentrification of this area, with its beautiful waterfront vistas in close proximity to Washington, DC. The wealthy of Washington and elsewhere have built summer and vacation homes there, contributing little to the local economy beyond what they spend on real estate. Yet, it is a pleasant place to be, and the weekend that Ricardo and Brianna and I visited, there was exceptional autumn weather, in the low seventies and sunny. The guestworkers we visited seemed happy, having worked only until three that Saturday and being free to meet with us most of the day on Sunday.

We were visiting to determine how much the guestworkers' living and working conditions in Virginia resembled those of North Carolina, but also to deepen our relationships with the families of Sinaloa, Mexico, where the women and men are from. While we were there, I was struck by the importance of telephones in the workers' lives—land lines, local cell phones, international cell phones, and phones capable of taking and storing photographs. One woman had three cell phones and access to the house's land line. One of her cell phones was for local calls to the plant and to other workers living nearby, another for calls across the United States to her children living in California and other parts of Virginia, and a third for international calls to her family in Sinaloa. She stored different images on each of her phones—family members, pets, scenic views. She was, it is true, exceptional. Most of the others had a single cell phone and access to the house's land line, using the land line for local and US calling and the cell phones for calls to Mexico.

Of the dozen workers we met that weekend, only one was a man. He was young, short, and pleasant, also from Sinaloa, a Jehovah's Witness who worshiped in a small town several miles from their house. The four women he lived with referred to him with the diminutive suffix, calling him Manolito (Little Manolo, Little Manuel).[1] He, too, had a cell phone, which he used not only to call home but also to take photographs inside the crab plant where everyone worked. He shared these photos with us. Ricardo downloaded them onto his computer and, using an image-editing program, annotated them with the help of Manolito and the women, viewing the interior of the packing plant and learning more about the different stations of production. It was, in a sense, a privileged view. Rarely in our work are we privy to the private, hidden spaces inside factories. Unless we take jobs in packing plants, which is often not possible because guestworkers have taken all the available work, most of our views of such places are monitored closely by tour guides.

Manolito had taken the photos to show his family and friends in Mexico what it was like where he was working. He had not anticipated sharing them with us, with people studying the industry, its labor supply, and its involvement with guestworkers, but he happily shared them nevertheless. My immediate thought on seeing the images was methodological. I thought that we could begin asking workers to provide such images as part of our efforts to understand in more depth the work process, conditions in the plants, and other aspects of production, perhaps using them as visual cues for interviews. Later, my thoughts turned political. I wondered about the potential role of cell phones in the continuing, if occasionally silent, struggle for an improved balance of power between workers and employers, between sending and receiving countries, and between labor and capital. Not we, I thought, but workers could use the tools of cell phones to document incidents of injustice, collect evidence of abuse, and initiate their own Arab Spring uprising—perhaps, in part, by taking photos and sharing images, each one worth a thousand of our words.

Note

1. Because Manolito was taking pictures inside the plant, perhaps without the owner's permission, we use a pseudonym to refer to him, although the women did refer to him with a diminutive of his real name.

Appendix

Chronologies and Selected Characteristics of
North American Guestworker Programs

David Griffith, Melanie Hamilton, Josephine Smart,
and Pablo Valdes Villareal

CANADA

1966 The Seasonal Agricultural Worker Program begins in partnership with
Jamaica, which becomes the first country to send migrant workers under
SAWP. Trinidad and Tobago and Barbados follow in 1967, and Mexico
begins in 1974. The Organisation of Eastern Caribbean States comes on
board in 1976. Bilateral agreements have been signed with each of the
participant countries.

The program is run by Human Resources and Skills Development Canada
and Service Canada but is administered by two private, nonprofit agencies:
Foreign Agricultural Resource Management Services (FARMS, Ontario)
and Fondation des Entreprises en Recrutement de la Main-D'œuvre
Agricole Étrangère (FERME, Quebec).

SAWP participants are not eligible for permanent resident status but can
be sponsored through an employer in the Provincial Nominee Program.
In 2004, fewer than 3 percent were women, but this has been increasing.

1973 The Live-In Caregiver Program begins. Work permits are issued for up
to three years three months; caregivers are required to live in their
employers' home and must apply for a new permit if they change employers. Caregivers may apply for permanent resident status after working for
twenty-four months within a thirty-six-month period. In 2005, only 5 percent of workers in this program were men.

1994   The New Democratic Party government enacts the Agricultural Labour Relations Act (ALRA), which grants collective bargaining rights to agricultural workers in Ontario for the first time.

Mid-1990s UFCW Canada begins outreach to seasonal agricultural workers in Ontario.

1995   UFCW Canada, Local 1993, is certified to represent approximately 200 workers at Highline Mushrooms in Leamington, Ontario.

1995   The Progressive Conservative government repeals the ALRA, denying workers at Highline farms and elsewhere the chance to bargain for a collective agreement.

1995   UFCW Canada takes the Ontario government to court to challenge the exclusion of agricultural workers under the Agricultural Labour Relations Act as a violation of workers' rights under the Charter of Rights and Freedoms in *Dunmore v. Ontario.*

2001   The Supreme Court of Canada rules in favor of UFCW Canada in *Dunmore v. Ontario* and gives the Ontario government eighteen months to comply with the ruling and include agricultural workers in the Ontario Labour Relations Act.

2002   The Temporary Foreign Worker Program is established. Both highly skilled and lower-skilled workers are admitted under this program.

The highly skilled are eligible for permanent resident status; their spouses can work in Canada under the Canadian Experience Program. Lower-skilled workers are not eligible to apply for permanent resident status; their spouses are not eligible for the Canadian Experience Program. This visa is good for two years but can be extended. After four years, the worker must return home.

Employers are required to cover recruitment and return airfare costs, provide suitable housing and medical coverage (until the worker becomes eligible for provincial coverage), and sign an employment contract prior to the worker's arrival in Canada.

2002   Ontario establishes the Agricultural Employees Protection Act (AEPA), which grants the freedom to "associate," but not collectively bargain.

2010   In Abbotsford, British Columbia, migrant farmworkers at Sidhu & Sons Nursery, members of UFCW Canada, Local 1518, successfully negotiate a collective agreement with their employer.

2010   UFCW Canada joins over 1,500 activists from around the world in Quito, Ecuador, to participate in the 4th World Social Forum on Migration.

2011   Filipino migrant workers file a $10 million lawsuit against Denny's in British Columbia, charging that the company did not live up to the employment contract the workers signed before they arrived.

2011 UFCW Canada and the Agriculture Workers Alliance applaud and defend the findings of two new reports that make a direct link between worker illness and the shortcomings of Canada's migrant worker system.

2011 UFCW Canada, Local 832, provides office space at its training centre in Winnipeg for Migrante Manitoba to build on its work for migrant workers.

2011 Charges allege that the Mexican consulate in Vancouver blacklisted unionized Mexican migrant workers in British Columbia; a leaked document is deposited with the British Columbia Labour Board.

2011 Migrant workers from Mexico and the Caribbean gather in British Columbia and Ontario to rally for human rights and to "celebrate" another Father's Day apart from their families.

2012 UFCW Canada leads a training session in Tapachula, Mexico, at the first Global Workers Defenders Network Forum.

UNITED STATES

1864 The Contract Labor Law allows recruiting of foreign labor.

1882 The Chinese Exclusion Act suspends Chinese immigration for ten years, bars Chinese from citizenship, and places a head tax on other immigrants. It also bars convicts, lunatics, and those unable to care for themselves from entering the United States.

1885 The Contract Labor Law makes it unlawful to import unskilled aliens from overseas as laborers, though the regulations do not pertain to those crossing land borders. The contracting of temporary workers is banned.

1917 The Immigration Act exempts guestworkers from the literacy requirement mandatory for immigrants.

1942–1964 The Emergency Farm Labor Supply Program, or bracero program, results from a formal agreement with the government of Mexico; several clauses favor guestworkers' labor rights. More than 4.5 million Mexicans participate over the years, despite reports of mistreatment.

1943–1947 The British West Indies Temporary Alien Labor Program attracts 66,000 workers principally in the fruit, vegetable, and sugarcane sectors. In 1952, it is absorbed by the Immigration and Nationality Act under the H-2 guestworker program.

1951 Public Law 78 requires employers who desire braceros to pay a fee in order to cover the costs of the program. Mexican workers are restricted to areas where domestic workers are not available, they should not adversely affect the wages and working conditions of domestic workers, and efforts should first be made to attract domestic workers. Employers who hire illegal entrants are excluded from the program.

1952   The Immigration and Nationality Act makes colonial subjects ineligible for quotas. The H-2 temporary visa establishes a large but generally unused guestworker program.

1964   Pressure from unions, churches, and human rights organizations leads to the cancellation of the bracero program, due to the abuses committed.

1965   Amendments to the Immigration and Nationality Act limit the number of Mexican immigrant admissions to 66,000 a year; the H-2 temporary worker program is continued.

1986   The Immigration Reform and Control Act requires employers to verify the immigration status of workers hired. The H-2 temporary worker program is split between H-2A (agriculture) and H-2B (non-agricultural) workers and now includes Mexican workers in both sectors.

1990   The Immigration Act prioritizes qualified admissions over those focused on family reunification. The percentage of immigrants annually accepted increases from 10 to 21 percent (from 54,000 to 140,000 per year). For non-qualified immigrants, the number is only 10,000.

2004   President George Bush proposes a temporary worker program, with strict duration (three years, with the possibility of renewing it once) and rules, and at the same time, the US government denies immigrant visas and strengthens border security.

References

Adams, Matthew
2006   Hybridizing Habitus and Reflexivity: Towards an Understanding of Contemporary Identity? Sociology 40(3):511–528.

Adler Hellman, Judith
2008   The World of Mexican Migrants: The Rock and the Hard Place. New York: New Press.

Agriculture Workers Alliance
2010   Migrant Workers Protest at Canada's Embassy in Guatemala. Agriculture Workers Alliance E-news, UFCW Canada. http://www.awa-ata.ca.

Alberta Federation of Labour
2003   Migrant Agricultural Workers in Alberta. Forty-Third Alberta Federation of Labour Constitutional Convention, May 1–4, Edmonton, Canada.

Ansley, Fran, and Jon Shefner
2009   Global Connections and Local Receptions: New Latino Immigration to the Southeastern United States. Knoxville: University of Tennessee Press.

Archer, Margaret
2007   Making Our Way through the World: Human Reflexivity and Social Mobility. Cambridge: Cambridge University Press.

Asis, Maruja
2005   International Migration and the Prospects for Gender Equality. *In* International Migration and the Millennium Development Goals. Pp. 113–125. Marrakech, Morocco: UNFPA.

Auditor General of Canada
2009   Report of the Auditor General of Canada to the House of Commons. Ottawa, ON: Office of the Auditor General of Canada.

REFERENCES

Austal

2009   Austal Opens New Shipbuilding Facility. Media release, November 10.
        http://www.austal.com/index.cfm?objectid=DB6E3AA2-65BF-EBC1
        -29AF6515E737B65A.

Austin, Diane E.

2006   Coastal Exploitation, Land Loss, and Hurricanes: A Recipe for Disaster.
        American Anthropologist 108(4):671–691.

2007   History of the Offshore Oil and Gas Industry in Southern Louisiana, vol.
        3: Morgan City's History in the Era of Oil and Gas: Perspectives of Those
        Who Were There. Washington, DC: US Department of the Interior, Minerals
        Management Service, Gulf of Mexico OCS Region.

Austin, Diane E., Bob Carniker, Tom McGulre, Joseph Pratt, Tyler Priest,
and Allan G. Pulsipher

2002   Social and Economic Impacts of OCS Activities on Individuals and
        Families, vol. 1: Papers on the Evolving Offshore Industry MMS 2002-022.
        Washington, DC: US Department of the Interior, Minerals Management
        Service, Gulf of Mexico OCS Region.

Austin, Diane E., and Rebecca Crosthwait

2013   Labor in the Gulf of Mexico Fabrication and Shipbuilding Industry. *In*
        Gulf Coast Communities and the Fabrication and Shipbuilding Industry:
        A Comparative Community Study, vol. 3: Technical Papers. Tom McGuire,
        Diane Austin, and Drexel Woodson, eds. Pp. 17–60. Washington, DC: US
        Department of the Interior, Bureau of Ocean Energy Management, Gulf of
        Mexico OCS Region.

Austin, Diane E., and Thomas R. McGuire, eds.

2002   Social and Economic Impacts of OCS Activities on Individuals and Families,
        vol. 2: Case Studies of Morgan City and New Iberia, Louisiana. MMS 2002-
        023. Washington, DC: US Department of the Interior, Minerals Management
        Service, Gulf of Mexico OCS Region.

Austin, Diane E., and Drexel Woodson, eds.

2012   Gulf Coast Communities and the Fabrication and Shipbuilding Industry:
        A Comparative Community Study, vol. 2: Community Profiles. Washington,
        DC: US Department of the Interior, Bureau of Ocean Energy Management,
        Gulf of Mexico OCS Region.

Bachrach Ehlers, Tracy

1991   Debunking Marianismo: Economic Vulnerability and Survival Strategies
        among Guatemalan Wives. Ethnology 30(1):1–16.

Baker, Margaret

2008   Indian Workers Unite against Signal. Company statement, March 7. Flier in
        possession of Diane Austin.

Barker, Kathleen, and Kathleen Christensen

1998   Contingent Work: American Employment Relations in Transition. Ithaca,
        NY: Cornell University Press.

Basok, Tanya

2000 Migration of Mexican Seasonal Farm Workers to Canada and Development: Obstacles to Productive Investment. International Migration Review 34(1):79–97.

2002 Tortillas and Tomatoes: Transmigrant Mexican Harvesters in Canada. Montreal: McGill-Queen's University Press.

Bernhard, Judith, Patricia Landolt, and Luin Goldring

2005 Transnational, Multi-local Motherhood: Experiences of Separation and Reunification among Latin American Families in Canada. Toronto: York University.

Beyerstein, Lindsay, and Larisa Alexandrovna

2007 Human Trafficking of Indian Guest Workers Alleged in Mississippi Shipyard: Contractor Defends 290-Man Camp. Raw Story, April 13. http://rawstory .com/news/2007/Human_trafficking_of_Indian_guest_workers_0412.html.

Binford, L.

2004 Contract Labor in Canada and the United States: A Critical Appreciation of Tanya Basok's Tortillas and Tomatoes: Transmigrant Mexican Harvesters in Canada. Canadian Journal of Latin American and Caribbean Studies 29:289–308.

Blanshard, Paul

1947 Democracy and Empire in the Caribbean. New York: Macmillan.

Boehm, Deborah A.

2008 "Now I Am a Man and a Woman!" Gendered Moves and Migrations in a Transnational Mexican Community. Latin American Perspectives 35(1):16–30.

Bolland, O. Nigel

1995 On the March: Labour Rebellions in the British Caribbean, 1934–39. Kingston, Jamaica: Ian Randle.

Bourdieu, Pierre

1990 The Logic of Practice. Cambridge: Polity.

Bourdieu, Pierre, and Loïc Wacquant, eds.

1992 An Invitation to Reflexive Sociology. Chicago: University of Chicago Press.

Brem, Maxwell

2006 Migrant Workers in Canada: A Review of the Seasonal Agricultural Workers Program. Policy brief, edited by L. Ross. Ottawa, ON: North-South Institute.

Briggs, Vernon

1992 Mass Immigration and the National Interest. Armonk, NY: M. E. Sharpe.

2004 Guestworker Programs: Lessons from the Past and Warnings for the Future. Center for Immigration Studies. http://www.cis.org/articles/2004/back304 .html.

References

Bump, Micah N.
2005   From Temporary Picking to Permanent Plucking: Hispanic Newcomers, Integration, and Change in the Shenandoah Valley. *In* Beyond the Gateway: Immigrants in a Changing America. E. M. Goździak and S. F. Martin, eds. Pp. 137–176. Lanham, MD: Lexington.

Burawoy, M.
1976   The Functions and Reproduction of Migrant Labor: Comparative Material from Southern Africa and the United States. American Journal of Sociology 81:1050–1087.

1985   The Politics of Production. London: Verso.

Bureau of Export Administration
2001   National Security Assessment of the U.S. Shipbuilding and Repair Industry. 003-009-00719-4. May. Washington, DC: US Department of Commerce.

Bush, M., and Canadian Farmworkers Union
1995   Zindabad! A History of the Canadian Farmworkers Union. Canadian Farmworkers Union. http://www.vcn.cn.ca/cfu.

Buzzanell, Peter, Ron Lord, and Nathaniel Brown
1992   The Florida Sugar Industry: Its Evolution and Prospects. USDA Sugar and Sweetener Report (June):11–34.

Calavita, Kitty
1992   Inside the State: The Bracero Program, Illegal Immigrants and the INS. New York: Routledge.

Canadian Civil Liberties Association
N.d.   Bill C-49 Punishes Asylum Seekers. http://ccla.org/our-work/focus-areas /bill-c-49.

Cancian, Frank
1969   Economics and Prestige in a Maya Village. Berkeley: University of California Press.

Carey, David, Jr.
2006   Engendering Mayan History: Kaqchikel Women as Agents and Conduits of the Past. New York: Routledge.

Carter, J.
2007   Thai Workers Disappointed with Canada's Welcome. Ontario Farmer, November 21.

Carter, Marion
2004   Gender and Community Context: An Analysis of Husbands and Household Authority in Rural Guatemala. Sociological Forum 19(4):633–652.

Castles, Stephen
2006   Guestworkers in Europe: A Resurrection? International Migration Review 40(4):741–766.

Castles, Stephen, and Mark J. Miller
1998   The Age of Migration: International Population Movements in the Modern World. 2nd edition. New York: Guilford.

CBS Business Network
2005   Gale Norton Holds a News Conference at the National Press Club on the Restoration of Offshore Energy Supplies Following Hurricanes Katrina and Rita. http://findarticles.com/p/news-articles/political-transcript-wire/mi_8167/is_20051004/gale-norton-holds-news-conference/ai_n50546669.

Chant, Sylvia, and Nikki Craske
2003   Gender in Latin America. New Brunswick, NJ: Rutgers University Press.

Chayanov, A. V.
1966   Theory of Peasant Economy. New York: Random House.

Chin, Christine B. N.
1986   In Service and Servitude: Foreign Female Domestic Workers and the Malaysian "Modernity" Project. New York: Columbia University Press.

Citizenship and Immigration Canada
2008   Facts and Figures: Immigration Overview, Permanent and Temporary Residents. Ottawa, ON: Government of Canada. http://www.cic.gc.ca/english/resources/statistics/menu-fact.asp.

2009a   Canada: Total Entries of Foreign Workers in the Low Skill Program by National Occupational Classification and Gender, 2007–2008. From RDM Facts and Figures 2008. Ottawa, ON: Citizenship and Immigration Canada.

2009b   Canada: Total Entries of Foreign Workers in the Seasonal Agricultural Workers Program by National Occupational Classification and Gender, 2007–2008. From RDM Facts and Figures 2008. Ottawa, ON: Citizenship and Immigration Canada.

2010a   Backgrounder: Improvements to the Live-in Caregiver Program. Ottawa, ON: Citizenship and Immigration Canada. http://www.cic.gc.ca/english/department/media/backgrounders/2010/2010-08-18.asp.

2010b   Backgrounder: Improvements to the Temporary Foreign Worker Program. Ottawa, ON: Citizenship and Immigration Canada. http://www.cic.gc.ca/english/department/media/backgrounders/2010/2010-08-18.asp.

2010c   Facts and Figures 2009: Immigration Overview: Permanent and Temporary Residents. Ottawa, ON: Minister of Public Works and Government Services Canada.

2011   Canada: Total Entries of Temporary Foreign Workers from Guatemala as Country of Citizenship by Sex and NOC Codes, 2003–2010. Ottawa, ON: Citizenship and Immigration Canada.

Coalition of Immokalee Workers
2008   CIW Media. http://www.ciw-online.org/media.html.

REFERENCES

Collins, Jane
1988   Transnational Labor Process and Gender Relations. Journal of Latin American Anthropology 1:178–199.

Commonwealth of Virginia
1989   The Commonwealth's Role in the Provision of Housing for Migrant Workers. General Assembly of Virginia, House Document no. 62. http://leg2.state.va .us/dls/h&sdocs.nsf/fc86c2b17a1cf388852570f9006f1299/be2c5508e58426a 785255fda0075c827/$FILE/HD62-1989.pdf.

Congressional Research Service
1980   Temporary Worker Programs: Background and Issues. Prepared for the Senate Committee on the Judiciary. February.

Contreras, Ricardo, and David Griffith
2012   Managing Migration, Managing Motherhood: The Moral Economy of Gendered Migration. International Migration 50(4):51–66.

Cotter, Amelia
2012   Stories from Camp Frederick: German World War II POWs in Frederick, Maryland. http://www.germanpulse.com/blog/2012/02/23/stories-from -camp-frederick-german-world-war-ii-pows-in-frederick-maryland-part-1.

Craig, Richard B.
1971   The Bracero Program: Interest Groups and Foreign Policy. Austin: University of Texas Press.

Crocker, Brad
2008   Congressman Wants Investigation of Workers' Charges. Mississippi Press, March 12. http://www.gulflive.com/news/mississippipress/index.ssf?/base /news/1205316925300060.

Crosthwait, Rebecca
2009   "I'm a Migrant?!" Mexican H-2B Workers' Perceptions of Industrial Work, Place, and Self. Paper presented at the Society for Applied Anthropology, March 19, Santa Fe, NM.

Daniel, Peter
1972   In the Shadow of Slavery: Debt Peonage in the South. Champaign: University of Illinois Press.

Darwin, John
1988   Britain and Decolonisation: The Retreat from Empire in the Post-War World. London: Macmillan.

Department of Labor
2006   Data Labor Certification Data Center Online Wage Library (maintained for the US Department of Labor). http://www.flcdatacenter.com/CaseH2B .aspx.

2007   Data Labor Certification Data Center Online Wage Library (maintained for the US Department of Labor). http://www.flcdatacenter.com/CaseH2B .aspx.

Díaz Mendiburo, Aaraon

2010   Matíces: Temporary Labor in Canada. DVD produced by Aaraon Díaz Mendiburo Studios, Quebec, Canada.

Dolin, B., and M. Young

2004   Canada's Immigration Program. Ottawa, ON: Library of Parliament, Fondation des Entreprises en Recrutement de la Main-D'œuvre Agricole Étrangère.

2011   Nombre de travailleurs étrangers qui ont eu recours à FERME de 1995 à 2008. Montreal, QC: Fondation des Entreprises en Recrutement de la Main-D'œuvre Agricole Étrangère. http://www.fermequebec.com/4-Realisations -et-temoignages.html#10.

Donato, Katharine M.

2004   Labor Migration and the Deepwater Oil Industry. MMS 2004-057. Washington, DC: US Department of the Interior, Minerals Management Service, Gulf of Mexico OCS Region.

Dooley, Channing R.

2001   The Training within Industry Report 1940–1945. Advances in Developing Human Resources 3(2):127–289.

Eddy, C. Vernon

2005   Winchester and Frederick County in War Time. War History Commission of Winchester and Frederick County. http://www.ls.net/~newriver/va/fredwwl .htm.

Eddy, David

2008   China Looms Large: While Juice Production Dips, the Introduction of Fresh Apples into the U.S. May Be Inevitable. American/Western Fruit Grower, February. http://www.growingproduce.com/americanfruitgrower/index .php?storyid=151.

Edwards, David

1961   Report on an Economic Study of Small Farming in Jamaica. Institute of Social and Economic Research, University of the West Indies. Glasgow: Glasgow University Press.

Edwards, Greg

2001   Uprooting Virginia's Apple Industry: Foreign Competition, Weather Causing Some Apple Growers to Get Out. Winchester Star, April 6.

Elgersma, Sandra

2007   Temporary Foreign Workers. Ottawa, ON: Parliamentary Information and Research Services of the Library of Parliament.

El Proceso

2011   Exigen al secretario del Trabajo explique "lista negra" de jornaleros en Canadá. August 10.

REFERENCES

Equal Employment Opportunity Commission (EEOC)
2011   EEOC Sues Marine Services Company for Labor Trafficking, Discrimination.
            Press release, April 20. http://www.eeoc.gov/eeoc/newsroom/release/4-20
            -11a.cfm.

Feuer, Carl Henry
1984   Better Must Come: Sugar and Jamaica in the 20th Century. Social and
            Economic Studies 33(4):22–34.

Field, Delbert
2010   Chief of Mission, IOM-Guatemala, April 26 interview.

Fischer, Edward, and Carol Hendrickson
2003   Tecpán, Guatemala: A Modern Maya Town in Global and Local Context.
            Boulder, CO: Westview.

Foreign Agricultural Resource Management Services
2011   How to Apply for NOC C&D (Low Skill Agriculture). Mississauga, ON:
            Foreign Agricultural Resource Management Services. http://www
            .farmsontario.ca/lowskill.php.

Frances, J., S. Barrientos, and B. Rogaly
2005   Temporary Workers in UK Agriculture and Horticulture: A Study of
            Employment Practices in the Agriculture and Horticulture Industries and
            Co-located Packhouse and Primary Food Processing Sectors. London:
            Department of Environment, Food and Rural Affairs.

Francis, Oliver James Claudius
1963   The People of Modern Jamaica. Kingston, Jamaica: Department of Statistics.

Franck, Anja, and Andrea Spehar
2010   Women's Labour Migration in the Context of Globalisation. Brussels: WIDE.

Frederick County, Virginia
2008   The 2008 Evaluation of the County's Rural Areas. http://www.co.frederick
            .va.us/planning/SpecialProjects/RA/RAstudy.aspx.

Friedland, W. H., A. E. Barton, and R. J. Thomas
1981   Manufacturing Green Gold: Capital, Labor, and Technology in the Lettuce
            Industry. New York: Cambridge University Press.

Fudge, Judy, and Fiona MacPhail
2009   The Temporary Foreign Worker Program in Canada: Low-Skilled Workers
            as an Extreme Form of Flexible Labor. Comparative Labor Law and Policy
            Journal 31(5):6–45.

Fuller, Varden
1942   The Supply of Agricultural Labor as a Factor in the Evolution of Farm
            Organization in California. PhD dissertation, University of California,
            Berkeley. Reprinted in Violations of Free Speech and the Rights of Labor
            Education and Labor Committee. Pp. 19778–19894. Washington, DC: Senate
            Education and Labor Committee.

Fussell, Elizabeth
2009   Hurricane Chasers in New Orleans: Latino Immigrants as a Source of a
        Rapid Response Labor Force. Hispanic Journal of Behavioral Sciences
        31(3):375–394.

Gabriel, C., and L. Macdonald
2011   Citizenship at the Margins: The Canadian Seasonal Agricultural Worker
        Program and Civil Society Advocacy. Politics and Policy 39:45–67.

Galarza, Ernesto
1964   Merchants of Labor: The Mexican Bracero Story: An Account of the
        Managed Migration of Mexican Farm Workers in California, 1942–1960.
        Charlotte, NC: McNally and Loftin.

Garcia, Juan Ramon
1980   Operation Wetback: The Mass Deportation of Mexican Undocumented
        Workers in 1954. Westport, CT: Greenwood.

Gardezi, Hassan N.
1997   Asian Workers in the Gulf States of the Middle East. *In* International Labour
        Migrations. B. Singh Bolaria and Rosemary von Elling Bolaria, eds. Pp.
        99–120. Delhi: Oxford University Press.

Gibson, J., D. Mckenzie, and H. Rohorua
2008   How Pro-Poor Is the Selection of Seasonal Migrant Workers from Tonga
        under New Zealand's Recognised Seasonal Employer (RSE) Program?
        Wellington, NZ: Centre for Research and Analysis of Migration.

Glaize, Phil
2003   Testimony before the Senate Appropriations Committee, Subcommittee
        on Commerce, Justice, State, the Judiciary, and Related Agencies, May 22.
        http://www.gpo.gov/fdsys/pkg/CHRG-108shrg89465/html/CHRG
        -108shrg89465.htm.

Glick Schiller, Nina, Linda Basch, and Cristina Szanton Blanc
1995   From Immigrant to Transmigrant: Theorizing Transnational Migration.
        Anthropological Quarterly 68:48–66.

Globe and Mail
2011   The Coming Conservative Court: Harper to Reshape Judiciary. May 13.

Goldring, Luin, and Sailaja Krishnamurti
2007   Introduction: Contexualizing Transnationalism in Canada. *In* Organizing
        the Transnational: Labour, Politics, and Social Change. L. Goldring and
        S. Krishnamurti, eds. Pp. 32–45. Vancouver: University of British Columbia
        Press.

Goździak, Elżbieta M., and Micah Bump
2008   New Immigrants, Changing Communities: Best Practices for a Better
        America. Lanham, MD: Lexington.

REFERENCES

Greenhouse, Stephen
2007   Low Pay and Broken Promises Greet Guestworkers. New York Times, February 28.

Griffith, David
1983   International Labor Migration and Rural Development: Patterns of Expenditure among Jamaicans Working Seasonally in the United States. Stanford Journal of International Law 19(2):357–370.

1985   Women, Remittances, and Reproduction. American Ethnologist 12(4):676–690.

1986   Peasants in Reserve: Temporary West Indian Labor in the U.S. Labor Market. International Migration Review 20(4):875–898.

1987   Nonmarket Labor Processes in an Advanced Capitalist Economy. American Anthropologist 89(4):838–852.

1993   Jones's Minimal: Low-Wage Labor in the United States. Albany: State University of New York Press.

2006   American Guestworkers: Jamaicans and Mexicans in the U.S. Labor Market. University Park: Pennsylvania State University Press.

2009a   The Moral Economy of Tobacco. American Anthropologist 111(4):432–442.

2009b   Unions without Borders: Organizing and Enlightening Immigrant Farmworkers. Anthropology of Work Review 30(2):27–39.

Griffith, David, and Manuel Valdés Pizzini
2002   Fishers at Work, Workers at Sea: A Puerto Rican Journey through Labor and Refuge. Philadelphia, PA: Temple University Press.

Gunewardena, Nandini, and Ann Kingsolver
2007   Introduction. *In* Gender and Globalization. N. Gunewardena and A. Kingsolver, eds. Pp. 3–22. Santa Fe, NM: SAR Press.

Hahamovitch, Cindy
1997   The Fruits of Their Labor: Atlantic Coast Farmworkers and the Making of Migrant Poverty, 1870–1945. Chapel Hill: University of North Carolina Press.

2003   Creating Perfect Immigrants: Guestworkers of the World in Historical Perspective. Labor History 44(1):69–94.

2011   No Man's Land: Jamaican Guestworkers in America and the Global History of Deportable Labor. Princeton, NJ: Princeton University Press.

Hangartner, Erin
2008   Signal Calls on Congress to Mandate Licensing Requirement for H2B Temporary Worker Program. Company statement. http://www.signalint .com/press.htm.

Helman, Christopher
2007   Labor Unrest: A Mississippi Oil Rig Builder Thought It Was Doing Itself and Some Immigrants a Favor by Paying $19 an Hour: It Ended Up Being Condemned as a Slave Driver. Forbes, June 4. http://www.forbes.com /forbes/2007/0604/124_print.html.

Henderson, Julia

1945   Foreign Labour in the United States during the War. International Labour
        Review 52 (December):609–631.

Hennebry, J. L., and K. Preibisch

2010   A Model for Managed Migration? Re-examining Best Practices in
        Canada's Seasonal Agricultural Worker Program. International Migration
        48(2):12–24.

Heppel, Monica L., Joanne Spano, and Luis R. Torres

1997   Changes in the Apple Harvest Work Force in West Virginia: Implications for
        the Community. Changing Face 3(4). http://migration.ucdavis.edu/cf
        /more.php?id=151_0_2_0.

Hill, J.

2008   Binational Guestworker Unions: Moving Guestworkers into the House of
        Labor. Fordham Urban Law Journal 35:307–338.

Hoefer, Michael, Nancy Rytina, and Bryan C. Baker

2008   Estimates of the Unauthorized Immigrant Population Residing in the United
        States: January 2008. Department of Homeland Security, Office
        of Immigration Statistics. http://www.dhs.gov/xlibrary/assets/statistics
        /publications/ois_ill_pe_2008.pdf.

Hollander, Gail

2008   Raising Cane in the 'Glades: The Global Sugar Trade and the
        Transformation of Florida. Chicago: University of Chicago Press.

Holley, M.

2001   Disadvantaged by Design: How the Law Inhibits Agricultural Guest Workers
        from Enforcing Their Rights. Hofstra Labor and Employment Law Journal
        18:573–621.

Hughes, Christine

2012   Costly Benefits and Gendered Costs: Guatemalans' Experiences of Canada's
        "Low-Skill Pilot Project." *In* Legislated Inequality: Temporary Migrant
        Workers in Canada. C. Straehle and P. Lenard, eds. Pp. 56–72. Kingston,
        Ontario: McGill-Queen's University Press.

Hugo, Graeme

2000   Migration and Women's Empowerment. *In* Women's Empowerment and
        Demographic Processes: Moving beyond Cairo. H. Presser and G. Sen, eds.
        Pp. 34–45. Oxford: Oxford University Press.

Human Resources and Skills Development Canada

2010   Number of Temporary Foreign Worker Positions on Labour Market Opinion
        Confirmations under the Seasonal Agricultural Worker Program, by
        Location of Employment. *In* Temporary Foreign Worker Program Labour
        Market Opinion (LMO) Statistics: Annual Statistics 2006–2009. Gatineau,
        QC: Government of Canada.

REFERENCES

2011a   Number of Confirmed Temporary Foreign Worker (TFW) Positions on Labour Market Opinions (LMOs) in Agriculture (non-SAWP), by Occupation, 2005–2010. Unpublished data request. Gatineau, QC: Human Resources and Skills Development Canada.

2011b   Total Number of Positions on Confirmed Labour Market Opinions (LMOs) for the Temporary Foreign Worker (TFW) Program Agricultural Stream NOC C&D Pilot. Unpublished data request. Gatineau, QC: Human Resources and Skills Development Canada.

2011c   Number of Temporary Foreign Worker (TFW) Positions on Confirmed Labour Market Opinions (LMOs) under the Seasonal Agricultural Worker Program (SAWP), by Province of Employment, 2006–2010 Seasons. Unpublished data request. Gatineau, QC: Human Resources and Skills Development Canada.

2011d   Number of Temporary Foreign Worker (TFW) Positions in Agriculture (Excluding SAWP) on Labour Market Opinion (LMO) Confirmations, by Province of Employment, January 1, 2006, to December 3, 2010. Unpublished data request. Gatineau, QC: Human Resources and Skills Development Canada.

Hurtig, Janise, Rosario Montoya, and Lessie Jo Frazier
2002   Introduction: A desalambrar: Unfencing Gender's Place in Research on Latin America. *In* Gender's Place: Feminist Anthropologies of Latin America. J. Hurtig, R. Montoya, and L. J. Frazier, eds. New York: Palgrave Macmillan.

Immigration and Naturalization Service
1955   Annual Report of the Immigration and Naturalization Service. www.archive .org/stream/annualreportfim1955unit#page/n5/mode/1up.

International Organization for Migration (IOM)
2008a   World Migration Report 2008: Managing Labour Mobility in the Evolving Global Economy. Geneva: International Organization for Migration.

2008b   Second Evaluation: Program Temporary Agricultural Workers to Canada. Working Notebooks on Migration 25. Guatemala City: International Organization for Migration.

Johnson, Fay Clarke
1995   Soldiers of the Soil. New York: Vantage.

José Alcalá, María
2006   The State of the World Population 2006: A Passage to Hope: Women and International Migration. New York: UNFPA.

Judge, Phoebe
2009   Shipbuilding Industry Hiring Despite Economic Downturn. Mississippi Public Broadcasting. http://www.mpbonline.org/content /south-mississippis-ship-building-industry-remains-strong-despite-recession.

Kalleberg, Arne K., Barbara F. Reskin, and Ken Hudson
2000   Bad Jobs in America: Standard and Nonstandard Employment Relations

and Job Quality in the United States. American Sociological Review 65(2):256–278.

Kammerzell, Jaime
2009   Jackup Count Increases Along with Uncertainty. Offshore, July 1. http://www.offshore-mag.com/index/article-display/8972010979/articles /offshore/volume-69/issue-7/drilling-completion/jackup-count_increases .html.

Kane, Jason
2008   Some Workers Delayed by Storm. Winchester Star, September 2. http://www .winchesterstar.com/showarticle_new.php?sID=6&foldername=20080902& file=workers_article.html.

Kasimis, C., A. G. Papadopoulos, and C. Pappas
2010   Gaining from Rural Migrants: Migrant Employment Strategies and Socioeconomic Implications for Rural Labour Markets. Sociologia Ruralis 50:258–276.

Kelly, P., and T. Lusis
2006   Migration and the Transnational Habitus: Evidence from Canada and the Philippines. Environment and Planning A 38(5):831–847.

Kramer, Peter
1966   The Offshores: A Study of Foreign Farm Labor in Florida. St. Petersburg, FL: Community Action Fund.

Kunz, Rahel
2008   'Remittances Are Beautiful'?: Gender Implications of the New Global Remittances Trend. Third World Quarterly 29(7):1389–1409.

Labrianidis, L., and T. Sykas
2009   Migrants, Economic Mobility and Socio-economic Change in Rural Areas: The Case of Greece. European Urban and Regional Studies 16:237–256.

Legendre, Raymond
2009   Recession Causes Drop in Foreign Workers. Houma Today, October 29. http://www.houmatoday.com/article/20091029/NEWS0101/910299950.

Levitt, Peggy
1996   Social Remittances: A Conceptual Tool for Understanding Migration and Development. Boston: Harvard Center for Population and Development Studies.

1998   Social Remittances: Migration Driven Local-Level Forms of Cultural Diffusion. International Migration Review 32(4):926–948.

Ley, David
2010   Millionaire Migrants: Trans-Pacific Life Lines. New York: Wiley Blackwell.

Lindsey, Linda
1994   Gender Roles: A Sociological Perspective. Englewood Cliffs, NJ: Prentice Hall.

REFERENCES

Lindsey, Lydia
1995   A Reexamination of the Significance of the MacCarran-Walters [*sic*] Act on Post–World War II Indian Migration to Britain: An Expository Note. Journal of Caribbean Studies 10(3):182–206.

Lindstrom, David, and Elisa Muñoz-Franco
2005   Migration and the Diffusion of Modern Contraceptive Knowledge and Use in Rural Guatemala. Studies in Family Planning 35(4):277–288.

Little, Walter
2005   Introduction: Globalization and Guatemala's Maya Workers. Latin American Perspectives 32(3):3–11.

Lovell, Terry
2000   Thinking Feminism with and against Bourdieu. *In* Reading Bourdieu on Society and Culture. B. Fowler, ed. Pp. 11–32. Oxford: Blackwell.

Lutz, Helma
2010   Gender in the Migratory Process. Journal of Ethnic and Migration Studies 36(10):1647–1663.

Luxton, Meg
2006   Feminist Political Economy in Canada and the Politics of Social Reproduction. *In* Social Reproduction: Feminist Political Economy Challenges Neo-liberalism. K. Bezanson and M. Luxton, eds. Pp. 11–44. Montreal: McGill-Queen's University Press.

Mackenzie, I. R.
1988   Early Movements of Domestics from the Caribbean and Canadian Immigration Policy: A Research Note. Alternative Routes 8:123–143.

Maclellan, N.
2008   Issues from New Zealand's Recognised Seasonal Employer (RSE) Program. Melbourne: Institute for Social Research, Swinburne University of Technology.

Mantsch, Stefan
2010   Program Manager, IOM-Guatemala, April 26 interview.

Marine Log
2006   For U.S. Gulf Shipyards, Labor Is the Thing. February 1. http://www.allbusiness.com/transportation-equipment-manufacturing/ship-boat-building/872480-1.html.

Maritime Administration
2008   Glossary of Shipping Terms. Washington, DC: US Department of Transportation. http://www.marad.dot.gov/documents/Glossary_final.pdf.

Marler, Dick
N.d.   Statement of the Chairman of the Board, Signal International, LLC. http://www.signalint.com/ceo.asp.

Marshall, Dawn
1987   A History of West Indian Migrations: Overseas Opportunities and "Safety-Valve" Policies. *In* The Caribbean Exodus. Barry B. Levine, ed. Pp. 15–31. New York: Praeger.

Martel, Andrew
2004   Apple Growers Take On Chinese Orchards, Weather. Shenandoah Valley Business Journal, September.

Martin, Philip
1988   Harvest of Confusion: Migrant Workers in U.S. Agriculture. Boulder, CO: Westview.

2001   There Is Nothing More Permanent Than Temporary Foreign Workers. Center for Immigration Studies. http://www.cis.org/articles/2001/back501. html.

2002   Mexican Workers and U.S. Agriculture: The Revolving Door. International Migration Review 36(4):1124–1142.

Martinez-Salazar, Egla
2005   The Everyday Practice of Guatemalan Women: Confronting Marginalization, Racism, and Contested Citizenship. PhD dissertation, York University, Toronto.

Massey, Douglas
2008   New Faces in New Places. New York: Russell Sage Foundation.

Massey, Douglas, Rafael Alarcón, Jorge Durand, and Humberto González
1987   Return to Aztlan: The Social Process of Migration from Western Mexico. Berkeley: University of California Press.

Massey, Douglas, and Chiara Capoferro
2008   The Geographic Diversification of American Immigration. *In* New Faces in New Places: The Changing Geography of American Immigration. Douglas Massey, ed. Pp. 25–50. New York: Russell Sage Foundation.

Matthews, Cedric O. J.
1952   Labour Policies in the West Indies. Geneva: International Labour Office.

McCoy, Terry L., and Charles H. Wood
1982   Caribbean Workers in the Florida Sugar Cane Industry. Gainesville: Center for Latin American Studies, University of Florida.

McDaniels, J., and V. Casanova
2005   Forest Management and the H2B Guest Workers Program in the Southeastern United States: An Assessment of Contractors and Their Crews. Journal of Forestry (April–May):114–119.

McGuire, Thomas
2008   History of the Offshore Oil and Gas Industry in Southern Louisiana, vol. 2: Bayou Lafourche: Oral Histories of the Oil and Gas Industry. MMS 2008-043. Washington, DC: US Department of the Interior, Minerals Management Service, Gulf of Mexico OCS Region.

REFERENCES

McKay, Deirdre
2001   Migration and the Masquerade: Gender and Habitus in the Philippines. Geography Research Forum 21:44–56.

McLaughlin, Janet
2009   Trouble in Our Fields: Health and Human Rights among Mexican and Caribbean Migrant Farm Workers in Canada. PhD thesis, University of Toronto.

Meissner, Doris
2004   US Temporary Worker Programs: Lessons Learned. Migration Policy Institute, Migration Information Source. http://www.migrationinformation.org/feature/display.cfm?ID=205.

MENAMIG
2006   Diagnóstico de menores de edad y mujeres trabajadores agrícolas temporales en Chiapas, México. Guatemala City: Mesa Nacional para las Migraciones en Guatemala.

Menjívar, Cecilia
1999   The Intersection of Work and Gender: Central American Immigrant Women and Employment in California. American Behavioral Scientist 42(4):601–627.

2006   Global Processes and Local Lives: Guatemalan Women's Work and Gender Relations at Home and Abroad. International Labor and Working-Class History 70:86–105.

Menjívar, Cecilia, and Victor Agadjanian
2007   Men's Migration and Women's Lives: Views from Rural Armenia and Guatemala. Social Science Quarterly 88(5):1243–1262.

Mexican Farm Labor Consultants Report
1960[1959] Reprinted in US Senate, Committee on Labor and Public Welfare, Subcommittee on Migratory Labor. Migratory Labor Hearings. Washington, DC: US Government Printing Office.

Mintz, Sidney
1957   Worker in the Cane. New Haven, CT: Yale University Press.

1985   Sweetness and Power: The Place of Sugar in Modern History. New York: Penguin.

Mitchell, D.
1996   The Lie of the Land: Migrant Workers and the California Landscape. Minneapolis: University of Minnesota Press.

Montes, Verónica
2009   Transformaciones de las relaciones familiares en el contexto migratorio transnacional: Pueblo Nuevo, Guatemala como caso de estudio ethnográfico. *In* V Congreso International Sobre Migración. M. Ugalde, ed. Pp. 12–29. Guatemala City: Instituto de Investigaciones Económicas y Sociales.

Monzón, Ana Silvia

2009   Mujeres migrantes en Los Ángeles, California: Comunicación, identidad y acción colectiva. *In* V Congreso International Sobre Migración. M. Ugalde, ed. Pp. 224–248. Guatemala City: Instituto de Investigaciones Económicas y Sociales.

Munroe, Trevor

1983[1944] Politics of Constitutional Decolonisation, Jamaica: 1944–62. Reprint. Mona: Institute of Social and Economic Research, University of the West Indies.

Nakache, Delphine, and Paula J. Kinoshita

2010   The Canadian Temporary Foreign Worker Program: Do Short-Term Economic Needs Prevail over Human Rights Concerns? Montreal: Institute for Research on Policy Study.

Nash, June, and María Patricia Fernández-Kelly

1983   Women, Men, and the International Division of Labor. Albany: State University of New York Press.

Nelson, Karen

2007   Signal Brings Recruits from India: Company Cites Widespread Shortage of Skilled Workers. Sun Herald (Biloxi, MS), January 2.

New York Times

2010a   A Bitter Guest Worker Story. Editorial, February 4 (correction appended). http://www.nytimes.com/2010/02/04/opinion/04thur2.html.

2010b   They Pushed Back. Editorial, June 28. http://www.nytimes.com/2010/06/29/opinion/29tue3.html.

Office of Technology Assessment

1983   An Assessment of Maritime Trade and Technology. OTA-O-220. October. Washington, DC: US Congress, Office of Technology Assessment.

Organisation for Economic Co-operation and Development (OECD)

2003   Trends in International Migration. Paris: OECD.

Otero, G., and K. Preibisch

2009   Farmworker Health and Safety: Challenges for British Columbia. Vancouver: WorkSafe BC.

2010   Farmworker Health and Safety: Challenges for British Columbia. Vancouver: WorkSafe BC.

Oubre, Shawn

2006   Memo to the Orange, Texas City Council. September 1.

Parks, James

2007   Guest Workers Exploited by Recruiters and Employers. Posted in "Organizing and Bargaining." http://blog.aflcio.org/2007/04/19/guest-workers-exploited-by-recruiters-and-employers.

REFERENCES

Penney, Lauren
2008   In the Wake of War: World War II and the Offshore Oil and Gas Industry. *In* History of the Offshore Oil and Gas Industry in Southern Louisiana, vol. 1: Papers on the Evolving Offshore Industry. MMS 2008-042. Diane Austin, et al. Pp. 37–66. Washington, DC: US Department of the Interior, Minerals Management Service, Gulf of Mexico OCS Region.

Pessar, Patricia
2003   Anthropology and the Engendering of Migration Studies. *In* American Arrivals. Nancy Foner, ed. Pp. 75–98. Santa Fe, NM: SAR Press.

Pessar, Patricia R., and Sarah J. Mahler
2003   Transnational Migration: Bringing Gender In. International Migration Review 37(3):812–846.

Piper, Nicola
2005   Gender and Migration. Geneva: Global Commission on International Migration.

Plewa, P.
2007   The Rise and Fall of Temporary Foreign Worker Policies: Lessons for Poland. International Migration 45(2):3–36.

Plewa, P., and M. Miller
2005   Postwar and Post–Cold War Generations of European Temporary Foreign Worker Policies: Implications from Spain. Migraciones Internacionales 3:58–83.

Polivka, Anne E.
1996   Contingent and Alternative Work Arrangements, Defined. Monthly Labor Review (October):22–35.

Pollan, Michael
2001   The Omnivore's Dilemma. New York: Knopf.

Post, Ken
1978   Arise Ye Starvelings: The Jamaican Labour Rebellion and Its Aftermath. The Hague: Martinus Nijhoff.

Pratt, Geraldine, and Brenda Yeoh
2003   Transnational (Counter) Topographies. Gender, Place and Culture 10(2):159–166.

Preibisch, Kerry L.
2004   Migrant Agricultural Workers and Processes of Social Inclusion in Rural Canada: Encuentros and Desencuentros. Canadian Journal of Latin American and Caribbean Studies 29:203–239.

2005   Gender Transformative Odysseys: Tracing the Experiences of Transnational Migrant Women in Rural Canada. Canadian Woman Studies 24(4):91–97.

2007a   Globalizing Work, Globalizing Citizenship: Community-Migrant Worker Alliances in Southwestern Ontario. *In* Organizing the Transnational:

Labour, Politics, and Social Change. L. Goldring and S. Krishnamurti, eds. Pp. 19–33. Vancouver: University of British Columbia Press.

2007b Local Produce, Foreign Labor: Labor Mobility Programs and Global Trade Competitiveness in Canada. Rural Sociology 72(3):7–36.

Preibisch, Kerry, and Evelyn Encalada Grez
2010 The Other Side of el Otro Lado: Mexican Migrant Women and Labor Flexibility in Canadian Agriculture. Signs 35(2):289–316.

Preibisch, Kerry, and J. Hennebry
2012 Buy Local, Hire Global: Temporary Migration in Canadian Agriculture. In Legislated Inequality: Temporary Labour Migration in Canada. P. T. Lenard and C. Straehle, eds. Montreal: McGill-Queen's University Press.

President's Commission on Migratory Labor
1951 Migratory Labor in American Agriculture. Washington, DC: US Government Printing Office.

Priest, Tyler
2013 The History of Gulf Coast Shipbuilding and Offshore Fabrication. In Gulf Coast Communities and the Fabrication and Shipbuilding Industry: A Comparative Community Study, vol. 1: Historical Overview and Statistical Model. Tyler Priest and John Lajaunie. Pp. 1–66. Washington, DC: US Department of the Interior, Bureau of Ocean Energy Management, Gulf of Mexico OCS Region.

Putnam, Lara
2002 The Company They Kept: Migrants and the Politics of Gender in Caribbean Costa Rica, 1870–1960. Chapel Hill: University of North Carolina Press.

Ramirez, Carlota, Mar Garcia Dominquez, and Julia Miguez Morais
2005 Crossing Borders: Remittances, Gender and Development. Santo Domingo, Dominican Republic: INSTRAW.

Raper, S., and K. Preibisch
2007 Forcing Governments to Govern in Defense of Non-citizen Workers: A Story about the Canadian Labour Movement's Alliance with Agricultural Migrants. In Organizing the Transnational: Labour, Politics, and Social Change. L. Goldring and S. Krishnamurti, eds. Pp. 44–61. Vancouver: University of British Columbia Press.

Rasmussen, Wayne
1951 A History of the Emergency Farm Labor Supply Program, 1943–1947. Washington, DC: US Government Printing Office.

Reed, Austina
2008 Canada's Experience with Managed Migration: The Strategic Use of Temporary Foreign Worker Programs. International Journal (Spring):469–484.

Reid, Sheryl Andre
1998 U.S.-Jamaica Relations: The Farm Work Programme, 1943–1962. MA thesis, University of the West Indies.

REFERENCES

Reigada Olaizola, A.
2009   Las nuevas temporeras de la fresa en Huelva: Flexibilidad productiva, con-
        tratación en origen y feminización del trabajo en una agricultura globali-
        zada. PhD dissertation, Universidad de Sevilla.

Reisler, Mark
1976   By the Sweat of Their Brow: Mexican Immigrant Labor in the United States,
        1900–1940. Westport, CT: Greenwood.

Resurreccion, B. P., and H. T. Van Khanh
2007   Able to Come and Go: Reproducing Gender in Female Rural-Urban
        Migration in the Red River Delta. Population, Space and Place
        13(3):211–224.

Richards, Glen
2002   Race, Class, and Labour Politics in Colonial Jamaica. *In* Jamaica in Slavery
        and Freedom: History, Heritage and Culture. Kathleen E. A. Monteith and
        Glen Richards, eds. Pp. 340–362. Kingston, Jamaica: University of the West
        Indies Press.

**Robinson, Terence, Stephen A. Hoying, Alison DeMaree, Kevin Iungerman,
and Mike Fargione**
2007   The Evolution towards More Competitive Apple Orchard Systems in New
        York. New York Fruit Quarterly (Spring). http://www.nyshs.org
        /fq/07spring/07SpringFQ.pdf.

Roche, Joe
2007   Signal's Guest Workers Add Productivity. Statement issued by Signal
        International, January 3. In possession of Diane Austin.

Rochester, Anna
1940   Why Farmers Are Poor: The Agricultural Crisis in the United States. New
        York: International Publishers.

Rogaly, B.
2008   Intensification of Workplace Regimes in British Horticulture: The Role of
        Migrant Workers. Population, Space and Place 14(6):497–510.

Roseberry, William
1989   Anthropologies and Histories: Essays in Political Economy. New Brunswick,
        NJ: Rutgers University Press.

Rubin, Leste
1970   The Negro in the Shipbuilding Industry. Philadelphia: Industrial
        Research Unit, Wharton School of Finance and Commerce, University of
        Pennsylvania.

Ruhs, Martin
2006   The Potential of Temporary Migration Programmes in Future International
        Migration Policy. International Labour Review 145(1–2):7–36.

Ruhs, Martin, and Philip Martin
2008   Numbers vs. Rights: Trade-Offs and Guest Worker Programs. International Migration Review 42(1):249–265.

Rural Migration News
2009   Canada: Unions and Migrants. Rural Migration News 12:2–6.

Rutherford, T. D.
2004   Convergence, the Institutional Turn and Workplace Regimes: The Case of Lean Production. Progress in Human Geography 28:425–446.

Rye, J. F., and J. Andrzejewska
2010   The Structural Disempowerment of Eastern European Migrant Farm Workers in Norwegian Agriculture. Journal of Rural Studies 26:41–51.

Sahlins, Marshall
1972   Stone Age Economics. New Haven, CT: Yale University Press.

Salley, George H.
1984   A History of the Florida Sugar Industry. Clewiston, FL: Sugar Cane League.

Schrecongost, Alyse
1999   The Changing Nature of Migrant Farm Labor: A Case Study of West Virginia's Apple Industry. http://www.rri.wvu.edu/pdffiles/alysereu99.pdf.

Scruggs, Otey
1960   The First Mexican Farm Labor Program. Arizona and the West 2 (Winter):319–326.

1961   The United States, Mexico, and the Wetbacks: 1942–1947. Pacific Historical Review 30(2):149–164.

Selwyn, B.
2009   Labour Flexibility in Export Horticulture: A Case Study of Northeast Brazilian Grape Production. Journal of Peasant Studies 36:761–782.

2012   Beyond Firm-centrism: Re-integrating Labour and Capitalism into Global Commodity Chain Analysis. Journal of Economic Geography 12:205–226.

Sharma, N.
2006   Home Economics: Nationalism and the Making of "Migrant Workers" in Canada. Toronto: University of Toronto Press.

2010   Manitoba's Worker Recruitment and Protection Act. Paper presented at the meeting of the Canadian Labour Congress's Temporary Worker Advocacy Group, Toronto, ON, March 23.

Sider, Gerald
1976   Culture and Class in Anthropology and History: A Newfoundland Illustration. Cambridge: Cambridge University Press.

Signal H2B Employees Organization
2007   Indian H2B Visa Workers Imprisoned, Enslaved in Gulf Coast. http://neworleans.indymedia.org/news/2007/03/9865.php.

REFERENCES

Siltanen, Janet, and Andrea Doucet
2008   Gender Relations in Canada: Intersectionality and Beyond. Toronto: Oxford University Press.

Simmons, Alan B.
2010   Immigration and Canada—Global and Transnational Perspectives. Toronto: Canadian Scholars' Press.

Simmons, Ann M.
2007   Guest Workers' Prospects Dim: Laborers from India and Mexico Say Gulf Coast Jobs Were Not as Advertised: Companies Cite a Lack of Skills. Los Angeles Times, March 14. http://articles.latimes.com/2007/mar/14/nation/na-workers14.

Siskind, Janet
2001   Rum and Axes. Ithaca, NY: Cornell University Press.

Smart, Alan, and Josephine Smart
2001   Local Citizenship: Welfare Reform, Urban/Rural Status, and Exclusion in China. Environment and Planning A 33:1853–1969.

Smart, Josephine
1994   Business Immigration in Canada: Deception and Exploitation. In The Reluctant Exiles. R. Skeldon, ed. Pp. 98–119. Armonk, NY: M. E. Sharpe.

1998   Borrowed Men on Borrowed Time: Globalization, Labour Migration and Local Economies in Alberta. Canadian Journal of Regional Science 20(1–2):141–156.

Smith, Barbara Ellen, and Jamie Winders
2008   "We're Here to Stay": Economic Restructuring, Latino Migration, and Place-Making in the U.S. South. Transnational Institute of British Geography 33:60–72.

Sohrabji, Sunita
2012   Judge Denies Class Action Suit by Former Signal Workers. IndiaWest, January 25. http://www.indiawest.com/news/2697-Judge-Denies-Class-Action-Suit-by-Former-Signal-Workers.html.

Soni, Saket, and Daniel Castellanos
2010   Letter to Department of Labor Administrator Nancy Leppink. Re: Protecting Guestworkers Facing Loss of Income in Relation to the Deepwater Horizon Incident. Alliance of Guestworkers for Dignity. New Orleans Workers' Center for Racial Justice. July 9. In possession of Diane Austin.

Southern Poverty Law Center
2007   Close to Slavery: Guestworker Programs in the United States. Montgomery, AL: Southern Poverty Law Center.

Standing Committee on Citizenship and Immigration
2009   Temporary Foreign Workers and Nonstatus Workers: Seventh Report of the Standing Committee on Citizenship and Immigration. Ottawa, ON: House of Commons Canada.

Stasiulis, D. K., and A. Bakan
2003   Negotiating Citizenship: Migrant Women in Canada and the Global System. Houndsmill, England: PalgraveMacmillan.

Stoler, Ann
1985   Capitalism and Confrontation in Sumatra's Plantation Belt. New Haven, CT: Yale University Press.

Stull, Donald, Michael Broadway, and David Griffith, eds.
1995   Any Way They Cut It: Meatpacking and the Transformation of Small Town America. Lawrence: University Press of Kansas.

Taylor, Don
1963   How Mexico Feels about the Bracero Program. California Farmer (April):20.

Taylor, Frank Fonda
1993   To Hell with Paradise: A History of the Jamaican Tourist Industry. Pittsburgh, PA: University of Pittsburgh Press.

Taylor, Matthew, Michelle Moran-Taylor, and Debra Rodman Ruiz
2006   Land, Ethnic, and Gender Change: Transnational Migration and Its Effects on Guatemalan Lives and Landscapes. Geoforum 37:41–61.

Thomas-Hope, Elizabeth
1978   The Establishment of a Migration Tradition: British West Indian Movements to the Hispanic Caribbean in the Century after Emancipation. *In* Caribbean Social Relations. Colin G. Clarke, ed. Pp. 66–81. Liverpool: Centre for Latin American Studies.

Times-Picayune
1997   Shipyard Crunch. November 13. Cited in Priest 2012:50.

1998   Foreign Workers Visas Are Approved: Shipbuilders to Fill 715 Slots. Times-Picayune, December 11. Cited in Priest 2012:50.

Tompkins, Kiltie
2007   The Core Issue: Virginia Farmers Adapt to a Changing Apple Market. http://journalism.wlu.edu/indepth/2007/Apples/core/mainstory.html.

Trumper, Ricardo, and Lloyd Wong
2007   Canada's Guestworkers—Racialized, Gendered and Flexible. *In* Race and Racism in 21st-Century Canada—Continuity, Complexity, and Change. Sean P. Hier and B. Singh Bolaria, eds. Pp. 151–170. Peterborough, ON: Broadview.

Trupo, Paul, Jeffrey Alwang, and David Lamie
N.d.   The Economic Impact of Migrant, Seasonal, and H-2A Farmworkers on the Virginia Economy. Department of Agricultural and Applied Economics, Virginia Tech. http://ageconsearch.umn.edu/bitstream/14836/1/rr980036.pdf.

REFERENCES

United Food and Commercial Workers of Canada

2009 UFCW Canada Report on the Status of Migrant Farm Workers in Canada 2008–2009. Mississauga, ON: United Food and Commercial Workers of Canada.

2011a Charges Allege Mexico Consulate Blacklisted Unionized Mexican Migrant Workers in B.C. United Food and Commercial Workers of Canada. http:// www.ufcw.ca/index.php?option=com_content&view=article&id=2353%3Ac harges-allege-mexico-consulate-blacklisted-unionized-mexican-migrant -workers-in-bc&catid=6%3Adirections-newsletter&Itemid=6&lang=en.

2011b History of Agricultural Workers in Canada. United Food and Commercial Workers of Canada. http://www.ufcw.ca/index.php?option=com _content&view=article&id=2012&Itemid=250&lang=en.

United Food and Commercial Workers of Canada and Agriculture Workers Alliance

2011 The Status of Migrant Farm Workers in Canada 2010–2011. Rexdale, ON: United Food and Commercial Workers of Canada.

United Nations Development Programme

2009 Human Development Report 2009: Overcoming Barriers: Human Mobility and Development. New York: United Nations Development Programme.

2011a Mexico: Country Profile of Human Development Indicators. http://hdrstats .undp.org/en/countries/profiles/MEX.html.

2011b Guatemala: Country Profile of Human Development Indicators. http:// hdrstats.undp.org/en/countries/profiles/GTM.html.

US Census

2007 NAICS Definitions: 336611: Shipbuilding and Repairing. http://www.census .gov/naics/2007/def/ND336611.HTM.

US Department of Agriculture

2005 Virginia Orchard Survey. http://www.nass.usda.gov/Statistics_by_State /Virginia/Publications/2005fruitpub.pdf.

2007 Census of Agriculture, vol. 1: U.S. Summary and State Reports. http://www .agcensus.usda.gov/Publications/2007/Full_Report/index.asp.

Vambery, Robert G.

1968a Proposals for a Long-Range Maritime Transport Programme for the United States. Unpublished manuscript.

1968b The Effects of Subsidies in the United States Shipbuilding Industry. Journal of Transport Economics and Policy 2(1):79–93.

Vandeman, Ann Marie

1988 Labor Contracting in California Agriculture. PhD dissertation, University of California, Berkeley.

Vargas-Foronda, Jacobo

2010a El Programa de Trabajo Agrícola Temporal en Canadá (PTAT-C): Mano de Obra Barata de Exportación. Diálogo 16:15–43.

2010b El Programa de Trabajo Agrícola Temporal en Canadá en su VII Aniversario

2003–2010: Una hipócrita negociación: Exportamos Mano de Obra barata con enormes rendimientos y altos lucros: Su cruda perversión y magnificada degradación. *In* Enlace Académico. Pp. 31–45. Guatemala City, Guatemala: FLACSO.

Verma, V.
2003   The Mexican and Caribbean Seasonal Agricultural Workers Program: Regulatory and Policy Framework, Farm Industry–Level Employment Practices and the Future of the Program under Unionization. Ottawa, ON: North-South Institute.

Vullnetari, Julie, and Russell King
2011   Gendering Remittances in Albania: A Human and Social Development Perspective. Gender and Development 19(1):39–51.

Waldinger, R., and M. I. Lichter
2003   How the Other Half Works: Immigration and the Social Organization of Labor. Berkeley: University of California Press.

Wallace, Barbara, James Kirkley, Thomas McGuire, Diane Austin, and David Goldfield
2001   Assessment of Historical, Social, and Economic Impacts of OCS Development on Gulf Coast Communities, vol. 2: Narrative Report. MMS 2001-027. New Orleans: US Department of the Interior, Minerals Management Service, Gulf of Mexico OCS Region.

Ward, Cherie
2007   Press Tours Quarters for Indian Workers. Mississippi Press, March 15. www.gulflive.com/news/mississippipress/index.ssf?/base/news/117395379885940.xml.

Washington State University
2009   The National Tree Fruit Technology Roadmap. http://arc.wsu.edu/researchimpacts/images/04page7.pdf.

Weinstein Bever, Sandra
2002   Migration and the Transformation of Gender Roles and Hierarchies in Yucatan. Urban Anthropology 31(2):199–230.

West, Candace, and Don Zimmerman
2007   Doing Gender. *In* Gender Relations in Global Perspective: Essential Readings. N. Cook, ed. Pp. 54–75. Toronto: Canadian Scholars' Press.

Wharton, Amy
2005   The Sociology of Gender: An Introduction to Theory and Research. Malden, MA: Blackwell.

Whitehurst, Clinton H.
1986   The U.S. Shipbuilding Industry: Past, Present, and Future. Annapolis, MD: Naval Institute Press.

Williams, Eric
1942   The Negro in the Caribbean. Westport, CT: Negro Universities Press.

REFERENCES

Williams, Leaford C.
1996   Journey into Diplomacy: A Black Man's Shocking Discovery: A Memoir. Washington, DC: Northeast Publishing House.

Williams, Robert
1991   Testimony before the Commission on Agricultural Workers, February 15. *In* Appendix I of the Report to the Commission on Agricultural Workers. Pp. 659–660. Washington, DC: US Government Printing Office.

Wolf, Eric
1982   Europe and the People without History. Berkeley: University of California Press.

Zlolniski, Christian
2006   Janitors, Street Vendors, and Activists: The Lives of Mexican Immigrants in Silicon Valley. Berkeley: University of California Press.

Zuñiga, Victor, and Rubén Hernández-León
2005   New Destinations: Mexican Immigration in the United States. New York: Russell Sage Foundation.

Index

Illustrations are indicated by page numbers in *italics*.

Great Depression: deportations of Mexican citizens and Mexican Americans during, 5; and economy of Jamaica, 9; and labor camps for homeless farmworkers, 5

greenhouse industry, and migrant labor force in Canadian agriculture, 93

Griffith, David, xix, xxi, xxiv, xxxi, 153–54, 230

growers associations, and privatization of guest-worker programs after World War II, 16–18. *See also* Frederick County Fruit Growers Association; North Carolina Growers Association

Guatemala: and Pilot project in Canada, 95; social remittances and labor migration of women to Canada, 161–81, 229–30; and United Nations Development Programme's Human Development Index, 96

guestworker programs: chronology and selected characteristics of programs in Canada and US, 233–236; contradictory positions of state toward, xxi–xxiii; and divergent interests of employers and workers, xiv–xv; future of in US and Canada, 225–232; and shipbuilding industry along Gulf of Mexico, 107–130. *See also* bracero program; managed migration; sending countries; temporary workers

Gulf & Western Inc., 25

Habitus, Bourdieu's concept of, 172, 173, 174

Hahamovitch, Cindy, xiii, xxiii, xxvii, xxviii, xxix, 23, 58n20, 91, 130, 137–138, 229

Haiti, and temporary labor force of apple industry in Virginia, 191–192. *See also* Caribbean

Hangartner, Erin, 123

Hart-Cellar immigration reform bill (1965), 23

Hatco, Inc. (Texas), 116

health care, and Pilot project in Canada, 92

Helman, Christopher, 123

Hendrickson, Carol, 174

Heppel, Monica L., 189

Holn, Rupert, 6

Hoovervilles, and Dust Bowl migrants, 37

housing: AgJOBS and allowance for, 54, 61n44; and development of farmland in Virginia, 198; for H-2B workers in shipbuilding industry, 119–120, 120–121, 127–129, 131n5; and labor activism in North Carolina, 218; and standards for bracero program, 38. *See also* labor camps

H-2A program (agricultural): and apple industry in Virginia, 187, 190, 191, 192, 193,

205–206, 208–210; chronology and characteristics of, 235, 236; and clearance orders, xxii; evolution, impacts, and future of guestworkers in US agriculture, 33–56; and history of labor contracting, xvii; and management of labor force by North Carolina Growers Association, xx; and organizational work of Juvencio Rocha Peralta, 219; and view of guestworker programs as alternative to illegal immigration, 3–27

H-2B program (non-agricultural): and clearance orders, xxii; establishment of, 236; and history of labor contracting, xvii–xviii; and seafood-processing industry in North Carolina, 152, 157, 223n3; and shipbuilding industry in US South, 107–130

Hughes, Christine, xxxi, 68, 229–230

Human Development Index, of United Nations Development Programme, 96

Human Resources and Skills Development Canada (HRSDC), 64, 88, 90, 233

hurricanes: and H-2B workers in South, 111–112; and immigrant activism in North Carolina, 216; and shipbuilding industry in South, 115–116; Thai workers and abuses in managed migration programs, 226

Immigration: and blue card holders, 53; Canadian government approach to, 65, 71, 75, 87; and development of H-2A program, 39–40, 42; and guestworkers in seafood-processing industry in North Carolina, 151–158; increase in legal and illegal from Mexico in 1920s, 36; of Jamaicans to US, 210n5; and quotas in US during 1950s, 23; Juvencio Rocha Peralta on need for reform of, 221; opposition of North Carolina Republican establishment to, 223n1; and state anti-immigrant laws, 55; temporary foreign workers in Canada and history of, 71; undocumented Mexican immigrants in US as percent of estimated population of Mexico, xxiii–xxvii; United Kingdom and Commonwealth Immigrants Act in 1950s, 22; view of managed migration as alternative to illegal, xxvi, 3–27, 158n1. *See also* Bureau of Immigration; Immigration and Naturalization Service; managed migration

Immigration Act (1917), 16, 35, 235

Immigration Act (1990), 236

Immigration and Nationality Act of 1952 (McCarran-Walter Act), 22, 40, 42, 235, 236

School for Advanced Research Advanced Seminar Series

PUBLISHED BY SAR PRESS

GRAY AREAS: ETHNOGRAPHIC
ENCOUNTERS WITH NURSING HOME
CULTURE
Philip B. Stafford, ed.

PLURALIZING ETHNOGRAPHY: COMPARISON
AND REPRESENTATION IN MAYA CULTURES,
HISTORIES, AND IDENTITIES
John M. Watanabe & Edward F. Fischer, eds.

AMERICAN ARRIVALS: ANTHROPOLOGY
ENGAGES THE NEW IMMIGRATION
Nancy Foner, ed.

VIOLENCE
Neil L. Whitehead, ed.

LAW & EMPIRE IN THE PACIFIC:
FIJI AND HAWAI'I
Sally Engle Merry & Donald Brenneis, eds.

ANTHROPOLOGY IN THE MARGINS
OF THE STATE
Veena Das & Deborah Poole, eds.

THE ARCHAEOLOGY OF COLONIAL
ENCOUNTERS: COMPARATIVE
PERSPECTIVES
Gil J. Stein, ed.

GLOBALIZATION, WATER, & HEALTH:
RESOURCE MANAGEMENT IN TIMES OF
SCARCITY
Linda Whiteford & Scott Whiteford, eds.

A CATALYST FOR IDEAS: ANTHROPOLOGICAL
ARCHAEOLOGY AND THE LEGACY OF
DOUGLAS W. SCHWARTZ
Vernon L. Scarborough, ed.

THE ARCHAEOLOGY OF CHACO CANYON:
AN ELEVENTH-CENTURY PUEBLO
REGIONAL CENTER
Stephen H. Lekson, ed.

COMMUNITY BUILDING IN THE TWENTY-
FIRST CENTURY
Stanley E. Hyland, ed.

AFRO-ATLANTIC DIALOGUES:
ANTHROPOLOGY IN THE DIASPORA
Kevin A. Yelvington, ed.

COPÁN: THE HISTORY OF AN ANCIENT
MAYA KINGDOM
E. Wyllys Andrews & William L. Fash, eds.

THE EVOLUTION OF HUMAN LIFE HISTORY
Kristen Hawkes & Richard R. Paine, eds.

THE SEDUCTIONS OF COMMUNITY:
EMANCIPATIONS, OPPRESSIONS,
QUANDARIES
Gerald W. Creed, ed.

THE GENDER OF GLOBALIZATION: WOMEN
NAVIGATING CULTURAL AND ECONOMIC
MARGINALITIES
*Nandini Gunewardena &
Ann Kingsolver, eds.*

NEW LANDSCAPES OF INEQUALITY:
NEOLIBERALISM AND THE EROSION OF
DEMOCRACY IN AMERICA
*Jane L. Collins, Micaela di Leonardo,
& Brett Williams, eds.*

IMPERIAL FORMATIONS
*Ann Laura Stoler, Carole McGranahan,
& Peter C. Perdue, eds.*

OPENING ARCHAEOLOGY: REPATRIATION'S
IMPACT ON CONTEMPORARY RESEARCH
AND PRACTICE
Thomas W. Killion, ed.

SMALL WORLDS: METHOD, MEANING,
& NARRATIVE IN MICROHISTORY
*James F. Brooks, Christopher R. N. DeCorse,
& John Walton, eds.*

MEMORY WORK: ARCHAEOLOGIES OF
MATERIAL PRACTICES
Barbara J. Mills & William H. Walker, eds.

FIGURING THE FUTURE: GLOBALIZATION
AND THE TEMPORALITIES OF CHILDREN
AND YOUTH
Jennifer Cole & Deborah Durham, eds.

TIMELY ASSETS: THE POLITICS OF
RESOURCES AND THEIR TEMPORALITIES
*Elizabeth Emma Ferry &
Mandana E. Limbert, eds.*

DEMOCRACY: ANTHROPOLOGICAL
APPROACHES
Julia Paley, ed.

CONFRONTING CANCER: METAPHORS,
INEQUALITY, AND ADVOCACY
Juliet McMullin & Diane Weiner, eds.

DEVELOPMENT & DISPOSSESSION: THE
CRISIS OF FORCED DISPLACEMENT AND
RESETTLEMENT
Anthony Oliver-Smith, ed.

GLOBAL HEALTH IN TIMES OF VIOLENCE
*Barbara Rylko-Bauer, Linda Whiteford,
& Paul Farmer, eds.*

THE EVOLUTION OF LEADERSHIP:
TRANSITIONS IN DECISION MAKING FROM
SMALL-SCALE TO MIDDLE-RANGE SOCIETIES
*Kevin J. Vaughn, Jelmer W. Eerkins, &
John Kantner, eds.*

ARCHAEOLOGY & CULTURAL RESOURCE
MANAGEMENT: VISIONS FOR THE FUTURE
Lynne Sebastian & William D. Lipe, eds.

ARCHAIC STATE INTERACTION: THE
EASTERN MEDITERRANEAN IN THE BRONZE
AGE
*William A. Parkinson &
Michael L. Galaty, eds.*

INDIANS & ENERGY: EXPLOITATION
AND OPPORTUNITY IN THE AMERICAN
SOUTHWEST
Sherry L. Smith & Brian Frehner, eds.

ROOTS OF CONFLICT: SOILS, AGRICULTURE,
AND SOCIOPOLITICAL COMPLEXITY IN
ANCIENT HAWAI'I
Patrick V. Kirch, ed.

PHARMACEUTICAL SELF: THE GLOBAL
SHAPING OF EXPERIENCE IN AN AGE OF
PSYCHOPHARMACOLOGY
Janis Jenkins, ed.

FORCES OF COMPASSION: HUMANITARI-
ANISM BETWEEN ETHICS AND POLITICS
Erica Bornstein & Peter Redfield, eds.

ENDURING CONQUESTS: RETHINKING THE
ARCHAEOLOGY OF RESISTANCE TO SPANISH
COLONIALISM IN THE AMERICAS
*Matthew Liebmann &
Melissa S. Murphy, eds.*

DANGEROUS LIAISONS: ANTHROPOLOGISTS
AND THE NATIONAL SECURITY STATE
*Laura A. McNamara &
Robert A. Rubinstein, eds.*

BREATHING NEW LIFE INTO THE EVIDENCE
OF DEATH: CONTEMPORARY APPROACHES
TO BIOARCHAEOLOGY
*Aubrey Baadsgaard, Alexis T. Boutin, &
Jane E. Buikstra, eds.*

THE SHAPE OF SCRIPT: HOW AND WHY
WRITING SYSTEMS CHANGE
Stephen D. Houston, ed.

NATURE, SCIENCE, AND RELIGION:
INTERSECTIONS SHAPING SOCIETY AND
THE ENVIRONMENT
Catherine M. Tucker, ed.

THE GLOBAL MIDDLE CLASSES:
THEORIZING THROUGH ETHNOGRAPHY
*Rachel Heiman, Carla Freeman, &
Mark Liechty, eds.*

KEYSTONE NATIONS: INDIGENOUS PEOPLES
AND SALMON ACROSS THE NORTH PACIFIC
Benedict J. Colombi & James F. Brooks, eds.

REASSEMBLING THE COLLECTION:
ETHNOGRAPHIC MUSEUMS AND
INDIGENOUS AGENCY
*Rodney Harrison, Sarah Byrne, & Annie
Clarke, eds.*

IMAGES THAT MOVE
Patricia Spyer & Mary Margaret Steedly, eds.

VITAL RELATIONS: MODERNITY AND THE
PERSISTENT LIFE OF KINSHIP
Susan McKinnon & Fenella Cannell, eds.

ANTHROPOLOGY OF RACE: GENES,
BIOLOGY, AND CULTURE
John Hartigan, ed.

STREET ECONOMIES IN THE URBAN
GLOBAL SOUTH
*Karen Tranberg Hansen, Walter E. Little,
& B. Lynne Milgram, eds.*

CASH ON THE TABLE: MARKETS, VALUES,
AND MORAL ECONOMIES
Edward F. Fischer, ed.

Timeless Classics from SAR Press

Participants in the School for Advanced Research short seminar
"Managing and Mismanaging Migration: Lessons from Guestworkers'
Experiences" co-chaired by Diane Austin and David Griffith, August 4–5,
2010. *Standing, from left*: Ricardo Contreras, Juvencio Rocha Peralta,
B. Lindsay Lowell, Philip Martin, Cindy Hahamovitch, and
Josephine Smart; *seated, from left*: Kerry Preibisch, Diane Austin,
and David Griffith. Photograph by Jason S. Ordaz.